ON THE
Fringe

A LIFE IN DECORATING

ON THE
Fringe

A LIFE IN DECORATING

Imogen Taylor with Martin Wood

PIMPERNEL
PRESS LTD
www.pimpernelpress.com

To the memory of my parents

The Hunting Lodge, Odiham, Hampshire.

On the Fringe: A Life in Decorating
Copyright © Pimpernel Press Limited 2016
Text copyright © Imogen Taylor and Martin Wood 2016
Photographs copyright © see page 224
Imogen Taylor and Martin Wood have asserted their right to be identified as the authors
of this work in accordance with the Copyright, Designs and Patents Act 1988 (UK).

First Pimpernel Press edition 2016
www.pimpernelpress.com

Designed by Becky Clarke

ISBN 978-1-910258-77-4

Typeset in Griffo Classico and Avenir
Printed in China

9 8 7 6 5 4 3 2 1

COVER 'Blue Leaf', a design by the great
nineteenth-century pattern maker Owen Jones,
produced as a wallpaper by Cole & Sons.

ENDPAPERS 'Stripe on Stripe', designed by John
Fowler and produced by Cole & Sons in many
different colours and widths of stripe.

HALF-TITLE PAGE 39 Brook Street in the 1990s.

FRONTISPIECE 'Berkeley Sprig', a design taken
from an eighteenth-century wallpaper found by
John Fowler in 1962 at 44 Berkeley Square, where
it was being used as a lining paper beneath a
Victorian red damask.

ABOVE John Fowler's country home, the
Hunting Lodge, painted by Donald Church.

Contents

PREFACE

When I decided in my late old age to write this book, it was because I had begun to realize that I had had a unique insight into a world that few knew about and that had changed dramatically. I thought I would be able to record a social history of almost a century, as well as my personal memories. It wasn't long before I realized this would be a huge task and would fill several volumes!

So this is just an edited edition of my life, leaving out so many people, so many happenings, all of the politics and what was occurring in the country, and nearly all of my personal and emotional life. However, I hope it gives a picture of those years and of the elite world I touched on, and that it is fair and reasonably accurate. I have had to delve into my memory, which at my age may be rather unreliable, and I hope my readers will forgive any mistakes.

Decoration is so ephemeral: it vanishes as soon as houses change hands, people die or marriages break down. We are fortunate when we have photographs to remind us of the taste and style of past years. Sadly, little of our work was photographed, much less published, for at the time interior decoration magazines were not ubiquitous, as they are today, and people valued their privacy.

In the end, for all it tells of war, political change and worries about the future of the world, this book is a record of a happy and fulfilling life.

OPPOSITE 'Leopard Stripe', an unusual design copied from an English document of about 1820.

ABOVE Watercolour of the garden at 39 Brook Street, by Marianne Topham, late 1990s.

1

MY FAMILY

I have often wondered what most influences one's life: is it the genes one inherits or the surrounding environment? Of course it is a bit of both, but perhaps the greatest influence is luck. In my life I have always felt I've had a great deal of luck, as though fate had it all planned out for me. Without doubt my greatest stroke of luck was my parents, whom fate somehow brought together against the odds.

In my father's family the dominant characteristic was a gift for music. My great-grandfather, Harry Taylor, was a professor of music and a military drum-maker in Islington, London.[1] He married an Italian singer from

My father with his parents, in about 1927.

ABOVE Great-aunt Trudi.

OPPOSITE 'Fern Chintz'. The neoclassical feeling suggests that this design is from the late eighteenth or early nineteenth century.

the Busoni family of northern Italy. My grandfather, Harold, and his sister, Gertrude (always known as Trudi), lost their Italian mother very early, when she died in childbirth, and suffered a difficult stepmother.[2] Because of the strong musical connections, Harold was sent to the Cathedral Choir School in Bruges, where he saw a little of his much older Busoni cousin Ferruccio Busoni, the renowned pianist and composer.[3] Unfortunately, when the First World War intervened he lost track of his Italian relations.

My great-aunt Trudi had a ghastly life because after the death of my great-grandfather she was left to care for her demanding stepmother. After her stepmother died she earned a rather precarious living sewing for various small companies. When I knew her she lived happily in a tiny crowded flat in Worthing where I often visited her with my parents. It was the first time she had had a home of her own. I remember that she sewed beautifully and was still doing piece work at home.

When my grandfather returned from his education in Bruges he took the civil service exams and became a Whitehall civil servant, not from choice but because it was a safe career. What he did in his work I was never told; his outside interests were more important to him. He married young and had a son called Duncan, but tragically history repeated itself when his young wife died in childbirth, leaving a fragile baby with a club foot. I always felt that it was because of his desperate position, with a new sick baby and a demanding job, that he married again in haste. His second wife, Rosina Webb, who was to be my grandmother, came from a fairly humble family. Her mother was the head housekeeper at the Regent's Street Polytechnic, but I believe her father was addicted to drink and sadly not a provider.

My father Edgar, his brother Howard and their sister Cecily, who were very close to each other in age, were all born in a house just off Clapham Common in London.[4] Their half-brother Duncan was said to be a charming and gentle little boy who loved his new family, but in a Dickensian way tragedy struck. He had a bad cold, yet his stepmother insisted he go to school, no doubt because she had three other children under seven. Duncan developed pneumonia and died at the age of eleven. My father never forgot his half-brother and I don't think my grandfather ever quite got over his unnecessary death. He was seldom home for his other children, and was a distant, rather secretive and remote figure. His main interests were the Musicians' Benevolent Fund, of which he was secretary, and his musical friends. We learnt after his death that he had also been involved with the Secret Service Bureau (forerunner of MI5 and MI6), which had been founded in 1909.

My grandparents moved to a larger house in Putney and my father and Howard were sent to Wandsworth Grammar School. Both boys were sporty and excelled in rugby football and swimming. My father was forbidden by his mother to high-dive and kept his rugger boots hidden for fear of recrimination. Boys will be boys and on one occasion my father, spurred on by others, climbed to the top of the local church spire and then could not get down again! To the horror of my grandmother, the fire brigade had to be called and as an ardent churchgoer she felt the publicity to be a disgrace. The family left the church in shame, They went instead to the Wesleyan chapel, but my father's belief in Christianity had been lost, never to return.

My father left school when he was not yet fifteen. The headmaster begged my grandparents to reconsider, as he was a very promising pupil, but I presume a lack of money was the reason. Not to be defeated, my father took evening classes in English literature and mathematics, which he was particularly interested in. I still have some of his amazingly advanced essays. He was, in fact, self-taught from that time on. My mother and I often wondered what he could have achieved had fate been kinder.

When war was declared in August 1914 my father and my uncle Howard enlisted. Although only seventeen, my father tried to join the Navy, but was rejected because he was short-sighted. He joined the Royal Horse Artillery Company at the very lowest rank, earning sixpence a day looking after the horses. His training was at Wentworth Woodhouse in Yorkshire where he had to deal with horses for the first time. He learnt to ride, and the experience made him a great animal lover all his life. While in barracks he befriended a dog, a Great Dane bitch, who became his constant companion and the regimental mascot. Known as 'Girlie' she seems to have been allowed in camp and on manoeuvres and was fed from shared rations with the help of the kitchen staff. In his innocence my father did

A very young soldier: my father aged seventeen, in early 1915.

not realize that 'Girlie' was pregnant, and the arrival of six Great Dane puppies added to the complications of army life. Their existence had to be kept secret, and they had to have additional milk, which on a sixpenny wage was not easy. Eventually homes were found for them before the regiment went to France. Alas, poor Girlie disappeared one day, and he never saw her again.

Following their brief training the unit was to embark for France. My father recalled riding all the way down from their training ground in Yorkshire to Sturry near Canterbury in Kent, ready for embarkation at Dover. It is difficult to imagine this journey now, along the traffic-less roads and lanes of England, camping en route, watering and feeding the tired horses, and living under canvas. He would recall that time with pleasure, seeing England for the first time, living with young friends, delighting in the pretty villages they rode through in the summer of 1915.

Like so many others, my father never talked about his experiences in the Great War. Nor could he ever read about them or look at television programmes showing photographs of the period. He was in the thick of battle, on a gun battery in the front line, and many of his friends were killed. My father was lucky, comparatively. The gun he was manning was hit by a shell, which killed all the other men and the horses, but he was only badly wounded. With shrapnel deep in his back and the back of his head, he was taken to the newly established American field hospital, which was using a new method of treating such wounds. They cleaned them out and packed them with wadding and sewed them up. This was very successful, although they left a little piece of shrapnel near his spine, which was to cause him agonizing pain from time to time for years to come.

He was invalided out of the army with hepatitis (then known as yellow jaundice), which made recovery a slow affair. It was the last months of the war, and he emerged from the experience, like so many thousands of men, with no career, no money, in poor health and scarred by hideous life-changing experiences. His mother had taken his paltry earnings while he was at the front and, worse still, she had thrown his beloved violin into the attic and broken it. The violin had been a treasured gift from his father, which he enjoyed, showing great promise before the war. He gave up music because of this, but remained addicted to opera and classical music for the rest of his life.

His father encouraged him to sit the civil service entrance exam, for which he had to study hard, and he succeeded in getting into the Home Office (prisons department) as

Walter and Alice Snelling, my mother's parents, in about 1920.

an accountant. It was a dull job for such a man, and it is a pity he did not have a more imaginative, inventive and interesting profession, because I am sure his life would have been very different. But he was lucky to have a job, to live at home and be able to take interesting evening classes. His brother also survived the war, having served in the Royal Flying Corps (it became the Royal Air Force in April 1918) and was to continue his flying career for a few years after the war.

As my father walked through the typing pool in the Home Office, he spotted a girl with blue eyes and curly hair with auburn glints. He was twenty-two and she six months older. He made a passing cheeky remark about her blue eyes. This was how he met my mother. Her family (the Snellings) lived in Upper Norwood, South London, which at the time was a prosperous suburb, occupied in the main by merchants and professionals, surrounding the very active centre of the Crystal Palace. My grandfather on my mother's side was one of seven children. His parents and his six siblings had all emigrated to Vancouver to start life afresh. They lived in a wooden cabin and farmed their land, and all remained in Canada for the rest of their lives. He never saw his parents again. He stayed in Norwood as he had just become engaged to a local girl, a Miss Alice Carbery, who became my grandmother, and together they started a large family. He ran a coal merchant's business on the Crystal Palace Parade, with its own stables and dray horses and quite a large staff.[5]

They lost their first child (probably a cot death) and as a result cosseted the next child, Walter. From then on, nearly every two years, a new baby arrived – two more boys and a girl, then my mother, Edna, followed by a sister who, because she had mental health problems, was never mentioned and the youngest boy, Charlie.[6] They were a noisy, happy, uninhibited family with devoted parents. The children were well educated, the boys being sent to Alleyn's School in Dulwich, and my mother and her sisters to a day school first and then to James Allen's Girls' School in Dulwich, where her music master was the composer Gustav Holst. She had a lovely singing voice and went on to take singing lessons with a French master (unfortunately he was more interested in his pretty pupils than the music and he had to leave in a hurry!). With the coming of the First World War the eldest boys, Walter and Eric, went into the army. Luckily both survived, but they were traumatized by their experiences. My mother took a typing course and joined the Home Office typing pool, where she made a particularly bad typist and loathed office work. My grandparents were horrified by what they regarded as a 'rebound romance' (she had been engaged to marry an army officer who had been killed in the war) and they forbade her to marry a sick, poor, wounded ex-corporal. They did not give up but remained secretly engaged for three years. My father pursued Edna at every opportunity. He would cycle from Putney to Box Hill or Dorking in order to get a glimpse of her if she was going on a family walking expedition. He would wait at the station in hope of seeing her, even though they were not permitted to speak. Luckily, they worked near each other in London and could spend illicit lunch hours together.

My mother has left me with the picture of my father from those days: a lean, curly-haired young man in glasses, crossing Whitehall without looking to left or right, so intent on his book – Cervantes' *Don Quixote*. She always identified him with Don Quixote, tilting at windmills and rescuing maidens in distress. She said she was his faithful companion, Sancho Panza. Eventually – after my father had won over his future mother-in-law with the present of a kitten to replace a recently lost cat – the family relented. My father had saved just enough money to pay the deposit on a tiny house in Wimbledon with a garden and a beautifully built Wendy house at the end of it. He spent every spare hour decorating it for his bride with up-to-the-minute schemes. This was 1923 and blue and silver were the rage, as were wallpaper friezes and art deco

My mother, Edna Snelling, on her wedding day, 23 July 1923. Her dress was *café au lait* chiffon.

china. Although I never saw this scheme, it was described to me as a child and we still had some leftover pieces of china. My father bought a Singer treadle sewing machine and made the curtains and cushions, built bookcases, laid carpets and hung tiles. He taught himself whatever skill was needed. They spent three happy years there, with my father sometimes dashing home at lunchtime to his home-based bride, because he could not bear to be away from her for long. But although both were born and bred Londoners they always hankered after country life and in 1926, when I was on the way, they made the move to Banstead in Surrey, which was then a small country village.

My parents' engagement photo, taken by my father in the early 1920s.

2

I ARRIVE

The first new houses were just being built in Banstead and Mr Bean, who already had a good reputation as a builder, agreed to build a small detached house for £850 complete. My parents raised the money by a private mortgage which was only paid off after the Second World War. Their new house was finished just before I was born and was named, rather romantically, Windflower Cottage, because my parents planted clumps of Japanese anemones along the front path, together with rosemary bushes as a namesake when I was born. I still have rosemary bushes which are descendants of these in my garden in Kent.

I was born there on the 29 October 1926 during a huge thunderstorm. My father went into the village to the only telephone and called the doctor from Sutton, who duly arrived and delivered me with forceps. It was a difficult and painful birth, as my mother had a spinal curvature. Because of this it was considered unwise for her to have any further children, so I never had the brother I longed for. A monthly nurse had been hired, as was then the custom. She was perfectly behaved in front of the doctor, but it transpired she had a secret drink problem and was a disaster as a nurse, leaving me uncovered in the cold and neglecting my mother. She was soon dismissed and my very inexperienced mother took charge, frail as she was. I thrived and was taken on daily walks in my second-hand pram along the country lanes. My very first memory is sitting up in the pram in our small back garden watching a blackbird on the handle of the pram. I must have been about two, but the memory is clear and I have been a passionate bird-lover ever since.

At the time Banstead only had a dairy and as soon as I could walk I would go up the road to the dairy with a little

With my mother in our small back garden in Banstead, Surrey, in 1927.

jug to fetch cream from a big bowl on the counter covered with a beaded muslin cloth. The milk was delivered in a handcart and scooped from a churn into a jug. When I was three or four, two more shops opened: Mr Tonge, the grocer, and a tobacconist's where sweets were also sold. The sweets were displayed at child height, but the counter was above my head, with a large Alsatian seemingly in charge of the shop. Mr Tonge had an assistant at one end of the shop, behind a cage: money was put into a metal capsule

OPPOSITE 'Geranium Leaf', a late nineteenth-century English design, which we found on an upholstered chair Tom Parr bought for the shop.

My parents on their wedding day in July 1923.

and a string pulled to send it flying across the wires to the assistant. Change came back promptly. The whole event was a thrill for a child. Even more thrilling was the glass jar of biscuits on the counter, and Mr Tonge would sometimes give me one free, although they really cost a penny.

My maternal grandfather sadly died of cancer just before my parents' wedding, and so it was a rather sombre event. My grandmother (who was in mourning) did not attend. My widowed grandmother, always known as Nana, lived in a large Victorian house in Upper Norwood and her son Warren and his wife, Nora, lived with her in the upper part of the house. They had a daughter, Edna, and a boy a few months younger than me called Michael. I would go to Upper Norwood every week with my mother to see Nana and play with my cousins. A further two cousins would join us, both slightly older, Peggy and David. It was a noisy, undisciplined group and we had a lot of fun and freedom in the orchard garden and basement of the house. I loved going there and adored my Nana and would often beg to stay overnight and share a bed with cousin Edna. It was on one of these occasions, when I was four and a half, that we were playing soldiers in the hall and Edna managed to stick the

metal ferule of a man's umbrella into my eye. I remember the event well, being rushed in a pushchair to the cottage hospital where the damage was too serious for them to deal with, so I was taken in a taxi to King's College Hospital on Denmark Hill.

Luckily I was seen by a fine eye surgeon, Mr Savin, and his young assistant, Mr Lyle. They operated immediately, using a pad of chloroform over my face as an anaesthetic, and I woke up with bandages round both eyes, completely unable to see. Parents were only allowed very infrequent visits and the fear I had in this lonely, blinded state in a big public ward and with a fierce matron is still very vivid. This was to be one of many visits to hospital and more operations to try and save the eye, if not the sight in it. The final outcome was not too bad as they were able to save my actual eye and although I had no sight in it except a sensation of light and dark, my good eye was excellent. I was to go on to be a one-eyed decorator, supposedly particularly good on colour!

Because of all these operations, I could not go to school, so I learned to read at home. I was read to every evening and particularly loved *Peter Pan* and *Alice in Wonderland*. When I was six I was taken to my first stage performance, a production of *Peter Pan*. This was the beginning of my love of theatre. My parents would often take me to grown-up theatre, but in order to get a cheap seat in the orchestra pit, you had to go early and rent a pit stool to form a queue outside the theatre. You returned later to wait for the doors to open and were entertained by buskers, fiddlers, ventriloquists and singers, almost as amusing to me as the play itself.

In those early years, as the Great Depression began to lift, Banstead grew hugely, with new bow-windowed, Tudor-esque, semi-detached houses for the commuters. With these houses came new roads – although the buses still had open tops – and new shops. In 1933 two young teachers, Madeleine Sabine Pasley and Patricia Wagstaff, bought a large house and opened Greenacre School. I was to be one of the first of its seventeen pupils and never went to another school. Greenacre School became a huge part of my life and Miss Pasley a great influence.

After an initial interview with Miss Pasley, which was an ordeal for my mother as well as me, I joined the tiny kindergarten. At six and a half I was older than the others. I enjoyed it greatly. I made friends with the only boy in the school – there were eighty pupils in the second term – and we became inseparable. After my rather solitary childhood with only occasional visits to cousins, I loved the

Me at London Zoo – with a friend!

My first school photo, from 1934. I am first on the right in the second row.

LEFT   With my grandfather Harold Taylor at West Wittering in 1930. BELOW   The coastguard's cottage at West Wittering, My grandfather rented it for holidays. Eric Gill lived in the house behind.

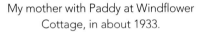

My mother with Paddy at Windflower Cottage, in about 1933.

companionship. Although I was immensely shy (and this shyness persisted until into my twenties), this did not stop me being a tomboy. I got myself and others into all sorts of trouble, but somehow I could usually talk my way out of it, which has proved a useful asset in later life.

My constant companion at this time was our Irish Setter, Paddy, a beautiful dog and totally faithful to his family. He would walk with me across the fields to school every morning, leaving me at the stile and returning home, just as he had earlier accompanied my father across the downs to the steam train at Carshalton. We also had two free-flying canaries, called Peter and Tinkerbell, and a large Belgian rabbit who was a close friend of Paddy's.

My grandfather Harold had a large car with a 'dicky' at the back and he would drive us inordinately slowly to West Wittering, where he rented a coastguard's cottage. It was here that I spent my earliest holidays, on the sands around Chichester harbour, collecting water from the well for my bathtub in front of the kitchen stove. Oil lamps and very simple primitive living, but magical. My parents would have preferred to holiday on our own, avoiding the constant criticisms of my grandmother Rosina. I was her first grandchild, but she did not like girl children, so consequently I was a great disappointment. My grandfather died unexpectedly of a heart attack at sixty-five. After that

my father bought a small Hillman car, and our holidays became camping trips to Devon and Dorset.

My father was always engaged in some project to enrich our lives. Some of my earliest memories are of playing with transistors in all sorts of colours that in my imagination became solders and farm animals. He was in fact making radios in elaborate mahogany cabinets for friends and family. Together with the local doctor, he spent hours perfecting these strange, elaborate machines made of parts he bought at specialist shops. He also constructed a gramophone and played crackly records of Caruso, Dame Maggie Teyte and many others. As another sideline he made objects in leather, copper and wood, and he also did elaborate bookbinding. He built me a Wendy house in the garden, using for the floor blue tiles from a redundant fireplace, and when I was six he made me a wonderful doll's house, complete with electricity and a lift. I papered the walls, carpeted the floors with tweed samples from tailors and lived an imaginary life with the tiny dolls who inhabited my house. Thus began my life as an interior decorator.

In about 1935 my father built a sailing canoe in the back garden. It had a frame in wood that was moulded to shape, covered in canvas, then primed, painted and made waterproof. He made the sails out of sailcloth on the sewing machine, and finally a trailer was constructed to tow the

My father built this twelve-foot canoe in
the back garden at Banstead.

boat. We set off for a sailing holiday on the rivers and coast
of Dorset, camping on a farm and sailing where we wished.
Even now I can smell the scent of the early morning,
waking in a tent with Paddy and sense the thrill of walking
across a muddy field to collect water, milk and eggs and a
slab of very yellow butter from the farmer's wife.

We also went sailing in the west of Ireland, around
Bantry Bay. We could not take the canvas boat, so a folding
rubber canoe with a small sail was bought. My mother was
rather apprehensive and with good reason. I was eight and
went out one afternoon with my father sailing and using
paddles in the bay. We were unaware of the strong currents
and as evening approached we were drifting further out
to sea despite efforts to get to shore. Eventually we drifted
to a headland and were able to land some miles down the
coast. By this time it was dark and a search party was being
mustered back at the B&B where my mother was staying.
We abandoned the boat and started walking, arriving after
midnight, just when the search party was about to set out in
a boat with lanterns. They told us that there were sharks in
the area, and we had certainly been surrounded by seals and
a few dolphins.

In 1937 my parents decided to take a trip to Venice by
train. We stopped on the way in southern Germany, and
again in the Dolomites in Italy. Apart from the battlefields

neither of my parents had ever been abroad and it was a
thrilling adventure. Our time in the beautiful Tyrol in a
village called Mittenwald was idyllic, with mountains and
lakes and wild flowers. My father did a bit of climbing
with some young Germans, all very Aryan, tall and blond-
haired, while my mother and I went to the lake and swam.
We all ate huge meals of sausage, veal and sauerkraut and
marvelled at the capacity of the Germans in the same
hotel. We continued by train to Cortina d'Ampezzo where
we stayed in a hotel high up in the mountains with very
different people and very different food. At last we went
through the Brenner Pass and down to Venice.

A child's view of Venice was very different from a
grown-up's, something that became clear to me when I
visited Venice later in life. But on my first visit, with my
teddy bear in my arms, I loved feeding the pigeons in
St Mark's Square, the trips by boat to the islands and the
Lido. Going to an Armenian monastery where the monks
would not let my mother and me into certain areas and
my father came back with tales of wonderful rather risqué
frescoes and mosaics. Unfortunately our time there was cut
short because my father was bitten by a poisonous fish when
swimming off the Lido in the early morning. By the time we
managed to get him back to the hotel he was unconscious.

A silhouette of me in 1933.

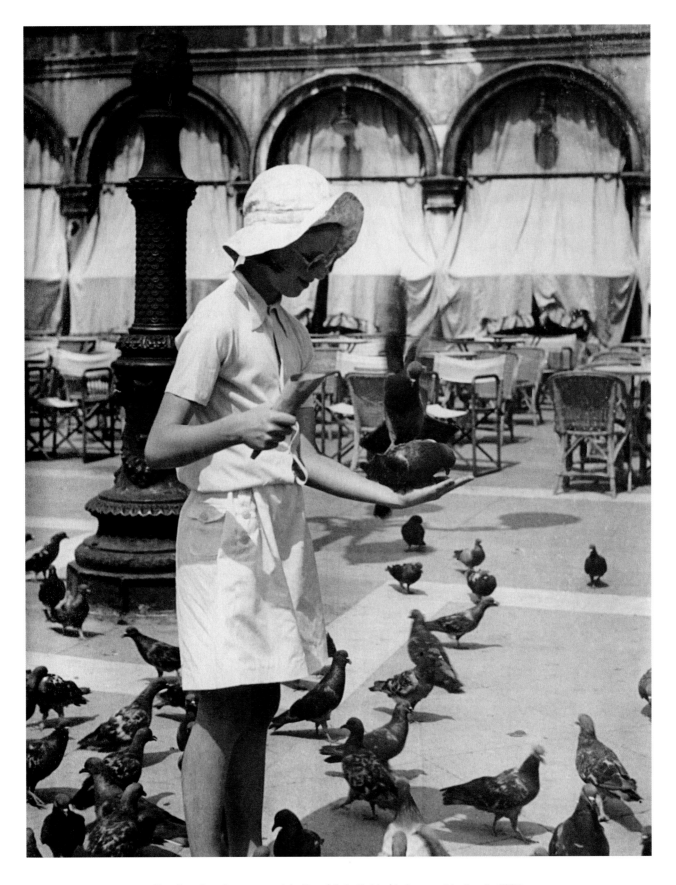

Feeding the pigeons outside Quadri's in St Mark's Square, Venice, in 1937.

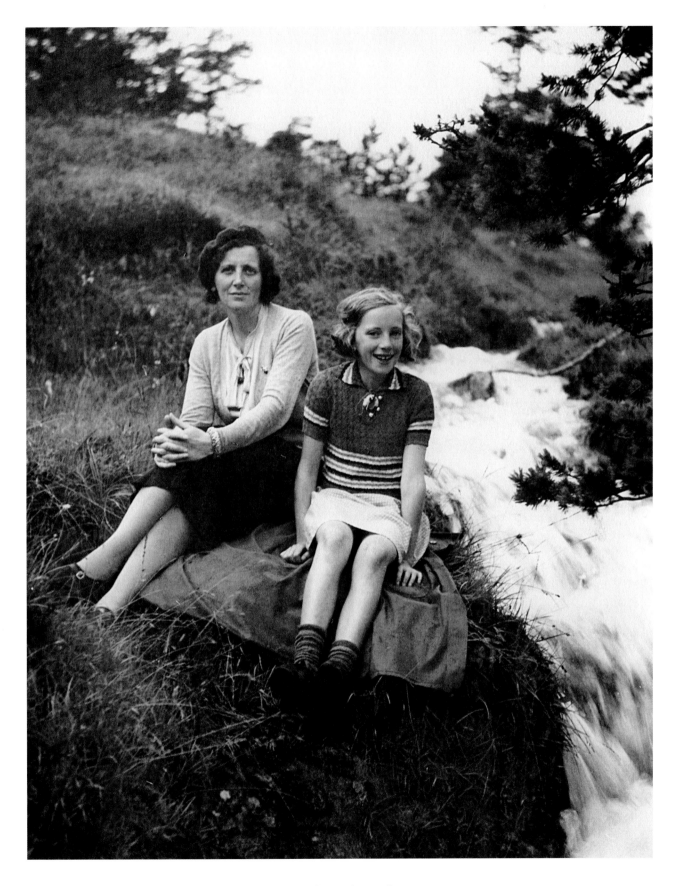

With my mother in the Tyrol in 1937.

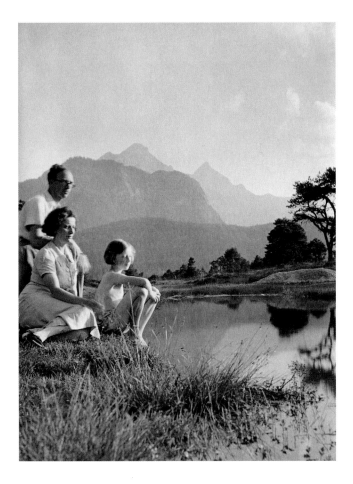

With my parents in the mountains above Mittenwald in 1937.
The photograph was taken and developed by my father.

A doctor gave him an antidote and he recovered over the next twenty-four hours, but this near-death experience had taken the charm from Venice, and we returned to Mittenwald to recover.

On the way through Germany we inadvertently got involved in a Hitler Youth rally in Munich, which was an amazing sight – a vast sea of young boys, Heil Hitler-ing and marching in formation. It made my parents very fearful of what was to come. I don't know if Hitler was taking the salute, but Berchtesgarten was very close so it quite probably was him. A year later Chamberlain came home with his message of 'Peace in our Time'; had he seen that vast rally I doubt he would have believed it. That first trip abroad left a lasting memory, but there would be no more for many years to come.

As the clouds of war gathered, our headmistress had to make plans to evacuate to somewhere safe those children whose parents wished it. We were told to prepare an emergency suitcase, to be ready at all times with sheets and blankets, clothes and gas mask. The moment came in the autumn of 1939 when war was declared, and a coach took us to a country house near Dorchester which had been requisitioned. Turnworth House seemed a lovely place, set in a valley with home farms. The poor owners had to move to a house on the estate and some sixty or seventy girls arrived to take over their home. The grand piano was still in the drawing room and some of their furniture, but the bedrooms were full of folding beds and the dining room was furnished from the school at Banstead. We had a few days before the term started and it was a beautifully hot summer so we made the most of our new country life, riding on the farmer's cart, playing in the hay barn and discovering the livestock. I vividly remember finding an overgrown dog's cemetery and clearing it up and decorating it with flowers. I was missing my best friend, Paddy.

Some of the staff came with us, but others were engaged locally. We had small classes of under twelve and learning, as far as I was concerned, was of secondary importance to a family of orphaned jackdaws that I nurtured and reared. They were very tame and lived in and out of my blazer pocket. They came to a tragic end, killed by a cat in the summer house where I had kept them. I also had a baby brown owl kept in the dormitory, which I fed on hard-boiled egg and grubs. It was a full-time job, but he was successfully released into the wild before the holidays came.

Letters from home told me that my father had been moved to Wormwood Scrubs Prison from Whitehall. The prison building was free because they had to move the prisoners to safety. He was moved to the new Ministry of Food, and his job was to find safe storage places throughout the country for the millions of ration books, which were more valuable than money. This meant he was permanently travelling, leaving my poor mother alone with Paddy in Banstead – alone for the very first time in her life, awaiting bombs and invasion. And the bombs duly came with the Blitz on London.

Not long after, the Ministry of Food was moved out of London to the hotels on the seafront at Lytham St Anne's, Lancashire. My father found a top floor flat where his family could live and the house at Banstead was abandoned. My mother and Paddy joined him and I went up for the holidays.

I did not return to school in Dorset, because of the difficulty of travel from Blackpool to London at the height of the Blitz and on to Dorset when invasion seemed pretty imminent. I vehemently refused to go to school locally, so had a whole year off and enjoyed myself in my new seaside life, taking riding lessons along the sands, fishing on land lines with my father and taking wartime cookery classes. My aunt Edith and my uncle Bryan had been moved to Lytham at the same time with their son, cousin David, who was only two years older than me. While waiting to join the RAF he had a job in the local cinema and was able to get cheap seats, so we spent a lot of time there seeing all the latest Deanna Durbin and Shirley Temple films. There were also some wonderful theatrical productions in nearby Blackpool, London shows with Laurence Olivier and Edith Evans, John Gielgud and others. This part of the war was good for us, out of danger and in a place that was pleasant although to us very foreign. The bombing of Liverpool was grim seen across the bay, but we picked up scraps of wood as it was washed ashore, some of which my father was able to use – I still have in my kitchen a two-tier table he made of driftwood. I also remember, on one wonderful occasion, masses of oranges from a bombed cargo ship, mostly edible despite the salty sea trip. These were the first oranges we had seen for at least two years and the sands were full of beachcombers.

After a year or so, when times were a little calmer, I joined a school friend from Cumberland and we had an adventurous trip back to Greenacre School, which had moved to a house near Wincanton in Somerset. Jill's brother, a dashing army officer, met us in bombed and blacked-out London and gave us a meal before putting us on a train to Somerset. It was a thrilling outing and we felt very grown up, but my principal memory of that day is of going down the Underground and seeing the packed masses of Londoners on the platform, lying almost to the edge, with children and bedding and food and hardly room to move, early in the evening, awaiting the night bombing. I realized how lucky I was to have escaped such a life.

The journey to Wincanton was very long and uncomfortable. The train was packed with many soldiers as well as civilians and the carriage had people lying up in the luggage racks and on the floor. Of course there were no lights and every station was blacked out with the names removed, so you relied on the porters shouting the station names. Finally we arrived and were met by the deputy head. I was too exhausted to take in the new surroundings and all my school friends were in bed, so I gratefully slipped into a temporary bed.

Because I had missed a year I was demoted to the form below, so joined a slightly younger group. Our classroom was the old harness room in the stables, the granary became

a gym and we had a tennis court. The food was very basic – my memory is of being endlessly hungry and eating thick slices of greyish bread with margarine and a scrape of Marmite and jam, ten rounds being a winning number at teatime. But we were never really deprived, and in fact the diet was pretty healthy.

We seldom saw our parents, and only the lucky ones went out at half-term. Our weekly letters were vetted and we were not allowed to write to anyone without permission. I couldn't write to my cousin David, for instance. As girls we saw no men or boys at all, except an elderly music master and the locals in church. The teaching generally was of reasonable standard and Miss Pasley was an excellent English teacher. We would sit around on the floor in her sitting room hearing her expound on the joys of Wordsworth, but hardly mentioning Byron, of whom she disapproved. None of us had ambitions at that time to go to university, though later a couple of my friends did get degrees.

We listened to all Churchill's speeches and were told versions of the news that were edited so as not to alarm us – Dunkirk was barely mentioned, but the D-Day landings were very exciting. My only brush with danger occurred when I caught a particularly bad dose of measles and after being near unconsciousness with a temperature of 104 degrees, I was moved to the local isolation hospital in Wincanton. One evening a bomb was dropped in the grounds of the hospital and I thought the end was nigh. I was able to go into the adjoining ward, which was full of children with scarlet fever, and get them under their beds for safety. It transpired that a German plane on his way home had offloaded the bomb.

My homeless parents had returned to the South of England, and rented temporary accommodation near Richmond, where I spent my holidays. They eventually found a new home that had previously been occupied by Canadian troops between Croydon and Westerham and purchased a 999-year lease with the little money they had. We moved there with our tattered furniture and Paddy at the height of the doodlebug raids and found we were in the path of the nightly raids on London. My father built an Anderson shelter into the chalky hillside garden, where we spent the nights while he was on fire watch in the city. I remember going into the shelter one night and shining my torch on the sleeping figure of my father, who had a large toad sitting under his chin! The war was drawing to a close, but, ironically, this was the most anxious and dangerous part of it for us. However, we survived unscathed.

3

THE WIDE, WIDE WORLD

In 1944 I left school with credits in every subject except maths. I never understood what algebra was about, or what possible use it could have, and luckily I have never had to find out! Although I would have liked to join the WRNS, by the winter of 1944 it was really too late in the war, so I decided to go to Croydon Art School. Our beloved Paddy had died of old age some months before and a golden Cocker Spaniel puppy was bought for me as a consolation. He was christened Trouble. Unfortunately I managed to slip and fall on ice while clutching my new puppy and I badly sprained my wrist. On my first day at art school my left arm was in a sling and I was dressed in a smock made by my father out of some material we had as kitchen curtains!

My art school friends Rita Campling and Audrey Oakden, in 1948.

ABOVE My mother with Trouble, our Cocker Spaniel, 1949.

OPPOSITE 'Josephine', a French dress muslin, probably Napoleonic, transcribed as a printed cotton.

My first life class was an eye-opener. The model was a man naked except for a G-string and red Cuban-heeled shoes. He was heavily made up and struck a dramatic pose. On my large sheet of paper I drew a rather small schoolgirl version of what I saw before me, finishing long before others. My neighbour was doing an enormous drawing in charcoal, contemplating between each stroke and chatting away merrily, and managed to take up the whole morning. I discovered that the model was actually Quentin Crisp, who later wrote his autobiography, *The Naked Civil Servant.*

I spent two years at art school doing a general course and finally specializing in textile design. I doubt if I learnt a great deal, but I enjoyed myself and made a few good friends, and with men returning from the services in 1945 to take up their missed education, I met older and more worldly men for the first time. My generation had a very innocent youth. In the normal way of things the height of frivolity was playing sport, going for long country rambles or joining a poetry reading group. Once a year there was a college dance and there were always concerts when we could afford it. My passion was the Royal Ballet and I used to go to London on the earliest milk train to set up a stool outside the gallery entrance at

Covent Garden for that evening's performance, returning to art school by nine thirty. My friend Rita Campling and I saw some marvellous performances with Robert Helpmann, Léonide Massine, Margot Fonteyn and many other famous performers. I also went to the theatre with my parents and saw John Gielgud, Ralph Richardson, Laurence Olivier, Peggy Ashcroft, Edith Evans and Sybil Thorndike playing some of the great roles. During those dark post-war days the theatre offered an alternative, magic world.

Those years at art school completed my education as I met all types of people and had some independence. I was living at home but earned a little money teaching small children in a private nursery school. Rationing was still severe, so there was no question of buying clothes. We ate as students in a lorry drivers' café, enjoying sausage and mash and jam roly-poly. I cycled to art school or cycled part of the way and left my bike in a newsagent's and bussed into Croydon. My father bought a huge Armstrong Siddeley car with a dividing glass between the front and back seats. It was in this car that I learnt to drive, from my father, but I failed my test when I did not know what was meant when asked to do a three-point turn. I attempted to turn in a narrow suburban road and the huge car reached from kerb to kerb, so it took at least six attempts to get round. After that I had one expensive driving lesson to learn what questions I would be asked and I passed the second time. Subsequently I had company cars and it was not until 1998, when I was seventy-two, that I actually bought my own car.

I took a holiday job which was to have an influence on the whole of my life. I answered an advertisement in *The Lady* for an au pair to help look after three children of ten, twelve and fifteen in Shere in Surrey. I went for an interview and was met at Gomshall station by the fifteen-year-old daughter Janet and her friend Una Mary. I liked Janet instantly, but found her mother rather awe-inspiring. She asked me what I did and I said I was a student. 'A student of what?' My reply of art did not impress her at all and she then asked what was my religion? Church of England, I replied. Had I been a Roman Catholic I wouldn't have had a chance. I got the job because I didn't look like a typical art student, and so became part of the Jones family – Audrey, Humphrey and their children Janet, Philip and Barbara remained close friends throughout their lives and those of their children. I encouraged Philip to draw and paint and realized he had a natural talent.[1]

At the end of my art school course I noticed an advertisement in the *Daily Telegraph* for an au pair to look after two children and a new baby in Paris. This seemed far more exciting than trying to find employment in fabric design. I went for an interview with a Mrs Salmon, who was the mother of the previous au pair and was selecting a replacement for her daughter.

Mrs Salmon lived in the Bayswater Road. I was very impressed with the rich and elaborate apartment and discovered she was a member of the Salmon and Gluckstein families who owned Lyons Corner Houses. I had no experience other than my nursery school job that suited me to look after small children and my French was at best schoolgirl, but I got the job. I was to live in a second-floor apartment overlooking the Seine and the Eiffel Tower and look after and teach English to six-year-old Patrick and four-year-old Dominique. The baby would arrive in two months.

My mother managed to buy some clothing coupons, and bought me a Dior-style camel coat, very full, long and extravagant, and some sensible flat leather walking shoes suitable for a nanny. With a beige beret on my head, I was ready for anything. Which was just as well. The day I arrived off the train in Paris in early November 1947 there was an all-out strike. No buses or Métro and no electricity. So Paris was pitch black and the queue for taxis was a mile long. People were sharing what taxis there were, and I got in with people going roughly in my direction. It all took ages as we dropped people off and I was the last to arrive. Alas, they had given me some money towards their fares, but it was not nearly enough and the taxi driver was greedy, so I had to give him everything I had, a meagre £5. The concierge came out of her candlelit room to tell me to climb the stairs in the dark to the second floor where Mme Formigé was expecting me. I staggered up with my suitcase a step at a time and banged on the door. Claude Formigé, the young mother, was pleased to see me as I was hours late and she had imagined me lost. She spoke little or no English and showed me round the candlelit flat and gave me something to eat before I collapsed into bed.

When I awoke the next morning, Dominique, aged four, was wide-eyed and standing in her cot in my bedroom. It was a surprise for both of us. Rosita, the Basque maid, arrived early and helped me dress Dominique and introduced me to a surly six-year-old Patrick, who was to be taken to school. The strike appeared to be over, and I was told how to take Patrick to school on the single-decker bus with the cage behind. I heard Claude telling her sister on the phone that I seemed quite nice, but did not speak a

Laurence, Patrick and Dominique.

Laurence at twenty months, dancing.

word of French. I could understand a little, but had never learnt to speak except at painful pre-breakfast conversations with a strict French teacher at school. The children chatted away and it was from them I learnt a baby French, using *tu* in all the wrong places, such as to their grandfather.

I count those two years in Paris as my finishing school, because they gave me so much. Post-war occupied France was emerging from great hardship and deprivation, but Paris had not suffered devastating bombing like London, and to my eyes it looked magical. The buildings were grey, but were already being cleaned and repaired. I was paid 10 francs – £1 – a week, all found, and I only had one free afternoon and evening a week and every other Sunday. So my scope was limited. However, I went to all the free museums and galleries and walked the streets admiring the beautifully dressed windows and the fantastic fashions, patisseries and delicatessens, the like of which I had never seen. I managed to go to the ballet very occasionally, to see Roland Petit and Zizi Jeanmaire in the tiny Champs-Élysées theatre, but most of my free time was walking, looking, admiring and absorbing. There was rationing, but also a thriving black market and I revelled in the delicious

food, some of which I had never tasted in my life. Going to collect bread at the baker's was a huge pleasure; the smells and visual delights I retain to this day. As for the dairy, where huge Brie cheeses were stacked on the counter between layers of straw, and yogurt and crème fraîche were ladled into your jug or bowl, this was another delight. I wrote home describing these strange and delicious foods to my poor parents, who were still on very stringent rations in England, even stricter than during the war.

The baby arrived in January and was christened Laurence – a tiny dark-eyed girl who was presented to me very shortly after her arrival. She was a sickly baby and could not keep down her food (a disgusting condensed milk I collected from the ministry offices on coupons). It was discovered that she adenoid problems and found it difficult to swallow. The operation for the removal of her adenoids was done in the apartment, but I refused to be present, as I could not bear to watch. After this, however, her condition gradually improved and I became better at nursing her.

The Formigés were a distinguished family of architects, and Grand-père Formigé had been responsible for the restoration of the Pont du Gard in Provence and the

Sainte-Chapelle in Paris. His son, the father of the three children, was also an architect and had married his cousin Claude at the beginning of the Second World War. Claude's mother belonged to an eminent military family and she ran her own business in the Faubourg Saint-Honoré. Claude's father was responsible for the French part of the Berlin airlift, which occurred during my time in Paris. The children called them 'YeYe' and 'Pape', and they were spoiling grandparents. YeYe would come every evening after work to see her grandchildren and she brought them extravagant presents – Patrick was her favourite so he always got the best presents. She was a charming, elegant woman with a good sense of humour and I learnt through her the extraordinary tight family loyalty the French have. Outside the family they seemed to have very few close friends. I only remember ever meeting one, who happened to be English.

They lived a rather old-fashioned way of life with several rituals. Every Thursday, when they had a half-day off school, my two elder charges had to be dressed in their very best, which consisted of white shirts, shorts, dresses, socks and shoes, which somehow had to be kept immaculate until lunchtime, when we all went next door to visit Grand-père Formigé for a family lunch party. Grand-père lived in an apartment crammed with good furniture and paintings – I remember particularly the Corots – and a dining room in dark panelling in the Dutch style with a great deal of blue and white delft in the form of tiles, plates, jugs and tureens. I sat at one end of the table with the children and marvelled at the most delicious food, cooked by Grand-père's excellent cook. Soufflés to die for, pheasant and partridge from the country estate outside Paris, potatoes cooked in cream, cheeses galore, chocolate desserts. I would sit silently taking in the conversation and the food, and relaying the experience in long letters to my poor deprived parents.

In the summer we spent time at the country estate, a large ugly rambling nineteenth-century house in woodland outside Paris. This was a relief for the children, who had more freedom, but I felt pretty lonely and isolated. During my last year in Paris I managed to get an au pair job for my school friend Jill, working with two small boys, cousins of my three children. Jill and I spent all our limited free time roaming Paris, taking a trip to Versailles, visiting museums and treating ourselves on our limited funds to wonderful patisseries. We were entrusted with the task of taking our five wards to a rented house by the sea at Jullouville in Normandy for a whole month. The Basque maid, Rosita, came to do the cooking and housework while we did the shopping and cared for the children in every way. Quite a responsibility for two young inexperienced and ignorant girls, as all the children were under eight, and the baby Laurence was only about eighteen months old. It was an idyllic time, full of sun and sea, and we had a great deal of fun with the children, who were very easy and disciplined and were put to bed in the early evening, with bedtime stories, just as an English nanny would have done. The parents came down at the end of the holiday for about a week and luckily found all was well. Jill's parents and younger sister Jennifer came to visit. My parents had managed a few days the previous year, staying in a little hotel near where I lived. This was their first sight of Paris and I was allowed a few hours off to be with them. I only saw them twice during the two years I spent in France, this visit to Paris and a week at Christmas, but we wrote constantly.

The time in Paris gave me a love of France and all things French, which has endured throughout my life. I had a dream that perhaps one day I would live again in France, but that was to take almost a lifetime to achieve. At the end of our time, Jill and I saved up £15 each to take a trip round France. We got a lift from one family as far as Narbonne, and from there took a train to Toulon. There we were lucky enough to hitch a lift with a young man in a dashing open sports car all the way along the Riviera to Saint-Tropez, sitting three in the front seat, feeling as though we owned that lifestyle, and were not retired au pairs with a few pounds in our pockets! We stayed that night in an *auberge* in Saint-Tropez, then a modest fishing village with a few yachts in the harbour. A night in a flea-ridden double bed cost us the equivalent of eight shillings for two and we lived on bread, cheese and melons, as this was all we could afford. In Beaulieu we were loaned an empty flat, empty except for a mattress on the floor and a few plates and cups, where we marvelled at the luxurious shops, beautiful villas and the sunshine and glamour of the South of France. We took the train to Annecy where we stayed for two days before returning to Paris – third class, wooden seats, and wrapping ourselves in newspaper to keep warm overnight.

I left my three young charges with great sadness as I had become very attached to them, particularly to the baby Laurence. Not long after I left their parents divorced and a little later, tragically, their father was killed in an accident shooting duck at sea off the Île de Ré. YeYe asked me to go back and help with the children, but by that time my new career had begun so I had to refuse.

A photograph of me taken in 1950, not long after I returned from France..

4

A NEW JOB: COLEFAX & FOWLER

I returned from Paris in September 1949 and desperately needed to find a job. Unfortunately, the only thing I had to sell was a small portfolio of poor fabric designs from my last year of art school. I had learnt about block printing and screen printing, the sort of dyes and mordants that were used, but I was no good because I wasn't properly taught how to design a fabric, and working out repeats and widths wasn't my strong point. I took my little portfolio to places like Heal's on the Tottenham Court Road and Liberty's, but was turned away almost as soon as I had crossed the threshold.

I had a little bit of luck: my father had a colleague, Lloyd Robert, whom we had met in Lytham St Anne's. He was then living in digs in Markham Square in Chelsea and he mentioned me to his landlady, who, it turned out, was a good friend of Gwen Gervis, who lived over the way in Smith Street. Gwen Gervis worked for a firm called Colefax & Fowler (Sibyl Colefax and John Fowler Limited as it was then), where she ran a studio restoring painted furniture. Not very long afterwards I was told I was to go to 39 Brook Street and meet Miss Gervis. Anything for a job, so I put on my best clothes (which were rather few) and, complete with gloves and a hat, of course, I sallied forth.

I had hardly ever been to London, except on an excursion to the theatre and to the park to feed the ducks when I was a child. I took the number 25 bus from Victoria to the top of Bond Street, and it was a great adventure for me to walk down and on to Brook Street. And there was this imposing shop window, beautifully decorated. I think I went to the side door, and was shown into what was known as the Blue Room on the ground floor – it had been Lady Colefax's office and she had always had it

39 Brook Street in the early 1990s.

painted blue. Eventually a lady appeared in an overall and flat shoes: 'So you're Imogen, are you? Well, what can you do?' I explained that I had just come back from being an au pair in France. That didn't get me very far! I then told her I had been an art student, and had specialized a little in fabric design, but had actually done a general course, which included anatomy, architecture and life drawing. This seemed to settle the matter: 'Oh well, we wouldn't be able to pay very much you know,' which didn't matter just as long as I was learning. 'You'd better come along and have a look at the studio.' So I went along a passage on the ground floor and there were a lot of people scraping at pieces of furniture and chatting away.

Miss Gervis turned and said, 'Well, I will give you a try. Would you start on Monday at £2.10s. a week? Bring your overall and some flat shoes, as it's pretty tiring. We work five and half days a week, Saturday till 1 o'clock. Oh and you won't get a holiday for six months, when you will have a week's holiday, and after that you will have to wait another six months for the next week's holiday.' I rushed home to tell my parents I had got a job! We were living in a leased house on Featherbed Lane, a sort of no-man's-land on the outskirts of Croydon on the way to Westerham, our own house having been requisitioned.

I started on 31 October 1949. I found the work boring, but I was absolutely goggle-eyed at everything around me. The house was full of lovely antiques. I ventured upstairs to see the pretty rooms, and I remember going into what was to become Nancy Lancaster's wonderful Yellow Room. It was terribly shabby then, painted a sort of grey-green and virtually empty of furniture because it was very expensive to buy the sort of furniture that would suit a room like that. I worked at Colefax for at least three weeks before John Fowler came into the studio and spotted me – 'Who is that girl? . . . What is this you are doing?' No conversation with him at all, just a brusque enquiry.[1]

In those days Colefax wasn't the huge business it is today. John had two personal assistants: Joyce Morant (known as 'Shearo') and Mrs Hourigan (known as 'Houri'), who ran the jobs he was doing. Barbara Heale (always called 'Heale') dealt with the fabrics. There was a packing room down below, and there were a couple of van men, and a man running the antiques department. The studio was run by Gwen Gervis, who for some reason was always known as 'Guide' (maybe she had acquired the nickname through having been a Girl Guide?). She had worked with John for many years before he joined Sibyl Colefax, as had Shearo and Houri. There was also a company secretary, Mr Carey, a bookkeeper, and I think Mr Carey had a secretary. In all there were nineteen of us in the business at the time, whereas there were over two hundred when I retired.[2]

I had just about got to know the girls and the boy in the studio, who were all attractive people with interesting backgrounds, when I heard that Elizabeth Winn, Nancy Lancaster's niece (Nancy owned the company), was leaving.[3] Elizabeth was the receptionist, which meant answering

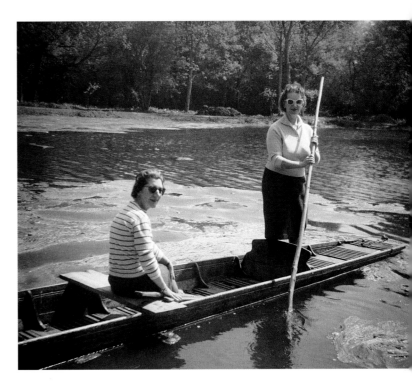

Boating at the Hunting Lodge, with Joyce Morant ('Shearo'), late 1950s.

enquiries from clients looking for a bit of wallpaper to go in their bathroom or a pair of chairs to go on their landing or some such. The receptionist would deal with any minor requests, but anything more elaborate would go to John, as he was the only decorator. I applied for the receptionist's job, which I got, together with a pay rise to £3 a week.

All these wonderfully glamorous people would come into the shop in their Dior 'new-look' clothes – lovely full-skirted coats and dresses, with beautiful fur trimming and fur hats. I would be probed with questions I could not answer, but I would refer them to Joyce Morant and to Mrs Hourigan. Both of these ladies were rather dismissive of me because I was young and probably rather stupid. However, they eventually thawed and once a week I was allowed to join them for lunch in a teashop in South Molton Street. It was the sort of teashop that sold nursery food. Lunch was three and sixpence and would be things like cottage pie with vegetables, and bread and butter pudding. I couldn't run to coffee and it wasn't easy to budget the three and sixpence out of my £3, which had to cover all my fares and everything. But having lunch with them was one way of getting into their lives, learning a little bit more about the business and the clients, and becoming friends with these rather superior beings.

Cyril Wopshott, Muriel Hourigan ('Houri'), Peter Atkins and me (lurking behind the tulips) at the Old Vienna restaurant, mid-1960s.

Barbara Heale, ('Heale'), on holiday in Portugal, mid-1950s.

Gwen Gervis ('Guide'), at the Hunting Lodge, mid-1950s.

Elizabeth Winn with Rachel and Corin Redgrave, mid-1960s.

One day John stopped me in the hall and said to me, 'I've got Lord Waterpark coming in with his fiancée.[4] They are going to live in the highlands of Kenya. She is French and only speaks French. I understand from Houri that you speak a bit of French, so I would like you to come in on the meeting and if we get the job you can do it.' They were a charming young couple and I spoke a little French to her and translated what John was saying.

The brief was very demanding. We were going to do a bedroom for them on a coffee plantation in the highlands of Kenya. They wanted to have a new four-poster bed made, but it had to be a termite-proof. It was to be hung with English chintz, but this mustn't touch the floor in case the termites whipped up the curtains. Paraffin was mentioned as a possible solution, because termites don't like paraffin, so I had little metal trays made for the legs of the bed to stand in and these were regularly filled with paraffin. I gather it worked. The bed was hung in a Regency Revival chintz, which had come from a document of trellis chintz with a border in dark green and white. Everything then had to be shipped from

John holding a piece of silk damask. He had Coles make a wallpaper from it using traditional wood blocks. This became known as 'Double Damask' design and was used extensively.

the Port of London and it was a huge learning curve finding out how to do this and complete all the documentation. The bed did eventually arrive and was set up but soon after the Kenyan estate had to be abandoned because of the Mau Mau uprising. I was rather sad that the young couple never came back to Colefax.

At this time I was also working as a gofer for Mrs Hourigan, which meant I learnt an awful lot. She sent me off to the City to the trimmings makers, to the dyers in Hammersmith, or the upholsterers in the Swiss Cottage. This was how I met many people who were to become very important in my life, and how I learnt the trade. But then John fell out with Mrs Hourigan. Houri had been with him for years, since the time when he was running a decorating business from his own house in the King's Road. (She did his accounts with a typewriter on the draining board of his kitchen sink, which must have been quite a change for her as she had previously worked at the 'Pru'.) But John was by nature intolerant and by this time he had probably tired of her and decided to get rid of her. He made life difficult for her, and she had to send messages via me. It was ridiculous and no way to run a business, but I ended up as the go-between. Eventually Mrs Hourigan left to work for Kenneth Villers and then started her own business, sharing a shop in the King's Road with Michael Raymond, who had an antiques showroom while she ran her decorating business upstairs.[5] She was very successful and did a lot of work for Her Majesty the Queen.

After Houri left I was given her job. I moved upstairs into her old office – my salary went up again, from £3 to £5, and I was allowed to have an assistant.

None of my friends understood what I did. People didn't know about interior decorators in those days as we were such a rare breed. You could certainly name them on the fingers of one hand (there was Mrs Monro, of course, but Syrie Maugham and Dolly Mann had retired by then).[6] There were the commercial decorators such as Keebles, Lenygon & Morant, and Hammond's. John Fowler, however, was definitely an haute couture decorator, and we thought of ourselves as the crème de le crème.

Becoming a client was a bit intimidating. The client would ring and make an appointment. When they arrived they were shown upstairs by the receptionist and I would meet them at the top of the stairs and take them into John's room. This was an extraordinary place. Lovely eighteeenth-century panelling, with John sitting at his desk by the window overlooking the garden – not ideal for seeing colours because there was a big fig tree outside the window and the light was slightly dim. There was a big set of shelves behind his desk with masses of things on them like bits of carving, lanterns and cornice mouldings – an extraordinary mixture of objects. Opposite his desk along the other wall were thousands of pieces of fabric he had accumulated over the years. There were off-cuts and antique pieces from the back of an old curtain (or, actually, anything) graded in colours – pale blue, dark blue, pink, red, scarlet, brown, green, purple, etc. – all the way down the wall. They were tied, knotted with a ribbon and hung on to hooks. In order to describe a colour for a wall he would pull down a pale bluey-green and say 'perhaps this green?' or he would say 'Find me the Eden green, or the Cliveden blue,' or 'You know, that red we had yesterday' – and from such a vague

description you had to know it was sealing wax red. There were hundreds of these colour samples and none were labelled. Only the ones he used regularly had names, which came either from some job, such as 'Rushbrooke pink', or were related to a painting – 'Nattier blue', perhaps, for the soft blue Jean-Marc Nattier often used in his paintings. That sort of thing.

John had a way of dealing with clients, although it rather depended on how the client had come to us. Many were Nancy's friends or relations, so there wasn't the vetting that would go on with an unknown client. If they were unknown to him, there was an initial interview to gauge what they were like and what they wanted. It was usually to help with a house they had inherited, but which had been requisitioned during the war, and they needed to make some alterations because you couldn't get staff as in pre-war days. It typically started off with them wanting help with the entrance hall and just the main reception rooms – the drawing room and the dining room. Often they would bring a photograph, but John would always ask them to describe at least the drawing room. You would get some vague reply like, 'It's a long room; there's a fireplace. I can't remember how many windows it has.' They could never remember whether it faced north, south, east or west; had three or four windows, or indeed no windows at all, nor exactly where the fireplace was. John would say, 'If you entered by the main door, did you go out of another door?' and they couldn't remember. It is most extraordinary how people live in a house and don't quite know it at all. In the end, if John liked them, he would say, 'Well, I think I should come and see it. Do you have a driver who could perhaps meet me at York station?' There would never be any mention of money, and we didn't charge a day fee in those days.

From the photograph we would see it was perhaps a nice Georgian house, maybe with wings on the sides, so John would know roughly the feel of the place and we would pack a little package of things for him to take. When he returned I would be brought in to take notes from the visit and to describe to the owner what the next move was to be – not an easy task, as John himself didn't describe things terribly well. Invariably I would get hopelessly confused. Later, I would go on trips with him, because it was easier. Later still, I would always make sure my staff came with me, because you can't do things 'blind'; and they would also remember things that I didn't remember, like the space above the window or the fact it was butting on to a wall – very important when it comes to curtains, etc.

By the late 1940s and early 1950s John was beginning to build up a reputation and we were getting clients like the Buccleuchs, the Haddingtons and the Ancasters, who had such lovely, important houses.[7]

One very important client was Nancy Astor, Nancy Lancaster's aunt, who was famous for being the first woman to take her seat in the House of Commons. When I knew her she was no longer an MP – her family had made her stand down in 1945 – but she was still living at Hill Street, Mayfair, in amazing style, with a butler, a footman, a housekeeper and a chef. She also had a lady's maid, who had been with her forever.

When Lady Astor's husband, the 2nd Viscount Astor, died in 1952 she moved from this enormous house in Hill Street, downsizing to what she thought was a simple pied-à-terre – two huge apartments on the first floor of an Eaton Square house. John created the prettiest of sitting rooms for her. She wanted a symphony of blues, something that can be difficult to put together, but he achieved it by combining a very pretty blue and white and light beige chintz with green-blue walls. Quite strong, and suitable for her, because she was not a pale character. It was full of her pictures and books, and was a lovely lived-in room.

Next door was the drawing room, which was used for receptions and was about sixty feet long, with tall windows overlooking Eaton Square. It had double doors between the two halves and the doors were being glazed with three tones of white, as usual. And, in a devastating way, I managed to walk through and kick the can of paint, which was very liquid, the consistency of milk, right down the centre of the carpet. Nothing would get that stain out. I had to break the news, first of all to Lady Astor and then – much worse – to John. Strangely enough, in really terrible dramas John didn't react badly. So instead of firing me on the spot – which he had good reason to do – he said, 'Well, dear, we've got to replace the carpet, that's all we can do.'

I contacted the manufacturer who had just woven this carpet, and told him the terrible story. As luck would have it they had over-ordered on the wool (which had been dyed especially), and there was enough left for them to be able to supply a strip that could be sewn in all down the centre.

Of course, a lot of John's clients stayed with him for years, and would come back to him if they moved. I used to think that some clients moved house just so they could employ him again! The actress Joan Dennis springs to mind.[8] John had already worked for her at Riverhall in Sussex, but at that time, because of the war and rationing, it had to be done using just whatever they could find. She had a store of a few bits and pieces of fabric, but the only things off ration were nurses' uniform cotton and a new fabric called noil, which was made of the slub ends of silk left over from making parachutes. John made an enchanting large cottage, using what they had very imaginatively.

Joan was a generous soul who worshipped the ground John stood on, and agreed with everything he said. Because she didn't stand up to him, he was awful to her – rude, dismissive and bullying. However, he did produce lovely things for her. After the war, she and her husband bought a mews house, 43 Hay's Mews, off Berkeley Square. I have to confess that I didn't think it had much potential. There was a nice entrance courtyard, but after that it was a series of rather low dark rooms on the ground floor, with a poor staircase leading to small bedrooms. But John transformed it into a delight.

First he suggested removing the ceiling in the drawing room to make a double-height room. This was an apse-ended room with a low ceiling, and it had an Eric Gill mural of some classical naked figures on the wall. I was incredibly impressed by this, but John dismissed it as being entirely unimportant, so we covered it up with bookcases to make a sort of library with a desk. The main part of the room was a beautiful warm blue. It had lovely arched windows opening on to the courtyard. For these John designed amazingly elaborate silk taffeta draperies – Dior-like ballroom curtains. John knew exactly how they should be cut so they seemed as though they were sort of blown up, pinned up, without much thought – whereas, on the contrary, an enormous amount of thought had gone into how they worked. He knew how to do this because he studied paintings of eighteenth-century rooms where the draperies looked as though they were pinned up casually, with a loose look. At Colefax we always made our draperies very loose. And it was John who taught the upholsterers how to do it.

Joan's mews needed a huge amount of work. For example, because the double-height room cut the upstairs in two, it was necessary to make a staircase at either end. But it ended up a remarkable house, beautifully detailed, Subsequently the house was bought by Drue Heinz of the Heinz tomato soup fortune and we redecorated it. That was a completely different job and far from being acquiescent, charming or easy, she was spoilt and difficult. The results were nowhere near as good as the first work. I have noticed that it is very difficult to redo a room you originally did,

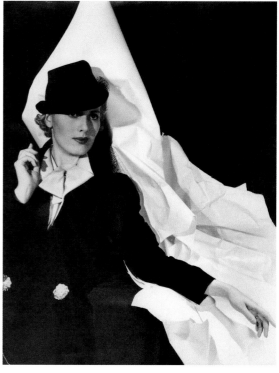

ABOVE John's old friend and client the actress Joan Dennis, in a studio photograph from the 1930s.
LEFT The drawing room John created for Joan Dennis in her Hay's Mews house by removing the floor above to create a double-height room.

even after a gap of twenty or more years, because you can never get that freshness of the first time: the ghost of the old scheme seems to haunt you.

We had quite a few theatrical clients. As well as Joan Dennis there were the Redgraves, who were old friends of John's. It was the Redgraves who introduced him to Laurence Olivier and Vivien Leigh, then at the top of their careers.[9] Laurence was extremely handsome, and Vivien

was very beautiful. But we soon discovered how difficult she could be – up one moment, down the next, and very demanding. They had bought a house near Aylesbury called Notley Abbey. This was by no means an easy house to tackle, and there wasn't a vast amount of money. In a roof area above a bedroom, we found something very interesting – some very early wall paintings of acorns and oak leaves. We had a fabric designed around these

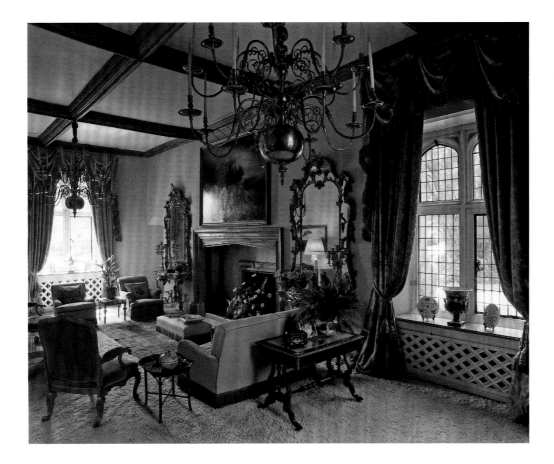

paintings – Nancy Graves did this for us.[10] We called the fabric 'Notley Nuts', and had it printed on rather coarse off-white cotton. This made attractive rustic curtains in one of the large rooms.

The Oliviers then bought a small top floor flat in Eaton Square, and Keith Irving, who had just joined the firm, helped John not only to decorate but also to put up with all Vivien's dramas. John devised a very different sort of bedroom, entirely hung in chintz, which was gathered loose to the floor and not stretched on the walls, as was the norm. The chintz covered doors and windows and had to be hitched back. As Laurence was in sort of regal mode, John did a purple dressing room for him, complete with velvet curtains. Fortunately for me, I didn't have anything to do with this flat; but Keith Irving dined out on the stories for years.[11]

Of course, the Oliviers were 'celebrity' clients, but at the same time we were working for clients from the old aristocracy, such as Anne Feversham, daughter of Lord Halifax. She was married to 'Sim' Feversham (Charles Duncombe, 3rd Earl of Feversham), who had inherited the Duncombe Park estates in North Yorkshire.[12] Duncombe Park was by then a school, and the Fevershams were

living in a large house on the estate called Norton Towers. 'Sim' Feversham was a collector of paintings and antique furniture, and was fascinated by the whole project. It's interesting to me, looking back through my career, how many men have been involved in the decorating of their houses. It's true that sometimes I dealt exclusively with the wife and the husband seemed to be there merely to sign the cheque. But this has by no means always been the case.

I remember going up to York with John, on a visit to the Fevershams, and as the train pulled into the station, I was busy gathering up the cases (I always had to carry the cases or shift pianos, so it's hardly surprising I have a terrible back!), John fell in the carriage, his foot having gone to sleep so it didn't support him. I heard him say, 'Oh, I think I've broken my ankle.' I had to wave to the guard to stop the train leaving and eventually found him a wheelchair, although I was sharply told, 'Don't be a fool, I'm not going to be seen going along York station in a wheelchair.' However, the guard had already brought one, a wonderful old-fashioned mahogany chair with a carpet seat and huge wheels, rolling towards us with John hobbling on one foot towards it. The Fevershams had sent a car so the chauffeur

coloured silk with the rose emblem in a paler shade, to use as a curtain edging. We also made the most magnificent cushions with tassels at each corner – every tassel was a work of art – for the Chippendale suite of furniture which the Queen already had. This was picked out in blue, so John did the walls in a beautiful pale shade of blue (the Queen likes blue) and brought in a great Aubusson carpet in browns, which complemented the silk. The room has since been repainted, but it remains exactly as John did it.

It was interesting to go from this room to working at Waddesdon for the Rothschilds. Mrs James ('Dolly') de Rothschild telephoned and asked to speak to John.[13] Her husband had died and she was leaving Waddesdon and moving to Eythrope, a house in the park which had been built by Alice de Rothschild – but only as a pavilion with no bedrooms. James and Dolly de Rothschild had added a wing with bedrooms, but they never lived in it. It was let to Syrie Maugham. After the war they decided to move there but they were still were doing alterations when James de Rothschild sadly died. Dolly telephoned to ask John to help her, but he was caught out and didn't realize who she was. Amazingly, he said to her, 'Er – do you have some pretty things?' She was appropriately taken aback, but replied, 'Mr Fowler, I have the best.' A great put-down. She did rag him about this later.

Dolly de Rothschild was an extraordinary character. She went into the most extravagant mourning when her husband died: even her car was blacked out – all the chrome on the wheels and on the headlights was painted black – and she wore nothing but grey or black for almost the rest of her life. Her clothes were always similar: a jacket and skirt, a silk shirt with a foulard collar, and handmade black lace-up shoes. She was probably, aside from the Queen, the richest woman in England and she had lived in one of the most magnificent houses in the country, filled, as she said herself, with the very best. But she was not in the least showy.

One of the first jobs we did for her was in Waddesdon itself – installing some display cases for buttons and Sèvres porcelain. Initially it was just John, myself and the architect. Dolly said, 'We're going to have lunch in the small dining room', which was a relief because the big dining room upstairs is huge. The small dining room, though a relatively modest room, had a large round table, beautifully laid with glass, a lovely table centre and little menus on ivory before every place written in French. There was Sèvres porcelain, silver and silver-gilt cutlery. Altogether, it looked rather grand – and this was, after all, just a working lunch for us.

took us directly to York General Hospital and John emerged with his foot in plaster.

When we eventually arrived at the Fevershams' after all this drama John said, 'I'm very sorry, Anne, but I can't possibly stay the night. I'm going to have to go back today because I'm seeing the Queen on Wednesday and I must get this sorted out.'

In the event, all they were able to do was fit a huge leather boot over the plaster, so it resembled an elephant's foot!

At the time (March 1960) John was decorating the Audience Room at Buckingham Palace for the Queen. It wasn't a major decorating task, rather rehashing an existing room, but as it was for the Queen even John was overawed. The Audience Room is where the Queen meets the Prime Minster every week and other important guests. The Queen was extremely kind to John. Although I didn't do the actual work on the room (Shearo did that), I seemed to get involved in various parts. It was a beautiful room, and the Queen was impressed because John brought with him a piece of ribbon which had belonged to Queen Victoria. It was a dark green ribbon with a rose in silvery white. He had it transcribed and especially woven in a sort of coffee-

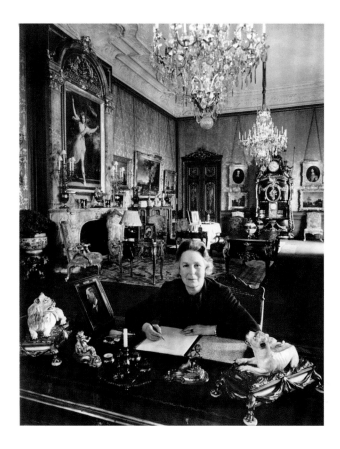

Mrs James ('Dolly') de Rothschild at Waddesdon, 1960s.

reds. They weren't used in the house, but were just there for the family and guests to walk through as they did a tour of the gardens.

Dolly had quite a few eccentricities. There was the endless mourning of course, but apparently she would also wash her own hair in rainwater collected from the roof. This involved bringing filtered rainwater through to her bathroom on a separate tap. You might have thought she would have a pretty four-poster bed, but her bed was more like a hospital or school iron bedstead, placed on plain floorboards with just a small rug by the bed. It was very austere, with a complete absence of comfort, prettiness or femininity. Her car was a Rover (when you might have expected a Rolls Royce or a Bentley) and she always drove herself, or seemed to, though I assume she had a chauffeur. She did have a lovely companion, Miss Brassy (Mary Brassy), always called Miss BB, who followed her anywhere. Everyone loved Miss BB. She was rather 'jolly hockey sticks' – a sort of Joyce Grenfell character, larger than life, large-boned and rather awkward – the absolute opposite of Dolly Rothschild.

Eythrope was an interesting project for us, as an empty house which was to be filled with amazing things to be brought from Waddesdon. At the same time, in Paris, Dolly bought two panelled rooms from eighteenth-century *hôtels*, and rooms were created to fit these boiseries. She had one comfortable room, not like a French château, and this was the library.

When the house was finished she very kindly asked my parents to tea to see what we had done. Rather to my embarrassment, my father rushed around saying, 'Hah! Mrs Rothschild, what beautiful Sèvres!' Or, looking at the chandeliers, 'Magnificent! I've never seen anything as good as that!' Which pleased her enormously.

What she wanted was a mini-Waddesdon, but in reality Eythrope wasn't a very exciting house. Driving down, she would leave her large London house in St James's Place, and the butler would alert the butler at the other house. As she drove up in her little black Rover the door would open as if by magic. Dolly would come into Colefax dressed in a mackintosh – but the mackintosh was lined in fur – carrying a Marks & Spencer shopping bag, She said she liked shopping in Marks & Spencer because they allowed you to change anything if it was wrong! I couldn't imagine what she bought in Marks & Spencer because her wardrobe, which seemed about fifty feet long, was full of skirts and jackets in grey and black, with row upon row of black shoes.

We were served by a butler and two footmen, which was quite unusual in those days. I think that was the first time I had ever been served by a footman. Lunch was not difficult, she was easy to talk to, and John was very reverential to her and flattered her, which she liked. Eventually we came to dessert: four comice pears were brought in, just as nature intended, but served on Sèvres plates. The table was laid with silver-gilt dessert knives, forks and spoons, and I wasn't quite sure how to tackle this. I held back and watched Dolly, who proceeded to cut the top off the pear like a boiled egg and, using the little pointy silver-gilt spoon, she spooned out around the core of the pear. I followed suit: it was indeed an absolutely perfect pear.

I remember being taken around the wonderful kitchen gardens, walking through the nectarine house, the peach house, and a hothouse with Muscat grapes. There was also a very large free-standing greenhouse filled with the amazing scent of myriad Brompton stocks, grown in pots, tiered on both sides, and graded from white at the bottom to purple at the top through all the shades of pinks and

She was always extremely nice to me, and obviously understood that John was by nature irascible and difficult – though never to her. He was on his best behaviour and, after his faux pas, was a contrite man. Of course, the whole thing was a bit of a charade, but Miss BB was the saving grace because she had her rather large feet planted firmly on the ground. In reality it was the end of an era, with Dolly trying to keep things going in the old pre-war way with footmen and Brompton stocks, but at the same time seeking to play down her life.

John loved France and all things French, so he was in his element at Waddesdon. Funnily enough, he never travelled much in France, except to Paris and Versailles, and aside from Château Latour (which he visited), and Château de la Croix des Gardes near Cannes (which he did not visit), he never worked in France.

In 1963 Lord Cowdray, in conjunction with Harvey's of Bristol, bought Château Latour – a small, extremely exclusive vineyard, and a nineteenth-century château.[14] As John had done the drawing room at Cowdray Park they asked him to decorate the château so it looked English – which was tricky in what was effectively a nineteeenth-century French box. It was not enormously big, but had an imposing drawing room and dining room, which were suitable for entertaining, and four bedrooms with bed alcoves. Sadly, John was ill at the time. However, he came over to see it and planned the decoration with Lady Cowdray. But then it was up to me to carry it all out, with George Oakes.

Having been left to our own devices George and I enjoyed ourselves enormously. I remember the arrival of all

LEFT TO RIGHT Château Latour, seen across the vineyards; John and George hard at work at Latour; the *vendange* at Latour, 1968.

the things we'd had made for the house in big containers. They were unpacked on the drive. Every single curtain needed ironing, because they had been in store. In my best French I asked if there was anybody who could help with some ironing, so a group of ladies who would normally be picking grapes set up the *vendange* tables (used to give the pickers their lunch), put blankets over them and ironed the curtains on the drive. The irons were flat irons with gas cylinders and very heavy. I looked at some of these curtains, which cost a fortune, and the irons heating up and I thought there would be a disaster, but they spat on their irons, got the temperature right and then worked away, laughing, chatting and thinking that this was a great joke. Somehow they got them looking pristine, and Peter Atkins hung them all.

When it was finished we celebrated with the opera and dinner in a grand hotel in Bordeaux. Lord Cowdray announced we were going to celebrate with a glass of Château Latour 1926 because that was the year his wife was born (it was also, as it happens, the year I was born). The sommelier came with a candle to decant the bottle, which was full of sediment. It was like drinking inky velvet, but Lord Cowdray drank only whisky with his dinner: although he had bought this famous estate, he didn't really like wine.

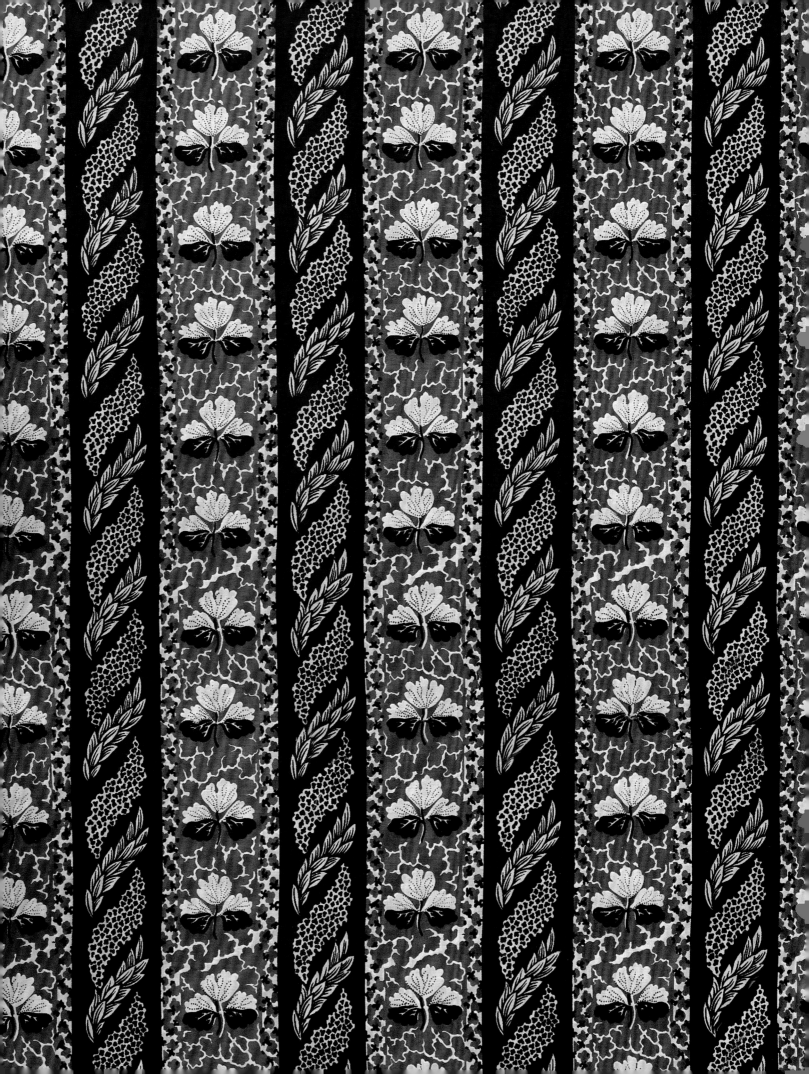

'JEKYLL & HYDE': JOHN FOWLER

5

John Fowler as a man was a mass of contradictions. He could be charming and he could be very cruel. He was often totally unreasonable, but within that unreason there was someone who was reasonable. He could be quite understanding (as, for example, when I kicked that can of paint down Lady Astor's drawing room carpet, when he could easily have gone berserk), but then he could be very silly about inconsequential things. He was all these things and more. A lot of the fun was the creating, and he was certainly very creative. Despite all the tantrums I grew to like John very much, not least because he was teaching me and introducing me to fascinating things. When he was in a good mood he would talk about history, fabrics or trimmings, architecture, porcelain or pictures, whatever it was, always teaching benignly, if slightly irritably – 'You fool, you don't know.'

John Fowler at the Hunting Lodge, 1960s.

ABOVE Pookie and me in 1952: the first of my five budgies and the only one to turn a somersault when asked!

OPPOSITE 'Strawberry Leaf', a Georgian pattern thought to date from about 1760. It was found by John Fowler, who gave the original document to the Victoria and Albert Museum.

He was a strange man really, one might say a 'mixed-up' person, but I think I sensed his vulnerability. I realized why he was as he was, though I didn't quite understand his childhood and its problems. To be homosexual at that time (homosexuality was illegal until 1967) was terribly difficult and that affected him deeply, but he always hid that side of his life, as indeed he had to.

However, he did take his frustrations out on other people, by bullying them – I suppose because he had been bullied. I have never really forgiven the sadistic side of his nature: hitting out at vulnerable people isn't attractive. But if you stood up to him and became invaluable to him – and I became invaluable, along with George Oakes – he began to respect you. Gradually he began to say, 'Come along, dear, we are going to have something nice with supper,' or 'Come down to the cottage at the weekend,' or 'I'll take you to Osterley Park,' or some such thing. To be honest, it was all a bit like being a dog with an irascible owner – we, the

dogs, waiting for treats but cowering in the corner when the master lost his temper.

The bullying and the bluster hid his insecurity, and he was always on the valerian, swigging it to calm his nerves. It's quite extraordinary that after years and years of experience, coping with all sorts of people, he would still dread dealing with a new client if he thought they might be difficult in any way. (On the other hand, with people like poor old Joan Dennis, whom he knew very well and for whom he didn't need a swig of valerian, if he was getting

LEFT John Fowler (plus parrot) in the sitting room at the Hunting Lodge.
BELOW The sitting room at 22 King's Road in 1939. It was still exactly like this when I first met John in 1949.

bored, or if they weren't behaving – by which he meant following his ideas – he would go and sort out his laundry.)

John was forty-three when I first met him, so a youngish man, but he'd had a lot of experience in the trade by then. Dressed in immaculate suits, with highly polished shoes, he always cut a very tidy figure. He was of medium height, trim, sort of light on his feet. He had enjoyed dancing as a young man – he possibly fancied himself as a ballet dancer – and he had this extraordinary way of entering a room. His old friend Alan Gore used to imitate him. He would do a sort of float as he came into the room. People have mannerisms and that was one of his. Nancy would fling open the door, come in and take over. John floated in.

When I first knew him he lived in a leasehold house, parts of which he let off, in the King's Road. It was a run-down, rather ramshackle late eighteenth-century house on an assured tenancy of £50 a year. It was falling around his ears. The kitchen had an old china sink with funny old taps that didn't quite work, a rather ancient gas cooker, really basic stuff, and a very basic bathroom on the staircase landing. Tenants on the top floor, tenants on the bottom floor, and John sort of sandwiched in the middle.

When he gave up the lease on the King's Road house in 1960 he came and lived at Brook Street, in the back room with a little wash place and loo. Mrs Roach, the Brook Street cleaning lady, was a good cockney lady and she would come in about six o'clock in the morning and take him his cup of tea. When I came in she would say, having sussed him out, 'I wouldn't go in there this morning: he's purple in the face!' Or she'd say, 'Quite good, actually.' He had high blood pressure, hence the purple face, so the bad mood could be a result of his health, or it might be too much drink the night before, or simply exhaustion from the journey he had made. He was very moody, and you didn't cross that bad mood or it wouldn't be worth your life.

He had a salary from Nancy. I have no idea what it was, but neither of them had any sense of money and I think he thought that money came from somewhere above, sort of grew on trees. John didn't have a champagne income, but he most certainly had champagne tastes. His shirts came from Turnbull & Asser: he liked to think big, so he would just say, 'Imo, would you order me twelve shirts like the ones I had last time.' He would have his suits made in Savile Row and always ordered his wine from Berry Brothers, by the case of course, and six gins – all things that were mind-boggling to me. He was perpetually in debt, though he never seemed to get into too much debt until the time came

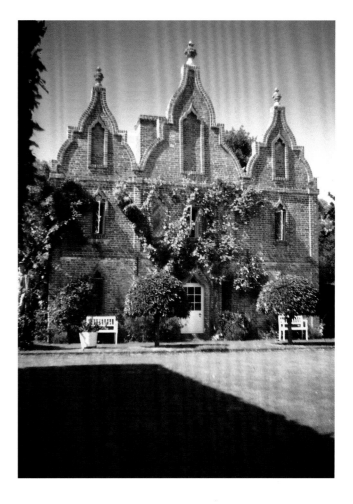

The Hunting Lodge near Odiham in Hampshire was John's home from 1947 until his death.

when he inadvertently didn't pay his income tax for three years! He didn't know anything about it and had probably torn up the letters as they arrived, assuming his accountants were dealing with them. It looked as though he would have to sell the Hunting Lodge, but when Lady Ancaster heard this she settled the £12,000 he owed.

This detachment from money and economic reality spilled over into his work. It was lovely to travel with him because we would be met by a nice car (having travelled first class on the train, of course). When we came back to London I would have to prepare estimates for the proposed works. I would write my estimates by hand on foolscap paper and then my assistant would type them out. Estimates were sent on everything, but John never appreciated that they had to be accurate, because the client needed to have some idea how much the work was going to cost. Money didn't come into the equation; he was just creating. Sometimes I would say,

'If we use that taffeta to line the tails it really will cost a fortune.' 'Well, never mind, they're rich,' he would airily say. Pressing the point, I would explain that they might just jib at the expense because after all it was only a lining, and you would just see a glimpse through the fringe at the bottom. It was never a question of economy with him, but in a funny sort of way he could create amazing things out of virtually nothing.

I had replaced Elizabeth Winn, who was a friend of John's, and they were forever going out to supper together and going to the theatre or the opera, so it was a different relationship.[1] My position was also different from George Oakes's. John had first employed George as a freelance painter and later offered him a job at Colefax, so they started on more of a friendship basis. I started as Houri's minion or her slave, but eventually I became indispensable to John and then it would be 'darling this and darling that'. The chaps were always called 'childies', whereas we girls were 'darlings'. There was a moment when I thought I've had enough of this. I saw an advertisement in the newspaper for an au pair in Rome to an Italian family with two boys and, as I had done it before, I applied but was turned down by *la contessa* because I was too young. I wasn't that young! But she probably thought I was too young to handle two boys in their early teens.

TOP A painting by Alexandre Serebriakoff of the red bedroom in about 1949.
ABOVE The sitting room, again painted by Serebriakoff. This was a rather small room, only twelve feet square.

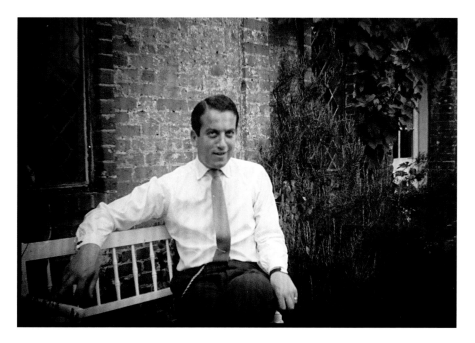

Tom Parr at the Hunting Lodge, in about 1961.

Tom after he had retired, in the late 1990s.

Eventually not only Houri but also Barbara Heale *had* had enough. But while John sort of forced Houri to leave, he gave Barbara his blessing and said he would send all his clients' children to her, which he did. For the next forty years she was never out of work.

Shearo had known John even longer than Houri: in fact, her family had lent him money to get started. He knew Maudie, her mother, from pre-war years and would occasionally go to drinks with her in their little house. During the war Shearo worked in an aircraft factory in Llandudno doing draftsman's work. She couldn't bear it. She was mixing with people she didn't understand, doing work she didn't understand, and stuck in a place she hated. Just before the war (in 1938) she married Basil L. Morant, but sadly her husband committed suicide a few months later. She was an only daughter and her parents decided to take her on a P&O cruise to South Africa to help get over what had been a very short and pretty hopeless marriage. I remember when I joined the firm (having never met her) I came in one morning and thought she was Lady Colefax! She was a middle-aged lady, rather grand, doing it on a shoestring. Not pretty but chic, sort of Chanel chic.

Guide was a little younger than Shearo, but not by much. She annoyed John because she would get in a flap about things. She had been in love with him in the Peter Jones days, which needless to say was completely hopeless. They'd been

young together, and gone to the ballet and theatre, but as he got grander she became a nobody. You knew John wouldn't be good with her, because she was nice and he wasn't. In 1963 she married an extraordinary deaf and dumb Russian, Alexander Bilibin, who had contracted scarlet fever and lost his hearing while escaping from Russia with his mother during the revolution in 1917.[2] He was a sort of Chelsea Bohemian and it was rather a funny arrangement, but I suppose she wanted to care for somebody. After he died she lived in South Harting in West Sussex, near Uppark where she used to be a guide when the house opened to the public.

I began to see a future for Colefax & Fowler when Tom Parr arrived in May 1960.[3] This was down to Michael Tree, who tried to sort out his mother Nancy's finances, which were perpetually distressed.[4] The firm was losing too much money, and when David Hicks and Tom Parr dissolved their partnership (Hicks was about to marry Pamela Mountbatten), Michael invited Tom Parr to join Colefax. The Tree family sold Tom 49 per cent, while they retained a controlling interest. (John didn't have shares at this point, though he got some later on.) Tom was in a way the ideal person because he had very good business sense, and also an enormous interest in the decorating world, which developed over the years. He became a very good decorator with a style of his own, rather nineteenth century in feeling, certainly heavier than John's eighteenth-century style of classical English decoration.

ABOVE LEFT George Oakes.
ABOVE RIGHT The mural painted by George Oakes in the
dining room at Sezincote.

Tom reorganized things and started to make the business work properly, including giving the staff a pay rise, since we were all, including John, grossly underpaid. We started charging fees, which we had never done, and charged for train fares. The business began to be properly managed, with accountants and people to deal with everything. Prior to that we'd had darling Mr Carey, whose schoolboy son John would come in to help in the holiday (John Carey is now Emeritus Merton Professor of English Literature at Oxford). Mr Carey was company secretary, but John could twist him round his little finger, getting him to settle his bill at Turnbull & Asser, or allowing him to borrow a bit of furniture for the cottage to impress a client, which somehow never seemed to be returned.

When Tom first arrived he seemed a very calm fellow – he didn't lose his cool at first. However, this soon changed. I think he also must have had high blood pressure because, like John, he used to 'go off' alarmingly. He would shout and bellow so the whole building heard every word – 'Get out you silly bitch. Go and leave at once, I can't have people like you in this firm.' Some poor girl had merely folded something the wrong way or done something very minor but he would get rid of her. The Duchess of Cornwall was one assistant who fell victim to one of his tantrums – I think she came in late having been to a dance the night before. Like John, he was awful to some of his clients, but in a different way. He was autocratic, dogmatic and dictatorial and although some people liked that, most wouldn't put up with it. I've always tried to be diplomatic with my clients, gently steering them in what I think is the right direction. Tom hadn't the patience and would get rid of clients if he didn't think they were going to toe the line.

Another very significant figure in the development of Colefax & Fowler was George Oakes.[5] He started with us in early 1959, doing murals, painted cushions, fire screens and all sorts of commissions. His cushions became very collectable. They were hand-painted velvet in a sort of nineteenth-century style, but not copies, entirely original. His talent at mural painting has rarely been surpassed. We talk in awe of Rex Whistler, but George's murals are equal to Whistler's in my opinion, if not surpassing them. There are two outstanding examples. One was for a

Cartoon and finished murals for the Lewis family in Atlanta.

dining room at Sezincote, and was inspired by India because of the connection with Warren Hastings. The other example was a more tropical design for the Lewis family in Atlanta. This was a house that had belonged to Margaret Mitchell, who had written *Gone with the Wind* in the upstairs bedroom. The house had been moved to what I call 'Coca-Cola Land' (it was close to the Coca-Cola heiress's mansion) and when I was asked to decorate it I commissioned George to paint a mural for the dining room. It had a tropical feel in keeping with the vegetation of Atlanta and the South. He really surpassed himself.

When Tom arrived he realized the potential to enlarge the sale of fabrics. Prior to this we were making a few one-off pieces of chintz for jobs and weaving a few special fabrics for clients, but nothing went on the general market.

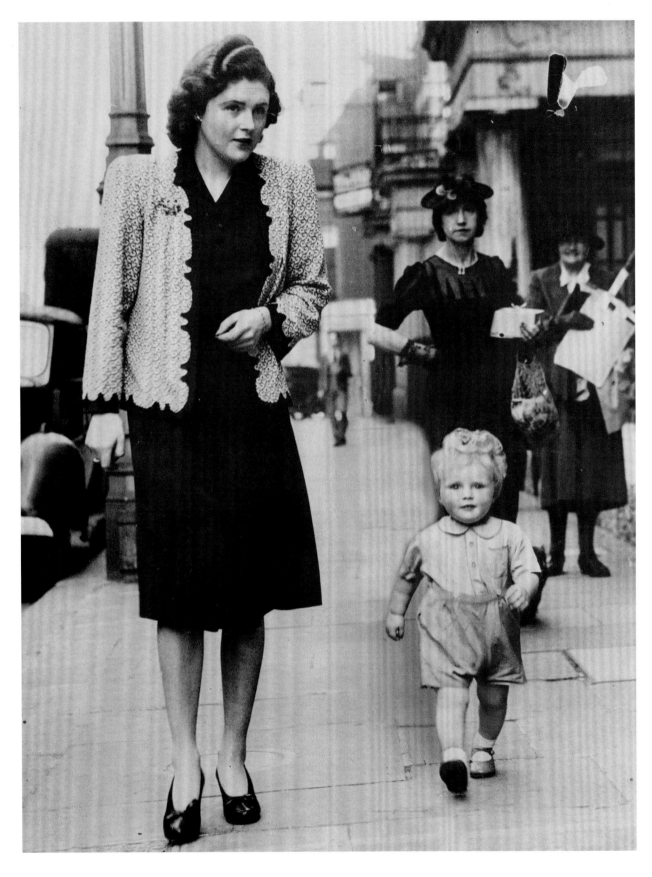

Pamela Churchill with a young Winston, in London in 1942. He was a little older when I met him!

Alongside his other work George established a studio to produce fabric collections, both woven and printed. The taste of the period, which John really created, was for mid- to late nineteenth-century fabrics. There were a few exceptions, such as some documents taken from the Regency period, and weaves that John evolved from old fabrics. Perhaps the most famous of these small weaves were 'Diamond' weave and 'Dalmatian' weave, which were inspired by eighteenth- century carriage cloths, and we had these woven in quantity and put into stock for sale within the shop itself.

George produced such an attractive range of colourways in the fabrics that it was only a question of a discussion between him and Tom as to whether this or that colour would be a good seller. Quite a few of the chintzes were produced in three colourways, but some like 'Old Rose' remained in just one original colour. Of course, changing colours alters the mood of a fabric. If it was in a darker, stronger colourway it could be used for a library, whereas if it's in a pale colour it becomes a bedroom fabric.

Throughout the 1960s and 1970s George was often producing two collections a year. Most of them were printed by Stead McAlpin in Carlisle, some with a Swiss company, and they were all on beautiful quality cotton. Sadly they were not as highly glazed as the old ones, but they've lasted for years. I have chintz curtains that I put up in my own house more than fifty years ago and they still look pretty fresh although they've been relined twice. I particularly remember the Jubilee collection to celebrate the Queen's Silver Jubilee in 1977. It was a lovely collection of fabrics, which sold very well, particularly the 'Jubilee' chintz he devised together with Pat Etheridge, a very good fabric designer. It proved to be an excellent seller and looked like a classic late Victorian chintz, but with a more modern colouring.

We were already selling our fabrics in the shop, but Tom was keen to develop this part of the business further and in 1973 we opened a charming little shop in Ebury Street. There you could buy off the shelf and even get a little decorating help, but usually people bought fabric and got it made up themselves. In later years we would hold a January sale in the RHS Hall in Westminster, which was hugely popular. When David Green joined the firm in June 1986, and it eventually became a public company in 1988, that side of it grew and David also bought some well-known textile companies in America (Cowtan & Tout, and Larsen) and France (Manuel Canovas). This all contributed to making Colefax the world-renowned fabric company it is today.[6]

You can't really overestimate George's influence in the world of fabrics. What has become Colefax & Fowler was essentially built on the basis of George's skills, his tastes in pattern and design and colour. Obviously he had the 'artist's eye', which he brought to the fabrics he designed himself and to those he recoloured. He didn't have an easy time because there was always a certain amount of opposition from Tom, but generally speaking George's collections were excellent and sold well.

Of course, at this time the crème de la crème clients usually went to John, but some jobs were so minor that however grand the client happened to be it wasn't worth John becoming involved. This is how one morning I found myself sent to see Pamela Churchill (Harriman, as she later became).[7] All she wanted was a new set of net curtains. She was already divorced from Randolph Churchill, living with her son (young Winston) and a nanny in a grand apartment in Grosvenor Square.[8] I was ushered into her bedroom to find her lying stark naked on the bed having a massage; I didn't know where to look! Pamela was totally unfazed by this but all I could see was her ginger hair and marble-white body. Winston kept running into the room, with nanny in hot pursuit. I used to tease him later about how I first met him when he was in short pants! Years later I ended up designing a library for 'Young Winston' at his house in Westerham to house his grandfather's collection, which is now at Cambridge University. Pamela Harriman, then United States Ambassador to France, invited me to go shopping with her for a few pretty things for the new library and I subsequently had a tour of the Paris embassy, much enriched by the Harriman pictures and her taste. Sadly, this was only a month before her untimely death in the Ritz swimming pool.

I suppose the passage of time has given me a perspective about John and today I bless him for opening my eyes to so much that has enriched my life. John might have been this 'Jekyll and Hyde' character but we all grew to love him despite the tantrums and the dramas, which are now the source of much merriment and mirth. Long after John died I met James Lees-Milne one Christmas at the house of mutual friends. He was at the time writing his book *Fourteen Friends*, one of whom was John.[9] Although Lees-Milne was a great friend of John's, he still wanted help to fill in some of the facts about John's life (these have been further explained by my friend Martin Wood in his book *John Fowler: Prince of Decorators*). I went to see Lees-Milne at his house on the Badminton estate, and we sat in the kitchen at tea reminiscing about someone who had touched both our lives but in very different ways. His portrait of John was accurate, though minus some of the many warts we observed in day-to-day contact.

6

GRANDES DAMES: SIBYL COLEFAX & NANCY LANCASTER

Ihad an image of Lady Colefax long before I ever met her.[1] She was a great socialite, the last of the grand *salonnières*, who shone in a world very different from our own. I had read many books where she seemed to appear on every page – in fact every biography of that period seemed to mention going to have drinks at Argyll House, Sibyl's house in the King's Road.

The sitting room at Sibyl's house in Lord North Street.

Sibyl Colefax (centre), with Violet Trefusis and Cecil Beaton, mid-1930s.

OPPOSITE 'Haseley Acorn'. Nancy had some curtains which she bought at the Ashburnham sale unpicked, and used the fabric to cover a bathroom wall at Haseley.

After her husband died she gave up Argyll House and went to live in a small house in Lord North Street, off Smith Square near to Parliament. When I was introduced to her she was far frailer and smaller than I had expected, more insignificant than I had imagined. We shook hands: 'This is Imogen, one of our new girls,' all very formal.

She missed the fun and the life of the shop terribly, and was very lonely. She had one son in England and one living in America, married to an American, and that seemed to be all the family she had. Today she is best known for being a hostess, a catalyst who brought interesting people together. Many people were horribly spiteful about her, as we so often read, but you knew you would meet interesting people at her

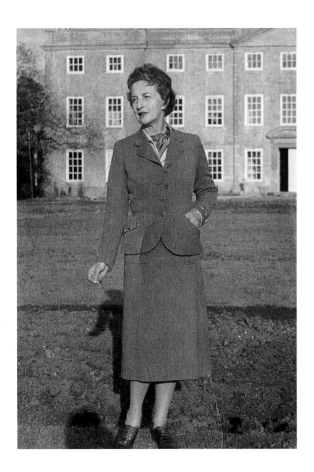

Nancy Lancaster in front of Haseley Court, in about 1955.

A painting by Alexandre Serebriakoff of the hall at
Nancy's Charles Street house.

parties because she would mix together politicians, writers, artists, people of importance of the day. She was brilliant at mixing people and you didn't go to pay court to her, unlike Emerald Cunard, but rather for the company she assembled.

John was very nice to her, although her influence on him was negligible decoration-wise: he was the decorator and she made nice rooms for people. She bought rather well for the shop, always interesting things, and she was a reasonably good businesswoman. She knew about fabrics too and several of the fabrics we were using in the 1950s were from her day. She had that ability to make an immaculate house, as demonstrated both in Argyll House and in Lord North Street. Quite pretty, by the standards of the day, with nice things and always very beautifully kept.

I can't say I remember my first view of Nancy Lancaster, who had bought the business from Sibyl in 1948. In the late 1940s and early 1950s she was living at Charles Street in Mayfair and came into the shop quite regularly. John and she would go on buying trips together, which was something

they both liked. They took the car and chauffeur and they set off around the London shops, or to Sotheby's to view the next sale or to a country house sale. The wonderful sale in Sussex at Ashburnham Place, held in June and July of 1953, sticks in my mind because they came back with the most extraordinary things — rolls of old Brussels carpet, which turned out to be the ancestor of the 'Roses and Ribbons' pattern, in that sort of dark brown colour with white roses. Of course, she outbid her own sister to get it! I remember the extraordinary arrival of the carrier from Ashburnham Place with boxes of hundreds of what I call toilet utensils from the bedrooms in Ashburnham — wash bowls and jugs, chamber pots and soap dishes. They all had to be put in the garden at Brook Street and it was an extraordinary sight. There were also *bourdaloues*, sort of sauce boats that ladies would use rather than a chamber pot, and I remember her using those to put the flowers in on the mantelpiece as a joke.

Charles Street, where Nancy lived, was just off Berkeley Square, so I used to walk round. She had three wonderful women servants. Winnie was her lady's maid (she wasn't quite as dotty then as she later became), and Beryl and Flo. They all thought they had come down in the world, working for Nancy. I seem to recall Beryl had worked for the Duke of Clarence as a chambermaid, Flo had been a lady's maid to a French lady and Winnie also came from somewhere grand. Ruby Hill was Nancy's companion and secretary – equally grand as she had been private secretary to the Viceroy.[2] 'Hilly' was always relaying muddled and confused messages from Nancy. We usually had to go back to source to find out exactly what she wanted.

Charles Street was a narrow house facing two ways on a corner, and the rooms were not spectacular in either size or scale. It was quite different from the sort of houses Nancy was used to, like Ditchley and Kelmarsh, and to her it was a sort of London pied-à-terre cottage. When she decided to sell Charles Street in 1957 she took a lease on part of Brook Street, basically one grand room with a few small rooms off, and that large room – which was to become the famous Yellow Room – was more what she was used to.

Nancy was adaptable, and had this wonderful way of treating everybody the same and on the same level. Although she did issue commands they weren't absolute; you could give a reason and explain it wasn't possible to do what she asked, and she would listen. You could never do that with John – he would think you were just making excuses.

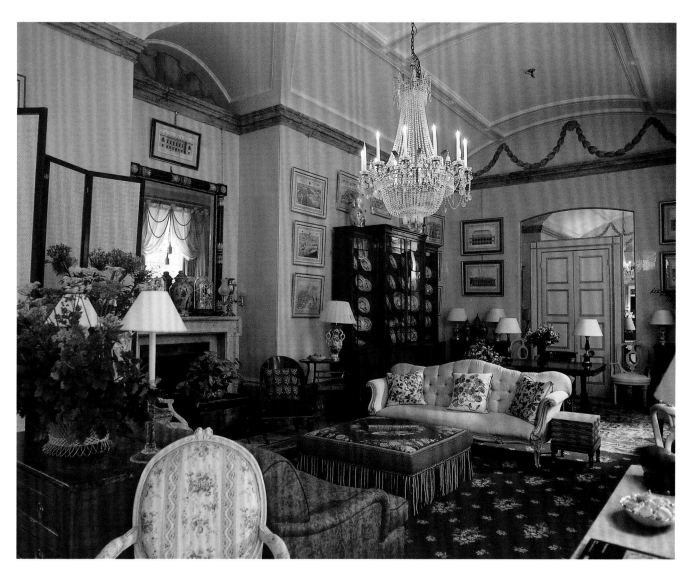

The Yellow Room at Brook Street after Nancy gave it up and we turned it into a showroom. It was repainted at this time: there was much discussion about which yellow to use but in the end we matched the taffeta of the curtains, as that is what had been done originally.

Nancy was more fair-minded. She wasn't easy to work for, though, because her instructions were always vague and invariably she would tell you only half of what she wanted. 'I'd like that cushion covered in a good yellow,' she would say – but wouldn't tell you exactly what yellow – and it should be 'trimmed with some of that stuff I had at Queen Anne's Gate', but never having been to Queen Anne's Gate you had no idea what she was talking about. She changed her mind too, of course, so something would be done only for her to say, 'Oh I don't like that', and we would have to do it again. She had to get it just right, to her taste, and would never settle for second best. That was really how she achieved the look that has become 'shabby chic'.

When she eventually bought Haseley I worked on the whole of that together with her and John, so I went through all the hiccups and all the rows! According to John she was unreasonable, but I think she quite liked sticking a pin in him and waiting for him to squeak – it was that sort of relationship. She was enjoying herself, but instead of laughing he'd get tense and rise to the bait like an old trout.

John respected her enormously, and respected her taste, and was a little bit in awe of the fact that she lived in such a grand way. She continued to live rather grandly after the war and especially after she found Haseley Court in 1954. I remember going down to see it with John and as we drove up I thought it looked pretty grim.[3] It had been empty for a long time, though the amazing topiary was neat and cut. Old Mr Shepherd, who had been gardener to the previous owner, Lieutenant Colonel Anthony Muirhead, was a wonderful man and he had kept it going right through the war. But it was set in a sea of long grass and nettles.

The rather grey flat facade didn't invite you to think this is a delicious house, and inside it was really run-down, but it had nice-sized rooms. Upstairs was what looked like a dilapidated village hall – the panelled Gothic room. I remember pushing my hand against a panel and the whole thing crumbling like cornflakes in my hand. I really didn't understand why she bought it because there were dozens of pretty houses in the country which she could have bought.

I believe it cost her about £4,000 (with 89 acres), but the renovations probably cost £15,000, a lot of money in the 1950s. And then began the decorating, which took up a huge amount of all our time – John's time, my time and the time of the staff as a whole. Nancy owned a decorating firm and she quite reasonably expected priority attention. Never mind all the duchesses who wanted things done!

BELOW LEFT Haseley Court just after Nancy bought it in 1954. BELOW RIGHT The saloon at Haseley, looking out on to the topiary gardens. The Jacobean portraits of the Fitton sisters reflected in the pier glasses were later used in the Yellow Room at Brook Street.

Working on Haseley was extremely taxing and difficult. With all the quarrels and the disagreements, it was certainly one of the hardest jobs I ever did. You never knew what the answer was, whether it was to be what John said or what Nancy said, and as the middle person I was always trying to get on and do things. The worst aspect was Nancy changing her mind, which she had every right to do, but which made it difficult to work for her. Equally John would go 'off the boil', because he had a row with her and suddenly he was no longer interested, but then he'd get on the boil and it was all right again. Nancy had a marvellous land agent, Kenneth Winterschladen, with an assistant called Jonathan Vickers, who would come to take notes.[4] Jonathan was tall, blond and good-looking. He and I would be giggling in the background: he was fascinated by the set-up between John and Nancy and loved the house.

There was a huge amount of building work and mess for months and months, but Nancy was brimming with ideas. I remember her coming in one day and saying, 'I've just been to the Villa Malcontenta and they are going to let me copy the chairs for the garden.' On another occasion she had been with

her aunt to stay with the King of Sweden, who let her copy a paper from a room at Drottningholm Palace for the small Palladian room, which George Oakes executed. She was always coming up with ideas, which were quite exciting, but sometimes she had wild ideas, which John had to control.

One thing I learnt from Nancy was an American insistence on comfort. Her beds were always lovely, especially the wonderful thin quilts made of down and covered in white Japanese silk. They were very impractical really, as things got spilt on them and they would tear. We used to have to recover them constantly, but they were also wonderful, light as a feather and the ultimate in comfort. She always had beautiful bathrooms too. She liked to use old-fashioned mahogany washstands with marble tops. It was very clever because it gave old-fashioned looking bathrooms with modern fittings. Nancy taught me a lot about bathrooms, making them comfortable with lights all over the place to give atmosphere.

It took two years to decorate Haseley and when it was finished Nancy invited the staff to go down to see it. She included the behind the scenes staff who normally never saw the end results of our decorating work. We were all amazed at what she was doing in the garden – laying out the big walled garden, and the topiary looking more and more splendid. The garden became very influential later on – David Hicks described Nancy as the most influential gardener since Gertrude Jekyll.[5] She adored gardening

BELOW LEFT The saloon, looking towards the fireplace. The girandoles, thought to be by Chippendale, came from the tapstry drawing room at Ditchley Park.
BELOW RIGHT The central path through the square garden at Haseley, from the gazebo.

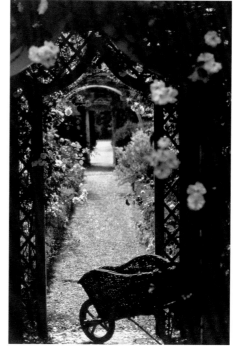

and she was always 'tail up' in the garden, bent over pulling out weeds. As you talked to her she would be, as gardeners always are, planning ahead and thinking about the garden, always with a hat on and a wonderful yellow or apricot scarf, very chic. She looked wonderful even in her gardening clothes.

Her lunches were always delicious in that sort of nursery way, not sophisticated, but something like an egg and cheese dish with a salad, and a bowl of fresh raspberries from the garden. I remember discussions about the dining table and the idea of putting wing chairs at each end of the table, which was very original to all of us, but John went along with it. John then devised rather wonderful curtains with swags attached, all in a wool rep, inspired by curtains Nancy had brought from Ditchley.

Nancy would have been about five foot six; her aunt, Lady Astor, was smaller but they had a very similar posture and fairly similar looks. She had that Virginian attitude, sort of outgoing, un-shy, which seemed to be shared by the whole family. Joyce Grenfell (Nancy's cousin) had that same attitude – the Wyndham girls have all got it, and Elizabeth Winn had it too.[6] There was something of the actress in them all. Nancy had a wonderful but sharp wit, with usually a slight sting in the tail. She would always describe things in a completely original and witty way. For example, she always described a particular grey colour as 'elephant's breath'. It seems a ridiculous thing to say, but we could all imagine it! I remember using the phrase to a journalist from *W* magazine, but unfortunately when the article came out it appeared as elephant's breasts!

I was fascinated by Nancy's way of dressing. She often wore tailor-made suits but it would never be a little black suit, but instead some sort of branded tweed, perhaps green tweed or something similar, and lovely silk shirts in bright yellow or emerald green. She'd often add a clashing colour, perhaps in the form of a scarf, which contrasted with the shirt so that it sort of gave you a little jerk when you saw it. There are pictures of her in a yellow dress, then a different sort of yellow round her hat, or a scarf, and then she'd wear amber beads or something, just to clash with the yellows. She did that in rooms as well – she would put in a highlight that gave you a tiny shock – very subtle, not blatant at all, but very clever.

She always use to wear hats, which she wore at a perky angle, together with good large jewellery, rings, brooches and necklaces. And always good shoes. She had aquiline features, a definite aquiline nose, and freckles and pale skin, which went with her auburn hair. She looked an outdoor girl because she was an outdoor girl. She loved riding and hunting, of course, and continued to hunt into old age. When I saw her in London she always had a slightly countrified air because she wore tweedy clothes and somewhat country colours. I didn't usually see her when she was dressed for smart events, but she did come in on one or two occasions and show us her latest evening dress. I particularly remember a wonderful Schiaparelli ball gown in emerald green, which suited Nancy so well with her auburn hair, and with it she wore a full parure of big emeralds. Stunning. She wasn't conventionally beautiful, but if she came in a room everybody's head turned: I suppose what she really had was presence.

One of the things I most remember about all the ladies who came into the shop in those early post-war days was their innate style. We'd been starved of anything, or at least anything to do with fashion, and austerity was the word. I particularly remember 'Debo' Devonshire coming in one winter's day in a waisted tweed coat with fox fur at the neck and cuffs and around the hem, and a little fox fur hat, together with a muff in her hand held on ribbons around her neck.[7] She looked angelic, and it was terribly stylish, all in browns and beiges with little leather boots, and very chic.

I suppose because of who she was I also remember the Duchess of Windsor coming to see John about a dining room in the mill outside Paris that they were doing up at the time.[8] When she came in I took her upstairs and she turned to the Duke, who was following her up the stairs, bounding like a schoolboy two at a time – and in a rather harsh voice she said, 'David, we don't want you.' He stopped abruptly on the half-landing and asked, 'What should I do?' 'Oh, why don't you go and buy some brushes at that shop at the bottom of Bond Street' – meaning Asprey's. And with that he was dismissed.

She was dressed totally in black – a black suit with an enormous diamond brooch on her lapel. I admired her dark hair, straight back and very petite figure – a very good figure. But she had a hard, rather marble face so that she reminded me, I hate to say, of a snake more than anything. She was very well mannered and good with John, and because the Duchess was Nancy's friend, they all went over to the Moulin together. John did a toile for her which he hand-painted himself, something he never did for anyone else. Canvas was prepared in distemper and on this he painted panels of bulrushes above a trellis dado.

The Duchess of Windsor in the dining room at the Mill, showing the bulrush paper John had painted for them. The Duchess had bought the furniture from Syrie Maugham years before.

The results were very pretty, in a sort of rustic style. But it is her appearance, the rather hard voice and her dismissive attitude to poor David that remain in my memory.

Aside from clients like the Windsors and members of her own family Nancy never did anything in the shop except buy furniture with John. He bought things which she disagreed with, and vice versa, but she would buy slightly quirkier things – although he became quirkier in his choice as time went on. He wasn't so good at buying to start with. It was new to him, bearing in mind that he wouldn't have been buying much good furniture when he was in the King's Road. From 1936 he started taking trips on the Golden Arrow to Paris to buy furniture, but as he never had much money he would buy chair frames. He had an excellent eye because he bought wonderful chairs, which we would do up in the studio. When I saw the shipment coming from Paris I would be amazed at the sort of ragged little collection of funny things. He was mad about tole, as indeed was Nancy, and he loved lanterns, always rather battered and requiring total restoration. Just occasionally he would buy pieces of fabric, which he would stuff in the drawer for future use.

I learned a huge amount from John and Nancy, who together produced a rather magical look that everybody knows and is mad about – this shabby chic, comfortable, interesting way of living, not very decorated. John taught me more about detail, but Nancy's influence was huge – it was from her that I learned about ambience and how to live. And I think that is really the key. People often don't know how to live, and I've spent so much of my life trying to teach them, which is essentially what Nancy taught me.

7

ON MY OWN

Eventually Tom decided that I ought to have my own clientele. I was made a salaried partner in 1966 when I was forty. Initially I had a staff of two, later growing to four, with up to seventeen jobs on the go at any one time. They would all be at different stages: some just at the beginning, some estimating, some in full swing, and some setting up.

I was determined to teach my assistants so they learnt and understood what we were doing and why. I'm glad to say many of them have gone on to be successful decorators in their own right, and they all remain friends.

One assistant, Lynette Hood (Pearson as she then was) came to me by chance when one of my staff left unexpectedly. She had been bound for a job at the British Film Institute, but somehow was seduced by the 'old world' charm of Colefax. One of the first jobs Lynette was involved in was a house in Mayfair for an American lady, Mrs Moffett, who was petite, brunette and about whom we knew almost nothing. She told us that she'd had a part in a Tarzan film and I seem to remember she had a daughter, but Mr Moffett never appeared. It was a sweet house – 46 Green Street, between Brook Street and Park Lane. (Sir Thomas Sopwith had lived there.) We did the house from top to toe. Lynette coloured a Mauny leaf design border, 'Parma', in citrus greens on shades of grey, which were very much the colours of the era. The highlight of the house was probably the mural of topiary trees on the staircase done by George Oakes – among the best he ever did.

At the same time I was finishing a house for Lady Manton. Plumpton Place in Sussex was an Elizabethan manor house that had been restored and altered by Sir Edwin Lutyens for Edward Hudson, the owner of *Country Life*. The interiors of Lutyens's houses are always difficult

Plumpton Place, Sussex.

to decorate, because he designed his houses from the outside in, and the architecture could overwhelm the ambience. Plumpton's rooms were typical as he had laid some bold black and white floors and built a music room looking out on to the lake with oak casement windows. I liked Lady Manton very much, especially as wherever she was she would be surrounded by border terriers and free-flying budgerigars, creatures which are equally dear to me![1] She was then married to Lord Manton, who died in 1968. Subsequently she married Lord (Perry) Brownlow of Belton in Lincolnshire. We did their London home, a house in Chesham Mews. It was pretty but very run-down, and rather incongruous because it was at the back of the German embassy, which was a modern and rather aggressive building. It was a typical mews house with small rooms. We incorporated a yard at the back to make a dining room.

OPPOSITE 'Climbing Geranium', an English block print design of 1830–40. The original document was in reds and dark greens.

The drawing room had walls painted in a soft coral colour, and we used hollyhock chintz ('Althea' by Lee Jofa) for curtains and a loose sofa cover with a dark green carpet. Either side of the fireplace were alcoves filled with a collection of Worcester porcelain decorated with birds. All very relaxed and very English.

I remember we discovered that Lady Brownlow's youngest border terrier was an expectant mother, and Lynette and I got very excited. Sure enough when she had her litter Lynette was offered one of the pups. Lady Brownlow then asked Lynette to house-sit while she and Lord Brownlow went off for the winter to his estates in Grenada and Jamaica. The challenge was getting John Fowler to agree to a puppy at 39 Brook Street, but I worked on John and persuaded him that it would be rather fun. His only condition was that the dog had to be house-trained. At last Colefax & Fowler had a dog. It seemed to sit in my room most of the time and was good at selling, particularly sofas! Having a dog brought out the softer side of John. He would feed the puppy his crusts at lunch –

there would be a great tease going on over the crusts. That was rather nice because John had been such a daunting figure to the junior staff.

Along with new jobs I gradually inherited some of John's jobs, and one such was Keir in Scotland. Susan Stirling was a very beautiful woman who had been a model for the London couture house Lachasse.[2] I could see why since she was still wonderfully slim and very tall with a lovely walk. She was quite a strange character in many ways, known not to particularly like women, but we seemed to get on well. As with all country house work of that period, ready money was not to hand – it was all in the estate. We used the contents of the house, rearranging them to give a different look, using old curtains or making new but using old trimmings. The effect was rich and had that essential country house look that people admired. It was of necessity, and luckily these people had an enormous amount of wonderful contents, which included both some very pretty things and some very ugly things too: nothing ever seemed to be thrown away.

Keir House, near Stirling, in 1975.

Susan Stirling in 1971.

If I was going up to Keir I would catch the night sleeper from King's Cross to Stirling. The train would arrive at Stirling early in the morning and remain in the station for a bit while we were woken by the steward with a cup of tea. This all seems very old-fashioned now. There would be a chauffeur waiting to take me to Keir. I was shown up into my bedroom with a blazing fire in the grate. I was always asked if I would like a bath, and the butler would run it for me – in this enormous cast iron bath with great big bath sheets. The butler would say on leaving, 'Breakfast is at nine in the dining room; you know the way.' It was quite difficult to know the way in a house that size! I was told that it had in all twenty-seven staircases.

When I went down to breakfast there were two side tables. On one would be hot foods such as porridge, which was served in wooden bowls and which you ate standing up. There would be bacon and eggs, scrambled eggs, boiled eggs, kidneys, kippers, kedgeree – in fact, anything you could think of. On the other buffet would be cold ham, cheese and fruit – again, anything you can imagine. It was a sumptuous breakfast, and there were only four of us! The Stirlings had a wonderful cook, a Mrs Thompson, and I don't think I've ever tasted such delicious food.

I went up several times over the years and got to know the family well. I remember on one occasion going with Susan on an expedition into the hills to fly her kestrel. Aside from her interest in birds, Susan loved gardens. Keir was famous for its collection of rhododendrons and azaleas, and there appeared to be acres of these plantations, which Susan restored and enhanced. She loved her Scottish life very much, but I also did an apartment for her in London. The house and estate of 15,000 acres were sold in 1975 for £2 million to Mahdi Al Tajir, an Arab businessman who also bought Mereworth in Kent from Michael Tree. It was very sad: the Stirlings had been at Keir since 1448.

It was Susan Stirling who took me to meet Lady Bute for lunch at Dumfries House. Lady Bute was very much a countrywoman, not really interested in decorating, architecture or anything beyond country matters. Dumfries had been little used, as the family had other properties on the Isle of Bute. It was a slightly dead house, but she showed me around saying, 'You know, this is all by Chippendale.' I looked at the dining room chairs and the furnishings, which at first sight appeared as though they must be reproductions as they still looked brand new! They had been ordered from Chippendale's pattern books and in one or two cases they must have got the sizes a bit mixed up because on arrival

Tyninghame House, East Lothian, in 1970.

some of the mirrors didn't fit quite over the chimneypieces, and had to be hung forward. I remember the dining room chairs were all covered, and when we went into the attic Lady Bute showed me some covers, which were the original loose covers that had gone over the dining chairs when not in use. They were rather coarse hand-woven and hand-sewn linen covers as supplied by Thomas Chippendale. They must be unique.

At the same time as working at Keir, I also worked for other people in the Lowlands of Scotland, again old clients of John's – the Haddingtons, at Tyninghame and Mellerstain House.[3] At Tyninghame, which was huge, the Haddingtons lived in just part of the house. I would go and stay and remember sitting in the great library one evening while Lord Haddington worked on embroidery. He was a total expert in needlepoint, both *petit point* and *gros point*.

Lady Haddington's bed at Tyninghame House, mid-1960s.

Lady Haddington at her desk.

It was extraordinary to see him stitching away. I now know that had I gone to Royal Lodge at Windsor before the war I would probably have found the King doing exactly the same, and the Duke of Windsor would be busy stitching in Paris, both having been taught by Queen Mary.

Lady Haddington was Canadian and both she and her sister (who married Lord Minto) brought with them fresh ideas and a fresh outlook. John had worked on a sitting room for Lady Haddington which was unique at the time because he chose to use a heavily ribbed yellow corduroy fabric on the walls. It was very strong and bold and had a sunshine quality. The sitting room was pretty and comfortable and furnished with pictures chosen from around the house, mirrors, curtains in 'Brompton Stock' chintz and plenty of needlepoint. John also designed two pyramid bookcases. Unfortunately, in transferring from one carrier to another on the way up to London, one of these fell off the lorry and broke, so we had to make a replacement. The room turned out to be a great success,

a sunny, chintzy and floral room in what was otherwise a rather austere house.

I carried on from John, working on other parts of the house, rearranging the contents and finding new uses for pieces that had perhaps been stored away. Later in my life, when I was working for Americans, there was nothing to start with, so they had to buy lots of eclectic furniture and pictures to achieve the country house look they were hoping for. It always meant a lot of searching and a good eye.

We didn't really work much in the Scottish Highlands, except for the Cowdrays at Dunecht House near Aberdeen. The Scottish baronial style wasn't our thing, but in the Lowlands they were going more for an English look. Probably our grandest Scottish clients were the Duke and Duchess of Hamilton.[4] John did Lennoxlove and later I did the dower house for the Duchess. This was a charming, slightly Italianate building designed by Philip Jebb.[5] The Duchess liked pretty things and was good to work with, very receptive to our ideas and also with ideas of her own.

LEFT The Duchess of Hamilton in the garden at North Port.
BELOW North Port, the Duchess of Hamilton's dower house,
designed by Philip Jebb.
BOTTOM LEFT The Duchess's bathroom.
BOTTOM RIGHT Looking through from the drawing room to the dining
room. The soft blackcurrant colour was an unusual shade to use.

Lady Kaye's bothy.
CLOCKWISE FROM TOP LEFT The bothy, almost at the end of the building process; the sitting room being boarded out – we built the interior walls to allow for window seats; the kitchen, pretty but practical; the sitting room, finished with just enough tartan!

With Elizabeth Kaye and Barley and Daisy in the garden of the Kayes' Hampshire home, mid-1980s.

I also did a mews house for her in London, which Philip Jebb had converted from a mews block behind their London house in Eaton Square. They had had a huge sale when Hamilton Palace fell into ruin (having been undermined by coal mining), but they kept many things and the furniture and pictures that survived were good. All the same, the mews house and the dower house were difficult to arrange because all the pieces had come from large houses and these were much smaller spaces.

It was always a pleasure to visit Lennoxlove; their children were young and the house was a bit ramshackle because of the five boys. She was the daughter of the Duke of Northumberland, and a great friend of the Queen Mother. She loved music and held a music festival in Haddington every year. I remember her being very agitated on one visit because the Queen Mother was coming to stay for the festival and she was making a patchwork quilt for her bedroom. She

was running late and the quilt wasn't finished, so she begged me to find someone to finish it for her. I managed to find a friend who finished it quickly, and we sent it back just in time for the arrival of the Queen Mother.

I think the only time I used anything vaguely 'Scottish baronial' was when I did a small bothy for Lady Kaye, who was an old friend and client of John's.[6] This was on the Buccleuch estate of Drumlanrig Castle. An L-shaped barn was demolished and the footprint used to build a bothy. I suggested we made the walls thicker, like those of an old stone farmhouse, which meant that you could have window seats. It looked like an authentic stone house, even though rendered and painted. We did have a slightly Scottish theme, and I did use a bit of tartan, but only in moderation. The dressing room was in tartan and I remember it looked very welcoming and charming because she had some pretty things sent from London. The main living room I recall was

Ramsbury Manor in August 1968.

Harry Hyams in the mid-1960s.

dominated by a wonderful Stubbs dog painting. It was nice to do because it was like a doll's house, a bolthole set in a beautiful landscape in the middle of nowhere.

I got to know many of my clients very well and they knew me, but they didn't enter into my private life. Most of them didn't enquire about my life at all. I was just somebody who came, discussed things they were interested in, joined in their lifestyle and met their family, but never really entered into their 'society'. I didn't want to: I liked being 'on the fringe'. Moreover, initially most of my clients were at least one generation older than myself. Lady Kaye was an exception, being just a year older than me. She wasn't grand like the duchesses, and was actually rather shy when she first came to meet John. I carried on working for her after John died and perhaps because we were a similar age a relationship developed that was more like a friendship.

Harry and Kay Hyams were also a similar age and again a friendship developed.[7] Hyams was a noted property developer at the beginning of the surge of development in London

in the 1960s. He famously built Centre Point in Tottenham Court Road, and his business, called Oldfield Estates, was doing extremely well. He came into Colefax and asked if we could help him with Ramsbury Manor in Wiltshire. It was a house we decorated three times in all for three different owners. Originally John had decorated the house for Lord Wilton after Ditchley became totally impractical for him. He had bought the house from the Burdett family in 1951 and brought with him from Ditchley many things the Trees had sold to him, including some of the four-poster beds. Lord Wilton in turn sold the house to Lord Rootes, of motor car fame, and again we did the house for him. After his death in 1964 Harry Hyams bought it for £650,000, then the highest sum ever paid for a private house in England – peanuts now, of course!

I had lunch with Kay and Harry Hyams in a little restaurant in Ramsbury and they asked if we would consider helping them. We then drove up to the house, which is very beautiful but seemed pretty sad, as empty houses are apt to be. It is a late seventeenth-century house, built in 1681. This is my favourite period because houses built then tend to have a sort of 'toughness' and 'earthiness' about them that later eighteenth-century houses lack. Somehow the architecture of the eighteenth century is more delicate and less bold.

OPPOSITE, CLOCKWISE FROM TOP LEFT The library; the dining room; a French bed which had once been at Ditchley; Harry Hyams's bedroom.

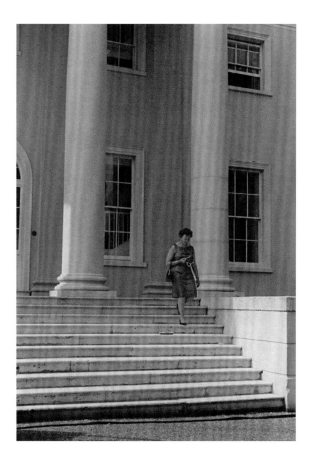

The hall at Howletts, late 1960s.

Beating a hasty retreat from Howletts!

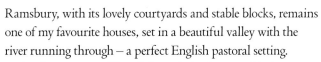

Ramsbury, with its lovely courtyards and stable blocks, remains one of my favourite houses, set in a beautiful valley with the river running through – a perfect English pastoral setting.

As time went on Harry's knowledge increased in leaps and bounds, and he assembled a remarkable collection. The quality was superb, including beautiful clocks and silver, amazing Chinese porcelains, a variety of wonderful objects. However, this can be a problem because a house can come to resemble a museum. I never wanted that, but rather a living house, which I think we managed to achieve. He turned part of the stable block into an indoor swimming pool with some extra guest rooms to have a place to entertain and have fun at the weekend. Harry had spent some time in the Bahamas on his yacht, the *Shemara*, and had met the architect Henry Melich, whom he brought over to transform the stable block.[8]

I also worked at the Hyams's Eaton Square apartment. I persuaded Kay Hyams to have a black and white *toile de Jouy* on the walls of her bedroom, which may sound macabre, but was a bit like putting an engraving on the wall. If you add some colour it's transformed. This lofty first floor room could

take such treatment and Kay always enjoyed her rather exotic bedroom. In the drawing room Harry had an enormous unfinished Burne-Jones painting. There is a charm to unfinished paintings, particularly of that period when things were usually so exact and realistic. The impressionistic look of the Burne-Jones was particularly attractive, and we formed the room around its monochromatic colours.

Harry was such a knowledgeable and perceptive person, and always very kind to me, with beautiful manners. He did have one minor problem in that he wasn't mad keen on paying the bill. He would always say 'It's like spilling my own blood to write a cheque!' In spite of this we worked for him for many years, and right up to his death he kept the house going and delighted in what John and I had done for him, which was touching.

Probably the most flamboyant, colourful and unusual client we ever had was John Aspinall.[9] In 1962 he asked John Fowler to decorate 44 Berkeley Square as a gambling house: he was already making a lot of money in the very top echelons of the gambling world. He was also obsessed with wild animals, and the conservation of Siberian tigers and gorillas in particular. Working on Berkeley Square gave John enormous pleasure (the house was designed by William Kent), as it is one of the finest houses in London and has a particularly grand and beautiful staircase, a beautiful salon and, of course, a rich history behind it. He allowed John his head and although rooms designed to play chemmy and roulette were not his normal field, he did a very glamorous job, working again with the architect Philip Jebb.

A few years earlier, in 1958, Aspinall had bought Howletts, a lovely eighteenth-century house near Canterbury, in order to give him space for his animals. I decorated the house and did the upkeep on it over the years. It was, I have to say, a rather eccentric household. I remember once being asked down because a young Siberian tiger, who had been in bed with Aspinall and his wife, had ripped down the silk hangings on the inside of their canopy bed. It was indeed in shreds when I saw it. That same young Siberian tiger had terrified one visitor out of his wits. The tiger had somehow managed to get into the bathroom while he was having a bath and had proceeded to get into the bath with him! The visitor survived the encounter to tell the tale, although some of the keepers were not so fortunate.

On another occasion I was asked to give advice about cleaning the stone flags in the hall as a wolf had unfortunately eaten his chicken there and made a very greasy mess. I arrived at the gatehouse where Lady Osborne, John Aspinall's mother, lived and she said would ring through to the house to let them know I was on my way.[10] It was a beautiful sunny morning, so I walked out onto the terrace, where I saw an old-fashioned pram. Imagining it contained a grandchild I peered in, only to be absolutely stunned by what I saw. Lying on its back was this shrivelled and wrinkled black-haired baby gorilla dressed in a nappy! I suppose I got off rather lightly. I recall Peter Atkins going down to Howletts and being taken to see the gorillas. One large gorilla seemed to take an instant dislike to him and digging into a large trough filled with ordure she proceeded to throw the contents at him. Needless to say when he arrived home he was in considerable trouble, so I had to send a note round: no one believed the highly unlikely story that his dishevelled state was due to a bad-tempered gorilla!

It came as a great surprise to us when suddenly the press was full of these amazing stories concerning Cliveden, a house we were very familiar with, the Astors, all of whom were clients, and John Profumo, also a client! We read the papers and lapped up this extraordinary story, which reverberated around the country. Profumo resigned his office and his parliamentary seat on 4 June 1963.

Jack Profumo was an old client of John's.[11] We did a house for him in Regent's Park – not one of the terrace houses, but a large corner house. His wife, Valerie Hobson, was a glamorous actress and we all knew of her as she often came to see John.

Another client of ours, Peggy Dunne, was a great friend of the Profumos and after the scandalous revelations she offered them a hideaway in a lovely little folly she had made on a hill above Gatley Park in Herefordshire. It was a beautiful oval tower. Raymond Erith had designed it, John Fowler had decorated it, and I carried out the decorations.

Years later I was asked by Valerie to come down and help them with some work in their house in Hertfordshire. I remember having lunch with them and I was very intrigued to see them after many years. It was sad really because all through lunch she would contradict practically everything he said, and in many ways it was embarrassing to witness. I realized that the wonderful public gesture Valerie had made in forgiving Jack's sins, so to speak, was a sham and in reality their marriage had been badly damaged by his infidelity. To me she was as charming as always, and I still have a lovely little shell butter dish she sent as a gift, together with a big basket of African violets.

One of our plum jobs arrived when I received a telephone call from Lord Jellicoe, who was then Lord Privy Seal and Leader of the House of Lords, asking if I could help redecorate Chequers.[12] Except for when John decorated the Audience Room at Buckingham Palace for the Queen, we had never done any work connected to the government, but I had worked for the Jellicoes and for his mother-in-law, Peggy Willis, and other members of the family, so the family knew me and were familiar with our style. As Lord Privy Seal and Leader of the House of Lords one of Lord Jellicoe's responsibilities was the Chequers estate. I went to look at it with him and it was a real mess. It had been occupied by prime ministers from 1921, when Lord Lee left it to the nation with all the contents – furniture and pictures, all pretty good, particularly the pictures – and a small endowment, which had probably been poorly invested.

Potentially it was a lovely job for us. Looking at the house I could see just about everything was needed, and it lacked a feminine touch. The place was run a bit like an embassy and was in embassy style, with grade one embassy colours of green and rust, as I recall. I suppose it wasn't helped by constant changes of prime minister. I remember the housekeeper telling me that Mrs Attlee had made the pink frilly lampshades, which were pretty disastrous, and others had added a cushion or two and tried to cosy it up a bit. Lady Eden probably had the most taste and she had tried to improve things, but without much success. Yet it was the official country residence of the prime minister of the day. It was a disgrace and needed a lot of work. George Jellicoe understood this and he was responsible for raising the funds, which he did by selling surplus farm property on the estate. I instantly knew I needed John to help me, but he had cancer and was really very ill at the time. Because it was for the prime minister he agreed to act as consultant, but we did most of the work and didn't trouble him about minor details.

John and I immediately saw that half the problem was the panelling, which made the house seem dark and gloomy. He suggested that the existing treacle-coloured panelling should be bleached to give a limed oak effect. Luckily George Jellicoe went along with the idea where many people might have considered it extreme and a violation of the panelling. John was trying to achieve the look panelling gets when left to age naturally and that is the effect the brothers from London who did the work managed to achieve, ending with a coat of wax to feed the wood. Against this background colours looked wonderful and the rooms came alive. In the Hawtrey room, which was the main reception room, we used a white and red linen 'Grande Arbre' *toile de Jouy*, which worked beautifully.

At the time Edward Heath was prime minister – Harold Wilson having just left, leaving his dog behind – but Edward Heath wasn't interested one iota, save for the display case for his model yachts.[13] He wouldn't allow us to do his bedroom,

The Long Gallery at Chequers as we decorated it.

which had to be 'shipshape' and was done by the lady who did his private work. It looked very bachelor-like – yachting and all that sort of thing. The other thing he said he had to have was his music, which meant big speakers and a music centre. Everything was very clumsy in those days, and they went into his study, but he insisted they were in the great hall too, which was a disaster, and of course he inevitably had to have a grand piano.

Perhaps the best room we did was the Long Gallery. It was a slightly truncated room – it didn't run the full length of the house – and as it had no panelling John decided to paper it. We used 'Berkeley Sprig', plain linen curtains, and John had the bookcases all painted in tones of white, which transformed the rather gloomy Elizabethan gallery into a room where you could gather to discuss things in groups or

sit and read books. After all, that was the point of the house: somewhere committees could meet and people could stay for weekends. There were often lots of people, so there had to be lots of seating in the gallery. Upstairs the beds had floral draperies, but when we arrived they were faded and tatty. We redressed them and renovated all the bathrooms, but John wasn't much involved with these. Eventually we were told it had to be finished as President Pompidou was coming to stay and I remember Lynette and I actually hoovering his bedroom, cleaning his bathroom and making up his bed at virtually the last minute before his arrival.

We got no feedback or comment, but when the house was finished Edward Heath gave a lunch party in recognition of our work. I was placed next to Mr Heath and immediately thought it was going to be a very sticky lunch. He wasn't

The back hall at Hunton Down House, hung with the 'Berkeley Sprig' wallpaper which for many years was used as the company's logo.

The anteroom at Hunton Manor, leading into the drawing room added by Raymond Erith.

LEFT The Mackinnons' drawing room, designed by Raymond Erith and decorated by John and myself.

OPPOSITE Mrs Mackinnon's sitting room: note the use of 'Venetian Blind' chintz as roller blinds.

interested in the house, and I didn't know anything about yachting, or much about music. He really had no small chat whatsoever and though I managed to scrape through it was the most unenjoyable lunch imaginable.

John and I worked again with Raymond Erith when he added a drawing room at Hunton Manor near Winchester for Mr and Mrs Angus Mackinnon. Erith was helping them renovate Hunton and extend it, while Russell Page was laying out the gardens. I carried out all the work John planned for the house and then continued to work with Marsinah Mackinnon over the many years that followed. She was a great animal and garden lover, so we had similar tastes. She kept her house in an immaculate state but her dogs were allowed to sleep on her bed and could do no wrong. (On the other hand, she was very strict with her staff!)

When her husband died she moved across the road to Hunton Down House, a dower house built to her tastes and requirements. She owned all the cottages in this little street.

I was brought in to help her decorate the dower house and some of the cottages, as well as a flat in Grosvenor Square, and she much enjoyed doing all of this. She became one of my best English clients as well as a good friend. Although 'on the fringe' of people's lives one became very involved and close to them, and I watched her two sons grow up and marry, and missed her greatly when she died.

The relationship between a decorator and client is an odd one. You become very intimate, but although you know the detail of their lives (down to which side of the bed they sleep on), and sometimes they might confide their problems, there is always a certain reserve, a certain distance.

Of course, our clientele gradually changed as society itself changed. I never counted the number of duchesses John worked for, but it was a very impressive tally. Gradually the duchesses departed and the old aristocracy and gentry gave way to a new generation, a new class with new ideas and new ways of living.

8

IN PRAISE OF CRAFTSMEN

I have always had the very highest regard for craftsmen and craftsmanship. This came to me first through my father, who was himself skilled at many crafts. And in decorating it doesn't take long to learn that you are only as good as the people who do the work for you.

One of my first jobs at Colefax was liaising with various workshops, following up on orders for curtains, upholstery, carpets, etc. I particularly remember visiting the curtain makers Chamberlain & Mason in Swiss Cottage.[1] The firm was run by Mr Chamberlain, who was an expert curtain maker, with skills developed over years of apprenticeship. He also lectured on the subject, teaching others some of his expertise. A skilled curtain maker, like a good couturier, has to understand cutting, because that is what gives 'the look'. What we always wanted was the kind of unstyled look you see in eighteenth-century paintings. This lovely loose,

John Mason's workshop in 1988, with Pat Cox finishing a frilled edge to a curtain, and June Andrews in the background.

ABOVE John and Ann Mason with me in Palm Beach in January 1993.

OPPOSITE 'Longford Toile'. This design is of unknown origin, but the strong Gothic Revival theme suggests it may date from the 1840s.

voluptuous effect is very difficult to pull off, both in couture and in drapery. It was Mr Chamberlain who taught John how to achieve it, as well as how to cut the fabric to create a swag or a tail, and all the extra things like bells and *choux*.[2]

John was very keen to bring the eighteenth century back into decoration. He had a huge knowledge of eighteenth-century paintings and engravings and could show you endless examples of how windows were dressed at that time. Much of our business involved quite elaborate curtain work in stately homes and large manor houses and John was meticulous about every detail, particularly the differences

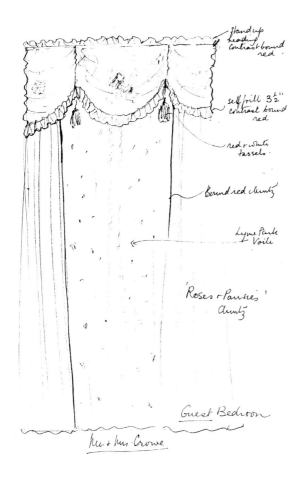

Stand up
heading
contrast bound
red.

self frill 3½"
contrast bound
red

red + white
tassels.

Bound red chintz

Lyme Park
+ Voile

'Roses + Pansies'
chintz

Guest Bedroom

Mr + Mrs Crowe

My sketch design for the curtains for the guest bedroom at Jack and Peggy Crowe's Chicago house,
and the finished curtains made by Masons.

between eighteenth-century and nineteenth-century drapery. For example, the tails of the curtains would be longer in a Victorian house than in a Georgian house. It was his attention to the smallest detail that made his work so exceptional.

Mr Chamberlain was a charming, rather plump, middle-aged man. I remember him with great fondness, as I do his partner Mr Mason, an expert in upholstery. Mr Mason was brilliant at cutting loose covers: he made covers that were neat and tight-fitting (unlike most). It was really because these two gentlemen were so skilled that John was able to start making upholstered furniture based on models from the past. He particularly admired the work of the firm Howard & Sons, founded in 1820 by John Howard.[3] Their sofas had tended to be heavily buttoned, but John pared down the style. He was determined to make sofas that were comfortable – to fit a human being – and he liked them deeper than average to allow for a cushion in the back.

He considered every detail, from the rake of the back, the length of the seat and the height and shape of the arms to the down and feather cushion mixture. He didn't approve of Chesterfield sofas, where the sides and back are the same height, because they don't allow the arm to rest easily; he liked sofas to have a 'P' arm, so called because it is shaped like a letter 'P' turned on its side.[4] Traditionally made sofas had hand-tied springs, jute webbing and a horsehair stuffing. There were different qualities of horsehair, and the very best white horsehair came from the tail of a grey horse (this was always used in mattresses by firms like Heal's). Gradually, with Mr Mason, John was able to work out a small range of upholstery styles; these went on to influence upholstery throughout Britain.

John became famous for elaborate curtains and beautiful draperies. He brought back festoon curtains, an eighteenth-century device he particularly liked, where the curtain was pulled up in daytime through a series of pulleys and let down as a straight curtain at night. He very carefully examined the eighteenth-century festoon curtains (then surviving, now sadly lost) at Uppark so that he understood precisely how much of the edge of the curtain should hang down, and where exactly the pulleys were placed across the curtain so they looked just right when they were drawn up. He was forever examining engravings of the period, so he could tell how things were done. It was really the looseness that he admired, the feeling that they had been sort of thrown up, or the fabric just tossed over a pole. He hated what he called 'cinema draperies', with regular swags or fabric pleated in a very neat way, feeling they lacked life and had a sort of dead look.

John also studied period costume, and he was fascinated by details on ladies' dresses. He invented a frilled effect on the edges of curtains and drapes. Single bound frills or double unbound frills made of silk taffeta were a sort of signature (and eventually became a joke). Somewhere John found a pinking machine, which gave a zigzag edge to the fabric, stopping it from fraying. We only had one machine, and it was always a bone of contention who got the pinking machine, as we all needed it to do double-pinked and scalloped frills! It sounds ridiculous today, but they looked good where we used them. We were working in elegant period houses with lovely high ceilings, and we dressed beautiful four-poster beds in what really looked almost like ball gowns. People kept these draperies for years, even though the colours of the specially dyed fabrics were fading and the edges were fraying, giving a sort of shabby chic look.

Today it is amazing to think that many of the workshops we used were in walking distance of the shop, situated in mews and back alleys in central London, still hanging on from the time of Dickens – indeed many of them were pretty Dickensian set-ups. For example, the other upholsterers we used had their workshops behind Selfridges. W. F. Atkins was founded by Walter Atkins, who, with John, developed a range of furniture which became a collection Colefax sold and indeed still does.[5] John might see a pretty chair in an auction, or a client would bring in a chair for recovering and he would ask if he could copy the frame. The famous Friar's chair is an example. This was an iron-back slipper chair but as it wasn't possible to do an iron frame we had it copied in wood. The trials of chairs that went on seem an extraordinary extravagance now. John would have a beechwood frame made and then have a part covered so he could try it. Then he might say, for example, that the rake

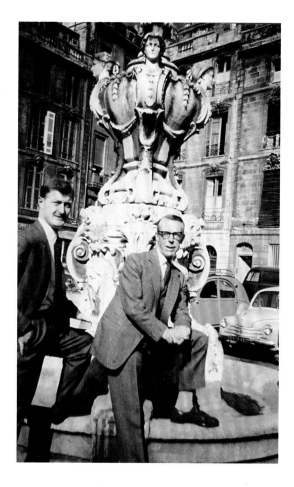

John with Peter Atkins in Bordeaux in 1968.

of the back wasn't quite right, or the arm should be a little higher or lower, which meant stripping out all the upholstery and starting again.

Walter Atkins's nephew, Peter, eventually took over his uncle's business and he became part of our lives. He was an expert at fabric walling, which is a very tricky process, because you have to join lengths of fabric for the whole wall before you put it up. If you have a twenty-foot wall, ten feet high, you've got a very large piece of fabric to hang (and there might be a door in the middle). You have to make sure that the wall is totally sealed, because if the plaster is cracked the heat of the room draws dirt (such as black lime dust from the old plaster) through the cracks and through the fabric, and you get dirty marks coming through. To prevent this we always put up a plastic lining before hanging the fabric. (You sometimes get a similar thing with carpets, where dirt comes through cracks in the boards giving awful lines, so we would cover floors with thin plywood.) After sealing the walls we

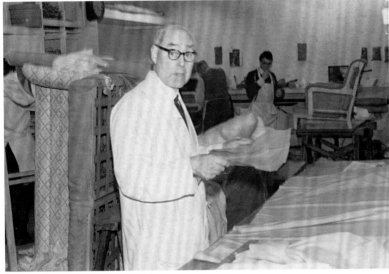

Reg Bayfield, the foreman at W.F. Atkins, examining fabric.

Mr Bayfield doing the decorative nailing for a felt door.

battened around the edges with small wooden battens for the nails, then we applied bump (a lint-like cotton cloth), over which we hung the silk, damask or whatever we were using, and then around the perimeter a gimp or, perhaps – as in the eighteenth century – a gilt fillet.

It was fascinating to watch the upholsterers on the ladders with their magnetic hammers, with which they would take the tacks out of their mouth. They would tack around the battening, stretching the fabric on the wall, and it would come out like a drum. The gimp (specially made to cover the tacks) was then glued in position. It was really an extravagant thing to have your walls covered in this way, since the damask fabric was always specially woven and the gimp made by hand. It is hardly surprising that it is now only very rarely done.

The people who provided the gimp, fringes and tassels were very important to John, indeed to all of us. Whatever fabric you had, whether very poor or very sumptuous, an extra trimming lifted it and gave it character, transforming the ordinary into the extraordinary.

There was the wonderfully Dickensian set-up of B.A. Clark Ltd in Little Britain, in the shadow of St Paul's Cathedral and then run by Bernard Clark.[6] When you opened the door you climbed a very, very steep set of wooden stairs, which went straight up like a ladder, with each stair worn away by the treads of time. At the top it opened into a very, very long and very narrow room called a ropewalk, with

people working on small looms on either side, making fringes and gimps of various kinds and in all sorts of materials. Down the centre was the winding gear for twisting rope and cord. They made everything from the heaviest bell rope for churches down to the very finest cord for the lapels of an officer's uniform.

John brought back the fashion for wool bullion fringes, a form of twisted cord fringe, and he used this on many of his pelmets and on chairs and sofas. If it was to be a solid colour it was made in natural white wool and then dyed to the colour we needed; if it was to be in two colours, then Mr Clark would have to dye the wool before it was woven. Subsequently we also had bullion fringes made in cotton and in linen.

By carefully examining illustrations, John was able to take models and modify them in some way, perhaps by enlarging them or using different materials. This was how he developed fan edging, for instance. I also remember Mr Mauny (of wallpaper fame) giving John a piece of silk edging fringe, which was an exact copy of one used by Marie Antoinette at Versailles. This was a cut-silk fringe one inch long, with an elaborate little picot heading. We had it copied to use as an edging on unlined muslin silk curtains or on lampshades. We subsequently had it made in linen, which was coarser but just as effective.

Bernard Clark would come to Brook Street with boxes of things all beautifully wrapped in tissue paper. It was like

Sewing fringe ornaments.

The ropewalk at B.A. Clark Ltd: the man is twisting cord — as he turns the wheel he pushes the carriage some 75 feet.

Trimmings made by Clarks for John Fowler.
TOP A curtain trimming; 'Embassy' gimp, copied from a guilloche pattern used at the former Dutch embassy; an ornament used to embellish draperies at Daylesford, Gloucestershire, for Lord Rothermere.
MIDDLE A fringe and gimp made for the painted cushions in the Queen's Audience Room at Buckingham Palace.
BOTTOM A copy of an early nineteenth-century gimp used in the drawing room at Haseley Court.

Christmas, unwrapping exquisite tassels. All my working life I would draw each tassel to scale, specifying every detail: the shape of the head and what the skirt should be made of — it might, for example, be in a cut silk. The heads were formed around wooden moulds, which came in different shapes and sizes. The shapes included 'mosque', which looked like an onion dome, and 'steeple', which, of course, looked like a church steeple. The moulds might be covered by what was called 'snailing', after the silky slime mark a snail leaves. Others were covered with plain fabric but with a netting placed over the top. The famous tassels at Buckingham Palace, for instance, which were pure silk with cut silk fringes, were made on netted moulds.

Then the tassel might have 'hangers', which were tiny ornaments which Bernard Clark had made by ladies in their homes around Southend. You might have 'mimosas', as they were known, which were made by winding cut silk around a little circular form (rather like making a woolly ball for a baby), then cutting it around the edge to make a bobble that looked just like mimosa. You might alternate a hanging mimosa with a different hanger made from parchment in the shape of a little five-petal daisy, with silk wound over it.

Eventually poor Bernard Clark went blind, and as his workers were elderly he retired and the looms were broken up. After his retirement we found Turners, who were an established firm making regular fringes, so we began to have fringes in stock rather than bespoke. People coming into

Brook Street to buy fabric to make up themselves could also buy fan edging, linen fringes or wool bullion fringe. We were going in a new direction and to a different market. Turners still had a few outworkers who could do very special work. When it came to the restorations at Windsor Castle, for example, they made all the passementerie, recreating Regency tassels and trimmings.

We were known for our lampshades too. These were specially made by an extraordinary lady called Miss Parks, who worked off Oxford Street in a rather cramped single room containing large tables and what seemed like rather large ladies. Miss Parks was also rather large and usually dressed in a sort of sporting tweed: it always seemed quite surprising she was making frilly lampshades. She made lampshades for the trade, most of which were pretty dire — awful shapes with nasty fringes and loops of stuff around them, and always in ghastly colours. John wanted something different, more straightforward, so he designed decent shapes that would give a good light.

Miss Parks did a lot of pleated shantung shades for us: these were hand-pleated and bound on to wire frames which

Betty Handley, our lampshade maker, with Tommy Kyle, one of John's clients.

Our principal cabinetmaker was Mr Bartell, a young man who had set up his own business in London doing high-quality work. He worked with John a great deal, developing things like bedside cabinets and cupboards, often copying old models from the eighteenth and early nineteenth centuries. Together they devised a variety of bedside tables that allowed you to have a lamp, your books and a little drawer for your pills together with somewhere to put your glass of water. They were capacious and had two tiers, or even three. These pieces look a bit dated today, but we must remember that a lot of John's work had been done in the 1930s and they were hangovers from that time.

Mr Bartell also made me a Regency bamboo desk chair in beautiful thin turning, with a cane seat and a swab cushion, which when painted in our studio looked like the real thing, because it was an exact copy from an original. We were into painting in a big way, especially creating distressed effects so that the furniture looked old. I'm sure much has subsequently come on the market which people have thought eighteenth-century painting when it was in fact from John's studio.

When we were restoring houses after the war the paintwork was usually in a parlous state. Complete repainting would often be needed and in the case of the grandest rooms this would also involve regilding. There are actually two types of gilding: water gilding, which is an extremely difficult

she had specially made. There were variations in the pleating, and we would specify the size of the box pleat, or double box pleating which revealed the under-pleat. Nancy Lancaster had broderie anglaise shades, though I don't know where she first came across them. The frame would be covered in Japanese silk over which she put a skirt of broderie anglaise, hanging loosely like a child's skirt or a ball dress, with a gathered and fixed top. These were charming for bedrooms. Then we had half-shades and shield shades. And we developed the famous card shade – no one had previously thought of making a shade by stretching cartridge paper over a metal frame. These card shades were made for all sizes of lamps, even quite large ones, and could be painted if you liked.

After Miss Parks retired we used Betty Handley, who was also a rather unlikely lampshade maker, being an American lady living in England. She had a small shop in Belgravia and used outworkers rather than employing a lot of people, but continued with the same shapes and styles, which by then were very much the Colefax style.

LEFT A column table lamp made by my father, with a card shade.
RIGHT A small round-ended coffee table painted in the studio.

process, and oil gilding, which is slightly easier. Water gilding creates the most sumptuous effect because it leaves the gilt absolutely pristine. When I worked in the studio I learned how to oil gild. The moulding is covered in size and sheets of gold that are beaten out thinner than tissue paper are pressed on to it. Then you clean off any loose gilt. We did a lot of this type of gilding in the studio, on picture frames and French picture mounts, and also on chairs, if it was necessary to touch up parts where the gold had rubbed off.

We didn't do really ambitious gilding work ourselves, though. We would employ a firm like Bellamy's of York, who were excellent at gilding plaster and woodwork. In grand rooms we might specify that a gilt moulding should be picked out on the cornice, or the moulding on the door cases and dado through the room could be gilded to create a white and gold effect. There was a lot of gilding when we restored the chapel at Grimsthorpe Castle, for example. Most of the work we did involved restoring what had been there originally, toning the new gilding down so it blended in and didn't look too flashy. There are two schools of thought about this: whether to allow the gilding to tone down naturally, or to tone it in. Gilding takes a long time to tone down by itself, so usually we toned it in.

We did a lot of picture framing, often using a young Bulgarian refugee, Mattei Radev, who had a studio near Oxford Circus.[7] In our English-style rooms, we had pictures all over the walls – in groups, in blocks up the staircases, everywhere – and we were always buying paintings, engravings and botanical prints. Framing is an art in itself, and you have to know your periods and your mouldings well. You can spoil a seventeenth-century painting or print by putting it in a nineteenth-century frame.

Colefax & Fowler became known for specialist painting really because John revived various methods of painting that had fallen into disuse. The Victorians did a lot of wood graining, which is a form of specialist painting, but they normally used solid paint colours. John revived an older tradition he had found on furniture and in paintings, where the colour was created with a series of glazes. On his travels he saw these techniques in French buildings, particularly the use of three tones of white (for which of course he was to become famous). He needed expertise for these effects and found a firm in Hay's Mews, behind Berkeley Square, called Haywood Brothers. John persuaded the foreman, a man called Cyril Wopshott, to experiment with glazed painting.[8]

Together they started applying three tones of white on panelled doors. The door was first given a coat of eggshell,

A bracket carved by my father and gilded by Mattei Radev. John Fowler left me the eighteenth-century original and my father made the 'pair'.

then a very, very thin glaze was dragged on top. The glaze was actually ordinary white undercoat tinted with pigments. John insisted that the pigments should be earth colours – raw umber, raw sienna, black, occasionally burnt umber. The tints were mixed into the white undercoat and the mix was diluted with turpentine to a milky-thin consistency. A coat was applied randomly over the entire surface of the door and then, using flat brushes, it was dragged down: the panels first, then the rails (the horizontal divisions between the panels), then the stiles (the verticals). The stiles and rails were of a slightly darker tone than the panel colour, and when they were dry the mouldings were picked out in a lighter white to give a sort of three-dimensional look. Finally, a coat of flat varnish was applied to the whole door for protection.

John would also pick out the dado and the cornice using the same tones of white. The ceiling would possibly be in lighter tones. If it was an ordinary flat ceiling it would be

Katie O'Looney painting a hall door in Fred Krehbiel's Hinsdale house (see chapter 13), using three shades of white, just as John Fowler had taught us all to do. Notice that the stiles and rails (uprights and horizontals) are in a slightly darker tone than the panels; and the mouldings are in a lighter white.

done in just slightly broken white, but if it was more complex and picked out it would be two or three tones of white.

I remember in the Marble Hall at Syon House John used twelve different whites, in a very complicated scheme of warm and cool whites.[9] When it was finished it was like a miraculous wedding cake, because it had light and shade and interest, whereas if it had been painted in the same white all over it would have lost all the detail. This was a tour de force of decorative painting, and probably the most complex scheme we ever did.

John very seldom flat-painted a wall – usually he would drag or stipple the paint. Dragging walls can be difficult because the mixture dries very quickly, and if you aren't careful you get joints. This problem is partly alleviated by adding a teaspoon of linseed oil to the mixture to help keep it 'alive'. John also usually 'smoked' his colours. If he was painting a wall pale blue, for example, there would always be a little bit of black or umber in the mix to break the

sweetness. It made the colour softer, and actually more like nature – which is all nuances of subtle colours. The blue would possibly be a mix of cobalt and cerulean blue together with a little raw umber, and white of course, which was then made thin – milk-thin – and put on with large brushes to spread it evenly and quickly. Then with a dry, soft badger-hair brush it would be dragged down the whole length to the floor, on and on around the room, while the paint was still 'alive'. The dragging can be done lighter or coarser according to your requirements and the coarseness of the brush and the consistency of the mixture. Local painters never knew how to mix the paint, so we would show them.

If you're working over a large area it can be difficult to complete the dragging before the paint dries. I remember when we did the staircase at Ramsbury John insisted on using the traditional method of dragging with distemper. The staircase was done in a wonderful sealing wax red distemper over a pink undercoat. It took three men to drag the distemper, one at the top, one in the middle and one at the bottom, passing down the dragging brush from top to bottom. It wasn't done as evenly as it would have been in a smaller space, but the coarse brushstrokes gave it great life.

Cyril Wopshott had a natural eye for colour and how to achieve it. John would say to him, 'I want the colour of that sky, can you see up there . . . that sort of blue . . . translucent blue' and Cyril seemed to know what should go into the mix to get it. Or we might show him a picture or perhaps a bit of ribbon and John would say, 'I want that sort of yellow or this sort of green.' It was never done with colour charts as it is today, but usually with a physical example of the colour he wanted, hence the famous 'colour wall' in his office. Cyril became a good friend. He later married Mrs Hourigan (they were both widowed), and a very happy marriage it was. He was devoted to Houri and they made a very good team, working at Buckingham Palace for the Queen and at important houses like Farmleigh, the Iveaghs' house in Dublin.

A while later I came across someone else who had a talent rather similar to Cyril's: a flamboyant and unusual lady called Mavis Long.[10] I met Mavis by chance, really, when a friend of my assistant's asked for some help. She lived at Squerryes Court at Westerham in Kent, which was fairly local to me, so I went along one Monday morning to meet the owner,

RIGHT, CLOCKWISE FROM TOP LEFT Painting the marbled floor of Kay Krehbiel's bedroom at their Palm Beach house; the finished floor (see also pages 152–3); painting a wall at the Palm Beach house.

together with a blonde-haired lady then living in a sort of motorized caravan. She and her assistant had undercoated the hall and were ready to put on the final coats, but didn't know what colour to use. I mixed gallons of stone white in three tones. Mavis looked on and applied samples of eggshell (not glazes) for me to test. She was intrigued by what I did and eventually asked if she could work for me and if I could teach her how to do things. I was moving offices in Brook Street and the new office was panelled, so I invited her to do my office and taught her how to glaze. It was just green on off-white, a sort of pale apple green, but she did it beautifully. She continued to practise and I began to use her on jobs. Subsequently Mavis had an immensely successful career and she has now been succeeded by her daughter Sandy.

When I started to work in America I needed a team to help me. By great good fortune I met Mark Uriu, who was then just setting up a painting firm.[11] I taught him my tricks of the trade – how to paint the sort of glazed finishes and colours that I required, effects that were little known in the States. Mark, who was Japanese American and a wonderful artist, quickly became very skilled. He learned how to marbleize and how to do beautiful graining, imitating any sort of wood. These finishes can be very effective in the right place. We often marbleized skirtings for instance, making them look as if they were real marble. Because Mark was so skilful I was able to extend my imagination beyond the work John had done. Of course, I wasn't constrained by the types of rooms and houses I was working on as John had been. Mine was a different challenge: I was often starting from the base of a rather bland apartment, which could be turned into something special simply by the way it was painted.

In the late 1960s scumble glaze came on the market. This was a gelatinous translucent medium into which you could mix whichever colour you wanted. It didn't dry quickly but stayed 'alive', so you could play around with it and drag it more than once if it went wrong. John actually lived to see the birth of scumble glaze, but he didn't like using it. It was greasy and sticky, and it also tended to yellow, so after a few years a pale blue wall would turn pale green. Subsequently, I worked with Colin Mitchell Rose, of Craig & Rose in Edinburgh, and we produced a flat varnish that didn't discolour to put on as a protective coat over glaze painting.

By the early 1980s specialist painting had become the in thing. Books were being written on the topic, a notable example being Jocasta Innes's *Paint Magic.* You could even buy a kit to do it. So anyone could attempt it, but to be honest we shrank in horror when we saw some of the results.

Very often in decorating a room evolves around a carpet: the pattern and colours on the floor dictate what you do in the rest of the room. It might be an antique carpet, or a copy of an antique carpet, or a rug. Or it might be Brussels weave carpet – a flat weave with an all-over pattern. We became known for our Brussels carpets, but this really happened by fluke. Just after the war John had bought an antique close stool (a portable loo for use in a carriage). It was typical of John to buy such a thing. On the top was a piece of Brussels weave carpet. The pattern – which was probably by Christopher Dresser – was like a mossy woodland floor. John liked it and thought it made a good contrast to the current vogue for plain Wilton carpet, which came in a limited range of colours (chiefly beige and eau de nil). So we approached Crossley's in Halifax to reproduce it. Amazingly, it turned out that they still had the cards for this very pattern.[12]

Fired with enthusiasm, John began searching for documents of similar Brussels weaves. At the Ashburnham sale there were a few Brussels carpets, among them the famous 'Roses and Ribbons' carpet which Nancy Lancaster bought for Haseley Court. We copied this in two colourways: one was a brown ground with white roses, while another was a dark blue ground with white roses. We gradually expanded the available range as we acquired further documents – a friend of John's even sent one from America (a very nice medallion design that we christened 'Higford', after the donor) – and George Oakes designed some new patterns. As Brussels weave is flat they are less luxurious than tufted carpets and give a completely different feel to a room.

New carpets meant we needed skilled fitters, and happily at the top of Bond Street there was G. Gerratts, an old-fashioned firm of carpet layers and fitters. They had a group of women who sat on the floor and hand-sewed together the Brussels weave, which came in 27-inch-wide strips. It was stretched and then the borders were sewn on: often quite intricate borders which went in and out around fireplaces, etc. These tough London ladies sitting sewing carpets were always cheerful and jolly, as were the carpet fitters. It's funny to remember different trades where some had cheerful workers and others gloomy. Carpet people were always cheerful, whereas the painters were usually morose – there must be something in the paint mix.

Aside from Brussels weave we used a lot of haircord, which is a mixture of horsehair and wool on a canvas ground. Again it's a flat weave, like Brussels weave, but because of the colour of horsehair, it is invariably in tones of beige, most often a brown-grey which Nancy christened 'dead mouse' – actually not a bad name for it, though I prefer 'grayge' myself! However, it's a neutral colour and because of the flat weave you can throw a rug on to it and it won't slip around much. We used fitted carpet a lot in bedrooms as a background. We'd add an antique rug or even a fluffy white rug to cheer it up.

In drawing rooms and the like we would often use antique carpets. We had particularly good suppliers in C. John in South Audley Street and Francis in Jermyn Street. They both had an excellent collection of carpets, including very rare English Axminsters and wonderful French Aubussons. I remember doing a job in Bedford, New York, a large, long drawing room, from scratch. There were no pictures, no furniture, nothing to hitch on to as a theme, which you really need. Very often in these circumstances the best thing is to find a lovely carpet to put on a polished wooden floor. I found a beautiful Bessarabian carpet, with very soft colours, particularly rose pinks, which by chance was the right size for the room. It was rather expensive, as that size of Bessarabian was rare, but it simply made the room.

Perhaps the carpets we used most were the rugs and carpets we had handmade for us in Portugal. Before the war

in Lisbon Lady Ellis had seen a need for women prisoners to be given an occupation which would allow them to earn a little money. She started to revitalize traditional carpet-making methods – including a particular stitch that is done on a rather coarse canvas – revived old designs and created quite a viable business. Somehow Nancy knew her, or knew of her, and she got her to copy a Directoire Aubusson from the saloon at Ditchley Park, which had fallen apart.

I would fly to Lisbon with my colour range and sizes, sometimes taking with me a design (a 'cartoon') done by George Oakes. Translating designs to rugs is actually quite a tricky business because you're choosing wool colours, and if you get them wrong you can upset the whole balance of the design. I never had a failure and some were exceptionally beautiful, particularly the ones George designed, which were less like the traditional rugs.

One of the things John particularly liked was tole, which is beaten tin that has been shaped and painted. It was very popular in late eighteenth- and early nineteenth-century France, where it was used for all sorts of artefacts.

ABOVE 'Roes and Ribbons', a Brussels weave carpet we copied from one Nancy Lancaster bought at the Ashburnham Place sale in 1953.
RIGHT A Brussels weave carpet in 'Mossy'. Originally produced by Crossley's of Halifax, this was probably a design by Christopher Dresser.

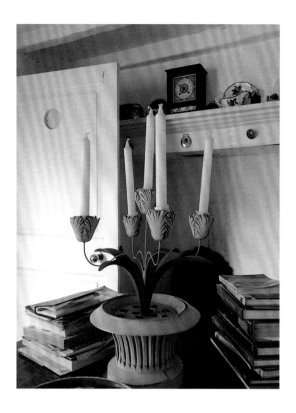

A 'Tulip' table centre in tole, copied from one John found in Paris.

A shell urn made by Gordon Davies for Fred Krehbiel.

When he got back from his sorties to Paris, aside from the furniture he bought, there were always pieces of Directoire-period tole, painted with pretty designs, rather like lacquer. He came back with names we didn't know – 'Would you send these *verriers* to the studio to have the inside touched up,' he would grandly say. A *verrier* was a bowl originally used to chill glasses – the serrated edges holding the glasses on a bowl of ice. He use to bring home wine coolers and jardinières, and also candle shades, which were very practical, being designed to shade a candle (or candles) so you didn't get the glare in your face. Tole wasn't very easy to discover, so John found two metalworkers, Mr Spering and Mr Best, and he got them to make copies of things he liked. I remember in particular a lovely metal-lined basket with a perforated plate for flowers, topped with metal candle holders in the form of tulips. The original John had found in Paris was broken, but there was enough there to have it copied. Mr Spering and Mr Best made the copies and they were painted in the studio, maybe a white and green basket with sort of dull green leaves and tulips painted in realistic stripes, perhaps white and mauve. They made wonderful table centres, with masses of flowers and candles.

Unfortunately, once tole became popular lots of cheap reproductions appeared, and we rather went off it.

When I started work we were undoing and repairing the ravages of the war and we often had to reinstate a room's architectural details, and occasionally to add them where they had never existed in the first place. I loved going to Putney to visit G. Jackson and Sons, the plasterworkers, at their workshop. It was a sort of Aladdin's cave, an enormous emporium. There were nets suspended from the ceiling and hanging from the nets were hundreds of plaster mouldings, covered in dust. All along the walls were racks of cornices, medallions, capitals, bases, flutes, every sort of plaster imaginable. Many of them had been taken from eighteenth- or nineteenth-century houses, and they were effectively the most wonderful documents.

This gave John the opportunity to do authentic eighteenth- and nineteenth-century rooms, because he could choose the right mouldings and recreate them in fibrous plaster, which he did on many occasions. It was probably done to greatest effect for Joan Dennis at Hay's Mews in Mayfair (see page 37). Here he made a double-height room with a bold cornice and he decorated the upper

Hand-printed Mauny wallpapers.

part of the wall with huge plaster swags and brackets which had come from old Northumberland House.

Visiting Jackson's was a revelation to me. I used cornices and dado rails wherever I worked. Today people live in plain boxes, stripped of architectural details, but I always feel the join between a ceiling and a wall requires definition, as indeed does the bottom of a wall, which is why skirtings are so important. Of course, standing in a plaster workshop in Putney it is not always easy to decide what will look right in a room in Yorkshire. Usually I would narrow the choice to two or three possibilities and Jackson's would lend me samples, which I would then get someone to hold up so I could judge if the dentil was the right size.

Of course, fabrics are an intrinsic part of all decoration. It was always a privilege to work with the printers and weavers. Going to the Carlisle factory of Stead McAlpin, who printed nearly all of our chintzes, was a thrill to me. It gave me a greater understanding of the techniques, how these multicoloured designs were created and how the cotton, which came from China in large unfinished and unwashed bales (what is known as 'grey' fabric), ended up as a perfect glazed chintz. Equally, learning the techniques of machine- and hand-weaving on site at the Walters factory in Sudbury

in Suffolk was not only very educational, but also helped me in my design work.

In the same way, working with Cole & Sons and Mauny, both wallpaper printers making beautiful handmade papers, opened up many possibilities when making exclusive papers for my clients. I found Mauny wallpapers particularly useful as they were handmade to order, so we could have special colourways done.[13] The background colour is usually hand-painted by two men. One brushes on the colour, using two brushes that look like scrubbing brushes but have soft bristles to apply the colour in interlocking circular strokes. The second man follows, brushing over the colour with a large straight brush to give an even ground with no graining. When the ground has dried, which takes a day or more, the pattern is hand block printed, one colour at a time. The paper has to dry properly after each blocking, before the next colour is applied. It is a very slow, labour-intensive process, but the the final result is very beautiful.

I always feel a special gratitude to all the various craftsmen I have known and worked with. Without them you really are nothing as a decorator. It was their skill, their talents and their knowledge which allowed me to create beautiful houses and rooms for my clients. My success was really their success.

9

ARABIAN ADVENTURES

It all began in 1977 with a telephone call from an architect in South Wales, Mr Alexander of Porthcawl. I didn't know him and he didn't know me, but apparently his secretary knew of us, and he wanted to ask if I would be interested in decorating a large family house in Saudi Arabia. Of course I would, but alas it was impossible because I was already far too busy, so I gave him the names of some other decorators. However, when he went back to his Saudi clients and told them I was unavailable for at least six months, they decided if I was that busy I must be rather good, and they were prepared to wait.

The job was essentially to decorate a large block of flats which Mr Alexander was building for Sheikh Salim Ahmed bin Mahfouz in what appeared to be desert just outside Jeddah on the road to Mecca. It was designed to hold the sheikh's family, which included his two wives, his five sons, and the wives and children of those sons who were married (as I recall one of the sheikhs was too young to be married, being only six).

I arranged to go to see them and I duly set off for Saudi Arabia, but when I got to Heathrow it was fog-bound and we were delayed, so I didn't arrive in Jeddah until the early hours of the following morning. Some poor soul had been waiting hours for me to arrive, but he recognized me very quickly – I suppose I must have cut an unmistakable figure walking alone through the terminal. We arrived at the residence about half past two in the morning, to be met by a sleepy Sudanese boy who carried my luggage up to the harem on his head. The harem was really a series of flats in a rather run-down building, which looked a little like an old-fashioned nursing home or guesthouse. I was shown into a bedroom, rather dusty, but with a bed, for which I was very grateful.

In the morning I was greeted by the extremely nice English-speaking wife of one of the young sheikhs, who was very welcoming: 'Come and have breakfast. We've got a room for you to work in.' There was a white tablecloth on the floor on which sat a large teapot, a jug of hot milk, a jar of Smedley's raspberry jam, Lurpak butter and some flat bread. They brought in a boiled egg and a knife. I crouched on the floor and grappled with my breakfast, the hot milk and the teapot, all done in my honour, of course, since they don't have breakfast like that. The problem was sitting on the floor, which I wasn't used to. When the young sheikh came up to greet me after breakfast he hoped everything was all right and said he was sorry my plane had been so delayed. He was very polite, as indeed were they all. 'Is there anything you need?' I asked if I could have a table and some chairs, as I would never manage to work on the floor all day. He simply snapped his fingers and in came chairs and a table for the ladies and me to sit down. I was then introduced to the sheikhs' wives. I asked them if they knew what their new house was going to be like. They didn't, so I produced the plans Mr Alexander had sent me. They had obviously never seen a plan and found them difficult to understand.

They were for a big building that would have various uses. It included a large area for festivals and big receptions, and also an area specifically for the men to entertain in. There was an apartment for the father, Sheikh Salim, and another for visiting guests. Otherwise, essentially, the apartments were all identical. The building had very high ceilings, I suppose over 12 feet high, and this doesn't make for easy decoration when the rooms are small – a small room, 12 feet long and 12 feet high, is very ugly. There were ways around these problems, but for the moment my main concern was finding out from the ladies how they would like their apartments to look. The architect had advised me to take lots of samples, magazines and pictures, because he thought the ladies didn't know much about decoration.

OPPOSITE 'Moiré Stripe', a design taken from a late eighteenth-century chancery silk found in an English pattern book. We increased the scale.

(Not that he really knew: being a man, he had never been allowed to meet the ladies.)

I soon found out that what the ladies wanted was westernized living. Many of them had lived in London and Paris (in fact the family had a house off the Bayswater Road in London, which they all used). And their husbands had been educated abroad, in England and America. So they had had a taste of the West, and they wanted western comforts.

The father, Sheikh Salim, had been born in the mountainous Hadhramout region of Yemen, but the story went that as a very young boy (it was said at the age of six) he had walked across the desert with only a jewelled dagger in his belt. Arriving at Jeddah he sold the dagger and started a sort of money-exchanging business, becoming a moneychanger to the King's agents. He was illiterate, could neither read nor write, but he could certainly add up and subtract! He went on to found the National Commercial Bank of Saudi Arabia and amassed an enormous fortune. I met him and his older wife, but I don't recall meeting the younger wife, who was kept somewhere else. There was a large staff, and all the servants, both male and female, were Sudanese.

I worked right through the day with the young ladies. They explained how they had guests and how they entertained ladies and how many people had to be catered for. In effect, I had to learn how they lived. I also very soon discovered that none of them wanted their apartment to look like any one else's: they wanted to be individuals. I pointed out that they could have whatever style they liked and they could choose what they thought was comfortable. One wife would say, 'Well, I like this look' (perhaps Spanish Colonial), while another one would say, 'I'd like it very French.' I think this was probably the first time they had ever been allowed a free choice in anything, except possibly their clothes.

In the evening, after supper, they all sat on banquettes around the wall, talking and smoking hookah pipes while the children played on the carpet. At about eleven o'clock I was summoned to go and see the sheikhs, who lived downstairs with their own servants. So downstairs I went in my Marks & Spencer's kaftan (I had bought several of them for this trip), where I was told to take my shoes off at the door before going into the sheikhs' presence.

They all sat around a huge round table in their white robes and headgear, and I recall that Mohammed, the eldest son, sort of chaired the meeting: 'We would like to know how you got on with the ladies today.' I explained that I had shown them how their apartments would be laid out and how big, and tall, the rooms were. And that we had looked at lots of magazines and some of them had chosen already the look they wanted. And that they were all very excited and enjoying it.

I did have one slight problem. It was specified that in the father's apartment I had to supply an Arab loo but I didn't know what an Arab loo was. One of the sheikhs led me along a passage and I peered down a hole in the ground with two footprints, and I realized I had seen something similar on the Continent. That amused them all. I was surprised he wanted that in a modern block of flats but the sheikh explained that was what he had been used to all his life and so he didn't want to change. Of course, everyone else wanted western-style bathrooms with showers and gold taps. (I tried to limit the gold taps!) It was going to be rather daunting to produce so many different bathrooms and cloakrooms – the total was something like fifty-seven. That also amused them.

On my first visit I spent five days with them, and this was to be the pattern: each evening I was summoned to give a daily report, which always seemed to greatly amuse the sheikhs.

As I had more conversation with the ladies and got to know them a little I found they were really very intelligent and bursting to know more about things. They were the first generation who had been educated. They had been to school and university, only to end up being so restricted, so closeted, and only allowed out veiled and in black. They thoroughly enjoyed our discussions and it was interesting that they wanted to be different from each other. It wasn't jealousy; it was merely that they wanted to express themselves and this was one way to do so.

During one of these sessions with the ladies a sheikh appeared and said, 'I've just had a telephone call from the British embassy. They've asked you to go to dinner at the embassy.' I didn't know anyone at the embassy so it was a great surprise. The sheikh kindly arranged for a car to take me, and one of the ladies accompanied me as my escort. When I got to the imposing embassy (actually the residence of the consul-general), I walked up to the door and as if by magic it opened and I entered another world. There was a butler with a small tray and on it a glass – 'His Excellency thought you might be longing for a gin and tonic!' How right he was. I was introduced to everyone and I asked the ambassador how he knew I was there. Apparently the Foreign Office had alerted him because it was unheard of for a British businesswoman to come to Saudi Arabia at that time – I suppose they were curious about what I was doing. The following morning the ladies were just as intrigued to hear about my trip out.

On another visit I went to Riyadh, catching a lift with a sheikh on his private jet, to see one of the ladies who was spending time there. Having read Wilfred Thesiger's *Arabian Sands* I was thrilled to look out and see the Empty Quarter of Saudi Arabia spread out below me. On the return trip I was on my own, apart from a Sudanese servant they sent with me. This poor woman had never flown in her life before and was terrified. Unfortunately, there had been some sort of incident at Jeddah airport, so we couldn't land and were diverted to Medina. I was taken to a grand hotel just outside the airport and given a suite, and my Sudanese servant was given a room. She was in tears, very frightened, and ended up sleeping on the floor of my room: she'd never slept in a bed before, either.

When I came home I realized that the job presented massive difficulties. I really couldn't see how it was going to happen. They wanted pictures of what the rooms would look like, which meant producing paintings, which was something we never did. I would sketch something for a client and give them a room plan, and do a sketch of the curtains, but a visual representation of how the whole room would look was something else. I knew I couldn't possibly do paintings of all these rooms on my own, so in June 1978 Pierre Serrurier came into my life as my assistant for this job. At the same time my colleague David Laws was working for another family in Jeddah, so it was decided we would share the new assistant between us.

When I went back to Jeddah in November the following year, Pierre came with me but had to live in the men's quarters of the old palace, while I was in the harem. Looking out of the window of the harem I noticed there was a completely empty swimming pool. It transpired that new buildings overlooked it, so it was impossible for the ladies to swim there. Few places are more depressing than an unused dirty pool, but this was where Pierre and I would take our breakfast so we could discuss things. I was doing all the upstairs talk with the ladies, and he was doing the business on site with the architects and the builders (he was forbidden from meeting the ladies). We would sit and be served breakfast (always over-boiled eggs) by a very distinguished Sudanese servant who must have been seven feet tall and was clad entirely in white.

Aside from the building itself my clients really had no furniture, so it would all have to be specially made – in the

Pierre and me, working in the street! We were choosing colours to go with this antique Zeigler carpet, which was so large we couldn't lay it out anywhere else.

climate antiques just fall to pieces. We went to a furniture factory north of Milan to source good-quality reproduction French furniture. We also went to Murano in Venice to plan lovely chandeliers and lanterns, and to Vicenza, where we visited a factory producing mosaic. It was fascinating to learn about the different sorts of mosaic, and how gold and glass mosaic are made in exactly the same way they had been for St Mark's in Venice. The huge reception rooms – 35 feet long and 12 feet high – that were used for entertaining needed the grand treatment.

In the end, though, I suppose I'm afraid I proved to be the apple of discord. My involvement really destroyed the whole project. Through me the ladies learnt a great deal about how other people lived, and they decided they simply didn't want to live in a block of flats using a central communal dining room. So they persuaded their husbands they wanted individual homes. After two years of intense work, producing dozens of paintings of each important room and each area, and hundreds of very painstaking and time-consuming estimates, it all came to nought. The sheikhs decided to sell the complete building to the Saudi government. We were suitably recompensed, but didn't make much profit because we never sold them so much as a stick or a stone: they actually bought nothing. The wives got their apartments or villas, but we weren't involved in the decoration. Our original specifications were so detailed they probably decided they could do it all themselves.

I never worked in Saudi Arabia again, but a few years later I went to work in Kuwait. Like many Arabs,

my Kuwaiti clients spent the summer in London and I was initially asked to do their London home in Regent's Park. Nadia Al Ghanim had read about us and as I had experience of dealing with Arab clients I was sent to meet her and got the job. I liked her enormously. After the London house was finished she asked me if I would help her with her house in Kuwait.

I flew to Kuwait to see this house, which was a large modern villa. Nadia liked French furniture, but she also liked Arab and other eastern artefacts, and bought old doors, pieces of pottery, sculptures and such things on her travels. She and her husband were both widely travelled and sophisticated in their taste. I did the whole house on budget and it was all shipped out. When assembled it was a comfortable and eclectic mix of furniture and objects. Nice carpets, some oriental, some rugs specially made for her, and good marble floors.

It was through Nadia that I was introduced to Princess Badria, who also had a house in Regent's Park. The princess was related to the Emir of Kuwait and had a palace in Kuwait where she had employed Hammond's to do some work for her. She felt that her main reception room – a room used by women for entertaining each other, and sometimes for royal receptions – didn't give her enough space, so she added an extension. On Nadia's recommendation I went to amalgamate the two areas and to slightly adapt what Hammond's had done – I suppose the idea was that I would jazz it up a bit.

Shortly after I had completed the job for the princess there came the First Gulf War. The princess was on holiday on the coast with her grandchildren and the children of other friends when the invasion began, and she was told to leave the country immediately, to head for Saudi Arabia and the safety of the border. Her palace was completely destroyed, and the entire contents looted and taken across the border into Iraq. All the work I had done had been in vain, and when she returned we had to start again on a completely new house.

Luckily Nadia was abroad at the time of the invasion, as were her husband and children. Nadia's house escaped almost unscathed. The only thing that happened was that some Iraqi soldiers who broke in left their mark by scratching a terrible gouge down the mahogany dining table.

After the liberation I was approached by a young Kuwaiti bachelor, Mr Emad Al Bahar, who was from an aristocratic family and must have heard of me through the princess. He had a college friend who wanted to be an architect, but who hadn't gone through the training. My client decided to allow him to design a house on a rather small plot of land in Kuwait City. It was the most eccentric house you could imagine; a sort of inside-out house. The facade was rather bland, but the interior was formed around a courtyard like in an old house, with the first-floor bedrooms behind mashrabiya lattice windows and an enormous cascade, made of fibreglass boulders, artificial ferns and palm trees, beneath a glass roof. The cascade, around which the staircase wound, stretched from the top of the house to the basement, the water cascading down into a pool at the bottom. Unfortunately, it proved to be so noisy it had to be turned off most of the time, so it was only a dribble not a cascade.

LEFT Nadia Al Ghanim's house in Kuwait. The Indian doors into the dining room; the reception room, showing the swag and tail draperies; the dining room. RIGHT The noisy water cascade running from top to bottom of Emad Al Bahar's house.

My client came to London and showed me photographs of things he had collected. He had many attractive artefacts. He loved oriental art, for which he had an eye, also porcelain, carpets, bronzes and paintings. He explained that he was going to be using the house as a bachelor. Accordingly we designed it around him, with a dining room, reception rooms and his master bedroom – all very comfortable. The reception rooms opened off the central hall with its pool and included a room for men to entertain and another room with mashrabiya lattice window screens of the type often found in old Arabian houses to shield women from prying eyes.

The windows were a real challenge for a decorator – some of them were 18 feet high and 6 feet wide. However, I managed to disguise them. We supplied a considerable amount of reproduction furniture, since antique furniture would never have survived the combination of the climate and the moisture from the cascade.

In the middle of everything, he told us he was getting married, to Afrah Al Sabah, a member of the royal family. This altered things considerably and we had to rethink to make it into a family home. His new wife came to London and chose some fabrics and styles with us. I enjoyed working with him enormously: he had a very good sense of humour and was generous, and we became good friends during the time we worked together. I have to say the finished job was like nothing I'd ever produced before. I think the architect who designed it was horrified, because he'd imagined a minimalist interior. But our client wanted

something more comfortable. Although the end result was a strange mixture, it looked quite good.

I cannot now recall who introduced me to Mr and Mrs Al Sagar, who wanted to build in the desert a new house to resemble a Nash villa in Regent's Park. Building something so totally out of context might seem surprising, but the suburbs and outskirts of Kuwait City were full of houses of every imaginable shape and size. It seemed that everyone just thought of a style they liked and reproduced it on the edge of the desert. There might be a Spanish Colonial house next to a classical building, or even some Tudorbethan. I suppose it was a bit like Beverly Hills, but on rather small plots of land. In any event this young couple, with their two young children, wanted a Regent's Park Nash villa and engaged a London architecture firm, John Beswick & Michael Robinson, to design one for them. It looked very good on paper. However, it was difficult to build because it had a modern steel and concrete structure, which was then clad in stone. The stone – a rather pale limestone as I recall – was cut and shaped in Syria. There were sash-like windows, as Nash would have had, but these had to be airtight because of the sandstorms and air conditioning.

Mr Al Sagar, who had an extremely successful clothing business in Kuwait, was very westernized and spoke excellent English and French. He would come to England with his wife, renting a house every summer, and I had quite a lot of meetings with them in London. First we discussed the styles they wanted, and then we went on

Derry Moore's photograph of the morning room at Heron Bay in Barbados, which inspired the coral room in the Al Sagar house in Kuwait.

shopping expeditions. We couldn't use delicate antiques, but we found pretty things to put in the house and she had a good notion of what she wanted. I was amazed when one day she pulled out of her handbag something she had taken from a magazine. It was a picture of Heron Bay, Ronnie Tree's house in Barbados. Ronnie Tree (Nancy Lancaster's second husband) loved Palladian architecture and having sold Ditchley Park he had built a copy of Palladio's Villa Barbaro in the Veneto. She particularly loved the coral stone walls and wanted to use the idea for their family room. Using coral stone itself was out of the question (it is simply unobtainable), but we found a supplier in Kansas who had stone that would give a similar look, being a light porridge colour, porous and with fossils. We sent over drawings for it to be cut into the necessary shapes for the walls, architraves to the windows and door casings, and even bookcases.

It was quite a feat to send the stone halfway round the world and assemble it to form a room in a house in Kuwait. I was horrified when I first saw it because the stones had been cut to about a quarter of the specified size. The cutters had read the detail wrong and it was clearly their fault. However, wherever the fault lay, having got the stone to Kuwait it didn't really matter – it was a disaster. I decided not to tell the client, but to put the walling up and make the grouting match the stones so you would hardly see it. This worked and didn't draw attention to the sizes of the stones. Actually, the final effect was perfectly acceptable and they loved it.

The room was furnished with French furniture, pretty mirrors and chandeliers, which were rather less glittering and ostentatious than a previous generation of Arab clients would have chosen. These young people had been westernized and wanted less gilt, but still needed a formal reception room like a French salon. Down in the basement we had a lovely indoor pool with changing rooms and a glamorous sitting area. It was enjoyed by the family for many years, but has now been filled in and replaced by a

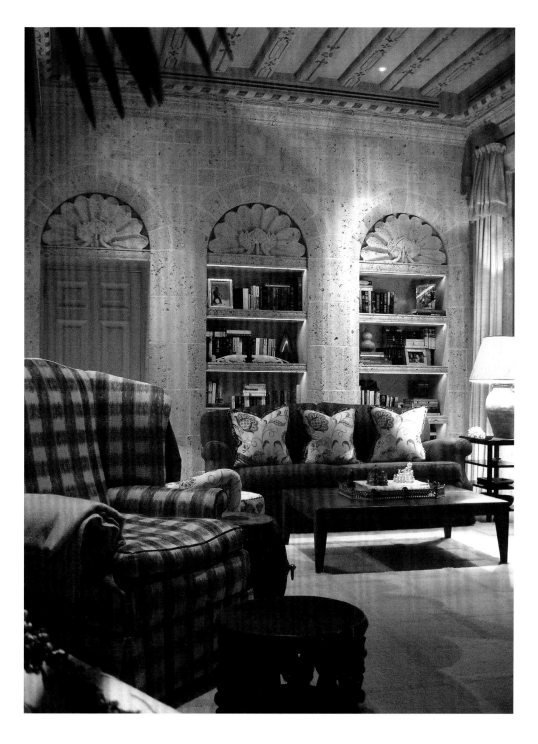

Our interpretation of the
Heron Bay room. The stone
came from Kansas.

big reception room. They also wanted a garden, which was
a little over-ambitious. Though she longed for little box
hedges and a parterre, it was pretty much impossible to
establish such a thing in Kuwait.

To decorate successfully for anyone you have to
understand how they live. The Kuwaitis, of course, had a
lifestyle that was very different from that of my English
clients. I needed to learn what they did each week and

how they entertained – in the older generation women
entertained women and men entertained men, although
the younger generation, who are more westernized, have
friends of both sexes and entertain mixed groups.

There seemed to be no indigenous interior style. When
I got my first commission I took pictures of Marrakech
riads, but they weren't thinking like that. They liked Paris
and wanted French things, and English things, and also

LEFT The garden door of the Nash villa in Kuwait, only the bougainvillea betraying the location.
BELOW LEFT The hall, painted in a soft Adam green.
BELOW RIGHT Banquettes in the saloon.

OPPOSITE LEFT Painted panels in the dining room.
OPPOSITE RIGHT A corner of the snug.

Indian things. They loved chintz, so I would do chintz bedrooms for them. We made furniture that looked antique and we also used painted things, which worked even though new (but we were clever with our paint finishes). We would add a genuine antique picture or a lamp or a big bowl to give a certain tone to a room because a house full of reproductions always looks rather dead – like a hotel, which was something we tried to avoid.

I enjoyed working for my many Kuwaiti clients. Their taste was rather eclectic: I would not normally choose to combine a French salon and an English bedroom. But they had all travelled a lot, and had seen beautiful Tuscan villas, lovely salons in Paris and English country houses. I was impressed by the sophistication of the younger generation of Kuwaitis, the women in particular. They admired and understood western-style living, and they worked with me to create a new style, which they have gone on to keep. An example is the Al Sagars' 'Regent's Park Nash villa', which is still exactly as I left it, apart from the pool area and the children's rooms, which were redone when the children left home. It is gratifying to me that the family still love and enjoy the house. And that really is the point of decorating: making a home for someone to live in.

10

GOING COMMERCIAL

All our work at Colefax was domestic and I had never done any commercial work. I always dreamed that one day someone would come in and want to have a hotel done or maybe a restaurant, but in the whole of my career neither of those things ever happened. However, although I might never have done a hotel, I did eventually do quite a bit of commercial work.

I had worked for one of the directors of Hoare's bank and he recommended me to his fellow directors. They approached me in 1973 and I was asked to go and see the directors of this extraordinary old-fashioned bank. It is

OPPOSITE 'Berkeley Sprig', a design taken from an eighteenth-century wallpaper found by John Fowler in 1962 at 44 Berkeley Square, where it was being used as a lining paper beneath a Victorian red damask.

actually the oldest established bank in the United Kingdom, and one of the oldest in Europe, housed in a beautiful building at 37 Fleet Street. It was not like any bank I had ever seen in my life. You went into an imposing entrance hall with a grand staircase off and then up to a reception room on the first floor. No sign of any cashiers or any banking going on at all. That actually took place in a large partners' room off the ground floor where stately gentlemen sat at partners' desks and worked. The directors wanted the reception room rejigged and redecorated, so basically I turned it into a drawing room where they could hold their receptions. It wasn't the normal sort of commercial job, but more a case of bringing a sense of domesticity to a commercial enterprise.

The next commercial job I did was for the Clerical Medical insurance company. They had a very fine building

ABOVE The Clerical Medical boardroom at Lichfield House.

The restored ceiling of the staircase landing.

The main boardroom of Willis Faber.

known as Lichfield House at 15 St James's Square. The house was designed by James Stuart, and dated from about 1765, with alterations by Samuel Wyatt in 1791. It had tall, elegant rooms and a very grand staircase. My main involvement was the staircase hall and the restoration of the plaster ceiling, which was probably by Joseph Rose and very important. We painted both the staircase hall and first floor landing, then moved on to the boardroom. Fortunately they already had a boardroom table and chairs, for which I was grateful because it would have been difficult to find a long enough table. We painted the room and supplied carpets, which I had specially woven by Mackay's in Durham. We found a design that seemed to fit the period of the house and ran it through the boardroom and the adjacent reception room. It was woven complete with border to fit the rooms,

and wasn't joined. Prior to this in most of our work we used Brussels weave carpets (John had led the way in reviving this type of carpet) but they were woven on narrow looms only 27 inches wide, which would have meant a lot of joins, and they wouldn't have been hard-wearing in a boardroom. The directors were pleased with the results, and I worked for them for a number of years. As the budget was limited, we would spend a year's budget on one room and then move on to the next.

I also did work at Schroders bank, where my client Gordon Richardson was chairman of the board from 1962 until he left to be Governor of the Bank of England in 1973.[1] He brought me in to do the chairman's office. I worked on the directors' dining room and various other reception rooms as well, but I concentrated mainly on his office.

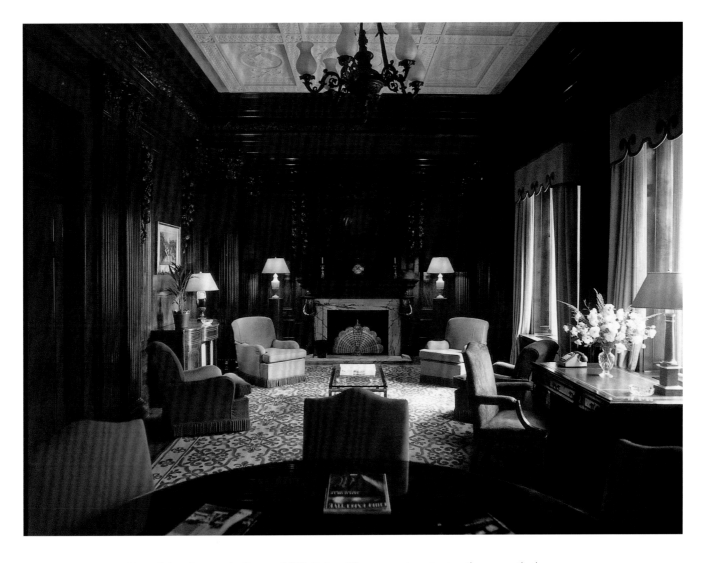

One of the directors' offices at Willis Faber. There were twenty-six others exactly the same.

One of the biggest commercial jobs I did was for the insurance brokers Willis Faber. They had bought the old Port of London Authority offices in Trinity Square Gardens on Tower Hill, an enormous Edwardian building facing the Tower of London. In this vast building the interior was virtually intact, although I think it had sustained some bomb damage during the war. It was extremely grand, and a daunting job for us: it took us about ten minutes to walk the length of the area we were engaged to decorate. There were fireplaces in all the directors' offices and large reception rooms with high ceilings and enormous windows overlooking the Tower. And as I recall there were twenty-seven directors who each had an office, and of course the twenty-seven men had twenty-seven wives, who naturally had ideas about how their husbands' offices should be.

There was a very long boardroom, which was panelled but very sad and run-down. Of course, there was no question of painting the panelled walls, but we had to find some way of lifting the gloomy atmosphere. The directors also wanted a dining room upstairs that could be used to entertain clients. The directors' dining room was interesting – and difficult – partly because it was so huge. We made what I would call very large window boxes, in which we grew hedges dividing areas of the room into separate alcoves. In these alcoves we would have a round table to allow for more private conversations. It gave a feeling of outdoor-ness, and since the room was on the top floor it was very light and airy. We even chose the cutlery and glass, which was fun. The room did look really very pleasant in the end and worked very well.

LEFT ABOVE The reception area at Lehman's. I commissioned the large paintings of Indian scenes.
LEFT BELOW The fabric-hung dining room at Lehman's.

At the same time a modern extension was being added at the back of the building. The architect in charge was Michael Hopkins, who subsequently went on to build the new opera house at Glyndebourne, a circular factory for David Mellor and many other innovative buildings. He was not involved in my part, nor I in his, but we had to discuss the main entrance hall to the building as it affected us both, and though we were on completely different wavelengths, we were able to agree on a scheme.

The job for Willis and Faber was difficult because of its scale, and because I had limited staff and limited time. The weekend before they opened we all worked into the night setting the whole thing up. It is perhaps not surprising that at the end of the job I was taken ill; after an x-ray it was discovered I had an ulcer.

We also did some work at Madame Tussauds, but it was a fairly minor job, involving a representation of the Queen on the throne. We had to produce a Cloth of State (the canopy over the throne) suitably braided and embroidered with the royal arms, and we also supplied acres of hard-wearing carpet, which was a very good thing for us financially.

With these and other jobs I was gradually making a name for myself, and that was how I came to work for Lehman Brothers. The young managing director from America, Stephen Bershad, asked which was the best decorating firm in London and we were recommended.[2] He came in to say he needed major work on a building they'd purchased, which had been the warehouse of the East India Company and formed part of the Devonshire Square development in Cutler Street. The warehouse, with its enormous floor areas (which had formerly been storage areas for all the things that came in from the docks, but were now redundant), was to be converted into a modern computerized dealing floor and general offices. It was a very interesting building and the fact it had belonged to the East India Company in the eighteenth and early nineteenth centuries gave a theme I could use.

They required us to create a trading floor, interviewing rooms and directors' rooms of varying sorts. It was too big a project to do on my own, so I turned to the architectural side of our business, Colefax & Fowler Associates, which was run by Chester Jones. It was one of Chester's assistants, Clive Butcher, who did the work with me. I had never seen a computer and had no idea what was required there, so he handled all that side. We had to work on the floor plan and divide the vast areas into rooms with partitions. The ceiling had to be lowered to accommodate all the wiring and the lighting, and I think the floor level was raised.

A Japanese-inspired dining room at Lehman's.

Following the theme suggested by the East India Company, I looked for pictures of Indian landscapes. I got an artist friend to paint two enormous paintings for the entrance. They looked like Thomas and William Daniell's paintings of scenes of India and gave some style to the rather boring reception room.[3] During my search for Indian artefacts I managed to find some Anglo-Indian furniture for the managing director's office, and that gave it an interesting look.

Subsequently, I helped Stephen Bershad and his wife with their house in Pelham Crescent, which was leased for him by the bank. He was pleased with what we did both in the offices and in his London house, so when he eventually returned to New York I ended up doing his apartment there. But that is, as they say, another story.

11

GOING TO AMERICA

When I worked for John Fowler we did some work for American clients, usually friends of Nancy Lancaster, such as David and Evangeline Bruce (for whom Fowler decorated part of the American ambassador's residence in Regent's Park), Bunny Mellon and the Whitneys.[1] Alas, John never went to America, which is a pity because I am sure he would have loved it, particularly the old plantation houses in the South. Incredible as it may seem he did all his American work by post. When I started to work on my own I also had a few American clients, but they were in London, not in America.

My first glimpse of America came in March 1980, when I went on a group trip organized by Ian McCallum, who ran the American Museum in Bath. It was a small, rather select group, including the restaurateur Robert Carrier, Stanley Falconer (a colleague from Colefax) and ten others. It was fascinating travelling, from Boston to New York, then down to Washington and Philadelphia. We saw some interesting houses and several museums. However, this was my only taste of America until Mr and Mrs Alan Dayton came in to Brook Street.

They showed me photographs of their house in Palm Beach, Florida. Alterations were underway to what appeared a fairly small house, and they kept saying, 'It's only a little house and we'd love the English look.' A comfortable sitting room and pretty flowery fabrics was what they were after. It's what Americans think of as English country house style, which is not quite the case. The English tend to have eclectic tastes. They have often inherited or acquired different sorts of things, which they combine together in their houses. Those who do it well create a lived-in comfortable look, while Americans generally have a more

formal approach to decoration. The voluptuousness of our curtains and the tailored looseness of our covers really appealed to the Daytons.

I flew to Miami to join the Daytons' architect, Henry Melich, who was an old friend (we met while working at Ramsbury). It was he who had originally advised the Daytons to come to me. He was in charge of the builders and I was to organize the furnishings.

When I arrived, having never been to Florida before I quickly realized that the light and atmosphere were completely different from the blue-grey light of England. Brighter, crisper and more like the light you get in Greece. I had to adapt the colour palate to this brighter light and suggested all sorts of fresh colours, brighter and sharper than the colours we used in England.

Not knowing what to expect in Florida I had brought over lots of chintzes. The soft reproductions of nineteenth-century fabrics just disappeared in that light. 'Honeysuckle' chintz, however, being on a white ground looked well there.

OPPOSITE 'Honeysuckle', an English mid-nineteenth-century block print design.

The sitting room at the Daytons' house in Palm Beach.

'Honeysuckle' chintz in the dining room.

The painted floor in the dining room.

I developed a scheme based around painted furniture using fresh colours and also painted floors. I had never done anything like that in England, but I had seen painted floors on my trip to the east coast. I felt they would give character and use the reflective light, and the Daytons liked the idea. We did a design for a painted floor which was geometric and made up of marbleized squares.

The problem was how to achieve the scheme. In England I knew exactly where to go to have things done, but I didn't know any craftsmen in America. I could only think to use the specialists I knew in England. I had a carpet made to my design and specifications in Portugal. Otherwise, except for the things the Daytons already had, everything – curtains and furniture and upholstery – was brought from London. This was all a new venture for me, buying furniture, tidying it, repairing it, possibly painting it, then shipping it to the States.

I brought over a team who had been trained in our studio in London to paint the house and the Daytons were very kind – they even took them to Disney World for the weekend. Sadly, I was considered too grown up and was left behind!

To be truthful I wasn't convinced that moving the English country house style to Florida really worked: it was a bit incongruous in what was essentially a seaside atmosphere. But the final result was pretty, and definitley different from what their friends had. The other houses in Palm Beach had a more American, Floridan look, with big, soft sofas and more blowsy prints: our look was more classical, using neat upholstered furniture of the sort

Colefax made at that time and still do. Our chairs and sofas had beautifully fitted loose covers, which was something they didn't do much in America.

Palm Beach is essentially just rows of houses all the way down to the sea. The Daytons' house was one block back from the ocean, on the lagoon side, not the sea side, so it didn't get direct wind or salt spray. They asked me how to deal with the front of the house, which was just a bare plot of land. I found a design from a Roman mosaic and made a small lemon garden, composed of lemon trees in Italian pots set in a little knot garden of box. It filled the space beautifully and was unique in Palm Beach. An artist friend of mine, Gordon Davies, had an extraordinary talent for modelling in terracotta and doing shellwork. Together we devised a little summer house to act as a focal point in the garden and to provide a home for a shell and terracotta mermaid. Henry's major contribution to the gardens was a beautiful gazebo dining room like an old-fashioned conservatory, with a sweeping roof formed from trellis.

Although everything was on a small scale the house and garden did have some panache when finished. It was pretty as you walked in at the front, through the mosaic lemon garden, then into the hall, then the painted flowery sitting room and the dining room beyond with its painted floor and 'Honeysuckle' chintz on the wall. I had been allowed a fairly free hand and more money than I would normally have spent on a small house. But the end result perhaps justified the extra expenditure.

CLOCKWISE FROM TOP LEFT The front garden being laid out; the completed front garden; a shell panel starring a mermaid, designed by Gordon Davies; the Slat House designed by Henry Melich.

The Daytons were very social and were always coming over to England. They subsequently bought a house in England, which I helped them decorate. I thought they might recommend me to their friends, but they liked being exclusive. They really enjoyed having something nobody had seen because a lot of the things I put into the house were English. They certainly weren't going to give away the telephone number of their decorator. This was true of practically every client I had in America. However, the Daytons did allow the house to be published in a book entitled *Summer Cottages and Castles: Scenes from the Good Life*, which came out in 1983.

It was lovely working with Henry Melich again and I was grateful for the introduction. Henry, who worked extensively in the Bahamas, also generously recommended me to Mrs Maria Davila, for whom he was to build a house. Mrs Davila was a young widow with ten children. The saddest thing was their youngest child was barely three years old when her husband died. He had left her a large fleet of cargo ships. She employed a young banker to help sort out the business, and they were extremely successful. She had a 1930s apartment in Madrid and a house in Miami, as well as the plot in the Bahamas. Later she bought a yacht from the King of Spain.

Mrs Davila came to Brook Street armed with a pack of photographs of the things she liked and owned. I took one look at them and didn't quite know what to say. One was a photograph of man-sized *cloisonné* vases, very vivid in colour. She said, 'I would like the room done around these. And I also have this – my jade collection.' There are two things in life I've tried to like and failed: one is *cloisonné* enamel and the other is jade. I know it is often beautifully carved, but it just isn't my thing. I knew I would love to work with Henry again, because he was an imaginative architect, and we had rather jokey conversations. Mrs Davila seemed good fun, and who would turn down a trip to the Bahamas? However, notwithstanding all the jade and *cloisonné*, I was very surprised to discover that Mrs Davila had told Henry she wanted a Roman villa.

Henry Melich

The Davila house at Lyford Cay in the
Bahamas.
ABOVE The entrance courtyard.
RIGHT The swimming pool, looking towards
the pavilions.
OPPOSITE, CLOCKWISE FROM TOP LEFT The
loggia; a corner of a guest bedroom; the
courtyard paintwork, showing the green
verdigris created using egg yolks; the dining
room, with the table laid for dinner.

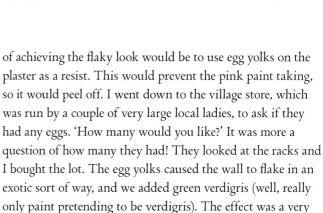

Her plot was at Lyford Cay, which is a very exclusive gated community. The plot wasn't on the sea, but set back on the edge of the golf course, within walking distance of the sea and not far from the Lyford Cay Club. We had to to wait a few months while the house was being built. In the meantime Pierre and I planned all the decoration. I had asked Mrs Davila if she had furniture and how we were to furnish. She explained she had some furniture, which turned out to be by Fornasetti with black and white faces on it.

Henry created a very exciting and unusual house. It was a single-storey building with a forecourt faced by a completely blank wall with a large gateway in the middle. No windows and no indication it was even really a house: just a wall, not a Palladian facade. The gateway opened directly into the courtyard around which the house was built on three sides. A large drawing room, a dining room and kitchen and some bedroom suites – not many, indeed just three, as I recall.

The courtyard had a lovely central fountain, bought in London, for which Henry made a base. Around this were arcades of colonnaded spaces leading into the rooms. As the instructions were to make it look like a Roman villa, I took Pompeii as the theme. I thought the walls of the courtyard ought to have the look of crumbling plaster in an Italianate pink. My lovely painter Mark Uriu and his team came to help me with the specialist painting. Mark thought the only way

of achieving the flaky look would be to use egg yolks on the plaster as a resist. This would prevent the pink paint taking, so it would peel off. I went down to the village store, which was run by a couple of very large local ladies, to ask if they had any eggs. 'How many would you like?' It was more a question of how many they had! They looked at the racks and I bought the lot. The egg yolks caused the wall to flake in an exotic sort of way, and we added green verdigris (well, really only paint pretending to be verdigris). The effect was a very Italianate terracotta pink, patchy and changing slightly in colour. It was all a bit of a gamble, but it worked beautifully.

The areas under the arcading around the three sides of the colonnade were furnished as outside rooms for sitting, for lazing and for dining. We had very exotic iron furniture with lots of big cushions on them. We also added white canvas blinds, like the blinds in St Mark's Square in Venice, which could be adjusted for the sun. The bar even had a Pompeian fresco behind it! And there were pots of ferns and exotic plants all around.

The courtyard led into the drawing room, which Henry designed as a typical Palladian room with double columns at each end. We painted it yellow, rather like the yellow of Nancy Lancaster's London drawing room. We placed the enormous *cloisonné* vases between the columns and I have to say they looked good.

BELOW The drawing room done in strong
Nancy Lancaster yellow.

OPPOSITE
LEFT A Fornasetti cabinet in the master bedroom.
RIGHT The iron four-poster bed with silk drapes.

Between the drawing and dining rooms there was a tiny octagonal anteroom, which we lined with lit cupboards to hold the jade; it did look exquisite. In the main bedroom, which had a painted and marbled floor, we used the Fornasetti furniture and just added an iron bed with forged iron posts hung with white silk. We papered the walls using a pale pink Mauny paper which looked like hung fabric, and added a very pretty Mauny border of grey doves as a finish around the top. It sounds a bit theatrical, but it worked very well with the black and white Fornasetti furniture.

Over the years I've worked with a lot of architects, but Henry Melich and Philip Jebb were probably the most gifted. For some architects the facades are so important that you find the interiors are problematic. Some have strange quirks, like Claud Phillimore, who always made enormous staircase halls and narrow drawing rooms!

One very interesting job was a house I did in Hobe Sound, Florida, for the Whitney Paysons. John, a nephew of 'Jock' Whitney, is a noted art collector and dealer. His then wife, Joanne, is Italian. They brought us plans for a house they had designed by a firm of New York architects. We needed to make considerable revisions to make the house workable, including altering the windows and their configuration so they could be properly 'dressed'. Pierre and I persuaded them to have murals of tropical gardens and forests in the dining room. John was hesitant

at first, but eventually he agreed. The murals were based on plants at Kew Gardens and they were painted on huge canvases by the scene painters at Shepperton Studios in West London. I was influenced by the Tobacco bedroom at Haseley, which had a paper by Dufour in sepia tones. I have to say that the room was very successful, as indeed was the whole house.

Sometimes what might at first sight appear to be a trifling job turns into a long and fruitful partnership. I remember being at Brook Street when reception asked if I could come down and talk to an American lady from Nashville. This led to me helping with two houses and an apartment in New York. At our first meeting Candy Leadbetter said she had repainted her large family room several times, but couldn't get the colour right and could I help. Not a very promising job, I felt, but she was a charming lady and as I was shortly going to Atlanta, I could fly on to Nashville afterwards. She agreed, explaining how she had come to be in Colefax & Fowler. She and her husband were college friends and married very young. They spent their honeymoon in London, staying at the YWCA as they had very little cash. Walking along Brook Street they had gazed into the windows of Colefax & Fowler and she had said 'When we are rich, I am going to come back here and buy some of their pretty fabrics.' Thirteen years later she walked through the doors!

The Whitney Payson house. CLOCKWISE FROM TOP LEFT One of the guest suites; the swimming pool pavilion; the dining room with the murals painted at Shepperton Studios.

The Whitney Payson house. CLOCKWISE FROM TOP LEFT A child's bedroom with a pretty painted floor; the master bedroom; the double-height drawing room. The master bedroom was very difficult to decorate and the clients were adamant that they wanted a canopy bed, which didn't really work in the space.

Solving the problem of the difficult colour in the family room was relatively simple and cheap, just a matter of applying a softening glaze over the existing red walls. I then went on to redecorate the whole of their lovely house in Nashville and together we went shopping to find pretty things and furniture in London. Later they bought a traditional old clapboard house on an island in Maine, and this became an exciting project for me. The children were young and they went up there every summer holiday, away from the heat of the South. We did the house very simply with fresh soft colours and lots of painted furniture. It was not the easiest place to get to because it involved a flight to Boston, then a small plane up the coast and finally a boat over to the island.

By then I had done several New York apartments, and had developed a team including Mark Uriu, Gordon Knox and their workforce. However, I had never done any work in the countryside outside New York. That all changed when Vivian Wyser-Pratte, for whom I had just completed part of a magnificent Park Avenue apartment, announced that they had bought a house in Bedford, New York State. We drove out to see it, through rolling wooded country that seemed remote from the hustle and bustle of New York. It was a large, attractive house, set in beautiful grounds with a large old barn, but was basically an empty shell with no furniture, pictures or objects of any sort and needed a complete redecoration, which was quite a challenge.

ABOVE LEFT The drawing room we did for Joseph and Candy Leadbetter in Nashville, Tennessee.
ABOVE RIGHT The main windows dressed with swag and tail draperies made by Masons.

Despite its location this was a house that could be given the English country house feel. The drawing room was a particularly handsome room, and I had a lucky find. You always need something to work around, and at C. John & Co., the carpet dealers, in London, I found a very unusual Bessarabian carpet – a flat weave with lots of formalized roses in the design, which I had never seen before. It was a perfect size and gave me a palette of colours to work around. We had many buying sessions around antique dealers in London to purchase furniture, pretty objects, pictures and mirrors and even the fireplace, which went to make a formal but comfortable drawing room. As I had done previously I had all the upholstered furniture specially made in England and sent over, which was unusual at that time.

I would frequently stop off in New York on my way to or from Chicago, where I gathered a number of clients. This came about through the generosity of Fred and Kay Krehbiel (see Chapter 13), who had no hesitation in recommending me to their friends and acquaintances. This was how I met Jack and Peggy Crowe, who lived in the same district outside Chicago as the Krehbiels and had seen my work. Their large family had grown up and left home, so they decided to move into the centre of Chicago.

The Wyser-Pratte house in Bedford, New York State.

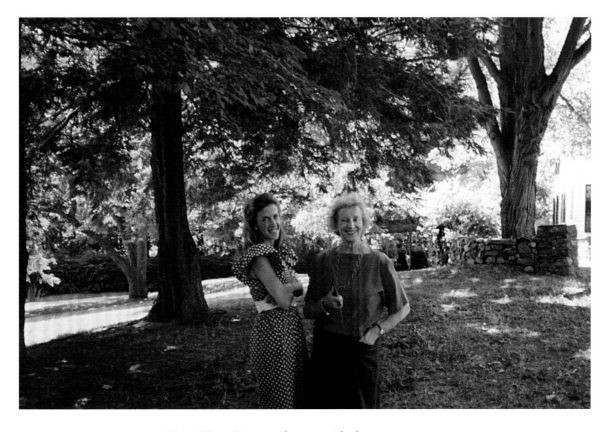

Vivian Wyser-Pratte and me, outside the guest cottage.

OPPOSITE
TOP LEFT The drawing room of the Wyser-Pratte house,
showing a corner of the Bessarabian carpet we bought for the
room, and around which it is decorated.
TOP RIGHT The staircase in the guest cottage, painted by Mark
Uriu and his team.
BOTTOM The sitting room of the guest cottage.

BELOW Jack and Peggy Crowe, with Rosemary Verey (left),
at Barnsley House, Gloucestershire. Rosemary helped them
with their garden in Lake Forest.

They had bought an exceptionally nice apartment in a classic building near the lake, with a library designed by interwar architect David Adler and an unchanged black and white 1930s kitchen. Great travellers, they thought nothing of coming over to London to meet me and discuss the project, and to go buying antiques for their new home.

It was good fun from the start and we created a classic traditional apartment using English and French furniture, English chintzes and fabrics to give a sense of a lived-in and happy place. The master bedroom was particularly attractive, with tall windows, the huge four-poster bed and a wonderful mirrored screen which no doubt dated from the same period as the building. The reflections of the room and the windows gave a great sense of space. I went on to decorate their beautiful home in Lake Forest, another classic where they were able to entertain their growing family of grandchildren. They have remained wonderful friends. Indeed, they were the perfect clients.

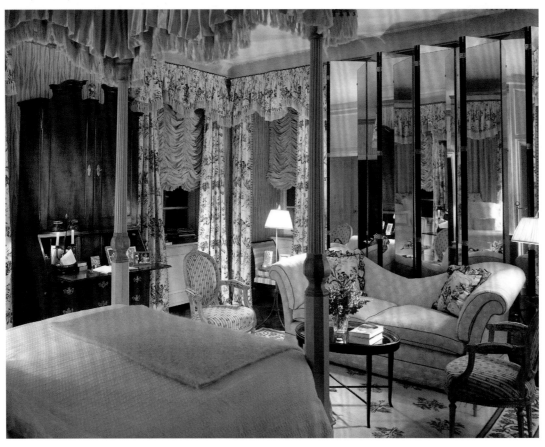

LEFT ABOVE The drawing room of the Crowes' Chicago apartment revolved around a Portuguese carpet I had made for them.

LEFT BELOW The bedroom with the mirrored screen. The walls were hung with a Mauny wallpaper that looked like fabric.

OPPOSITE The dining room had another Mauny paper allied with painted Louis XIV chairs, a Regency chandelier and elaborately draped silk curtains.

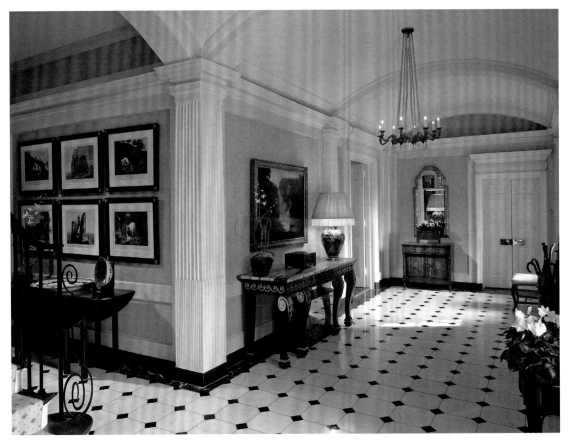

The Crowes' Lake Forest house.
LEFT The classical entrance hall with marble floor. All the furniture and fittings were bought in England.
BELOW LEFT The sun porch with a specially made needlepoint carpet designed to go with the walling and sofa.
BELOW RIGHT The breakfast room. We used trellis work on the walls and ceiling to give a garden room effect.

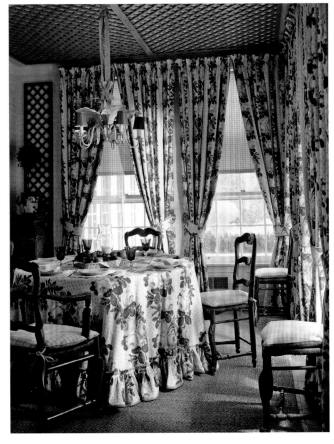

The Crowes' Lake
Forest house.
ABOVE RIGHT
The panelled
drawing room.
BELOW RIGHT
The bedroom has
English 'Maryport'
chintz, a Mauny
wallpaper and a
Brussels weave carpet.
Gordon Davies painted
the panel screen.

12

NEW YORK, NEW YORK!

The only job John ever did in New York was when Bunny Mellon asked him to decorate her brownstone house.[1] He wasn't prepared to go to New York, partly because he was timid about flying, but also because he did not like to be out of his own bed for more than one night, so Mrs Mellon had the painters and everybody sent to London for him to train, while I did all the soft furnishing for the house. It was actually Mrs Mellon who introduced John to her friend Jackie Kennedy. She came into Brook Street, having just moved into her apartment at 1040 Park Avenue in 1964, and she just wanted some simple curtains like the ones we had made for Bunny. Of course, simple is very expensive when you have to have a silk specially woven and the poles from which they are hung specially made, and everything totally handcrafted. They were unlined silk faille curtains basically, but they had a certain style. Jackie Kennedy had seen them and wanted a couple of pairs of similar curtains, but in cheaper simple shantung. We made these for her, but with great difficulty. She had the measurements sent, but as so often they had measured the wrong thing, and we never had a full set of measurements. People often forget to tell you how long the curtains should be for instance. Anyway, I made some simple curtains for Mrs Kennedy but, perhaps rather typically, it was Bunny Mellon who paid the bill!

Working in New York was actually to come later in my career through the work I did in London for Lehman Brothers. When their managing director, Stephen Bershad, moved back to New York in 1985 he asked if I could help decorate their new apartment. Luckily I was going to America anyway, to see Fred Krehbiel in Chicago, so I altered my plans to include a visit to New York.

I flew into New York on a Sunday morning I seem to remember, and on arrival got the key from the concierge to look at the empty apartment on the second floor of 80th or 81st Street. I had a little tape recorder with me, and as I walked around the rather dismal apartment I recorded my impressions as I went. 'Well this is a room about . . .' and I walked across the room pacing it out, 'about 16 feet wide by 20 feet long. It has three windows on one side', etc. 'And I must say it is about the dreariest room I've ever seen!' And then I would go to the next room announcing, 'Ooh! But the outlook is just a blank wall', and then the kitchen, 'Oh! That's so small. Oh! My gosh! The bathrooms!' I was very derogatory about the whole place.

After I came home I met the Bershads in London and naturally they wanted to know my impressions. I explained I didn't know much about New York apartments, but expressed my views about the rather small bathrooms and the fact the kitchen wasn't much to write home about, having a view out of the window of a brick wall. Rather embarrassingly, he made me play my tape recording, which I had made purely as a reminder for myself. Luckily they were amused by my comments and 'the terrible dismal apartment with its blank walls' remained a joke with us ever after. Even though I had been so rude about the apartment they agreed to employ me and we certainly managed to eliminate the gloom over the next year.

My big problem, of course, was how on earth to do the job, as I didn't know any builders or painters in New York. Fortunately, one of my assistants, Ursula, knew someone at Cambridge, who knew a student who was hoping to set up a painting business. That student was Mark Uriu, who became a superb specialist painter and worked with me throughout the United States. His friend Gordon Knox was setting up a contracting business and, while I must have been pretty foolhardy to take on a couple of students just out of university to help with an important job in New York, I liked them, and I knew they'd do their very best.

'Chilham', a floral chintz taken from a fabric printed in the 1920s which was in turn taken from an early Victorian design.

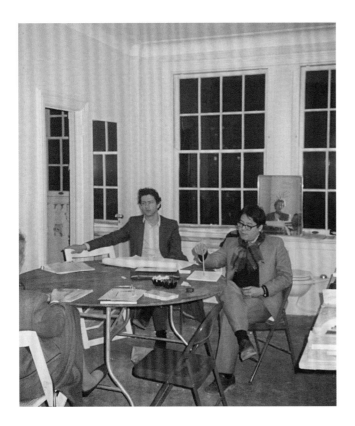

Mark Uriu, Gordon Knox and I in conference at the Schwarzman apartment in New York, January 1986.

Happily, Gordon built up other trades to work with him – masonry and carpentry, plumbing and electricity – and he ended up with an excellent team.

I produced quite an adventurous scheme for the apartment, for which Gordon and Mark had to prepare estimates. I created a library in one of the smaller rooms, which I lined with bookcases, doing the whole thing in a sort of dark emerald green lacquer, combined with a black background chintz which was really rather daring. We found a painting which became the mainstay of the sitting room, and from which the colours of the room were taken. In the kitchen, about which I had been so sniffy, we knocked down a wall (easier said than done in a New York apartment block). This made a great improvement and we were able to create a kitchen diner. Mrs Bershad also wanted a simple dining room, so we did one on a country theme – not at all 'New Yorky'. The clients took little interest in the progress of the job – he probably didn't have much time, he was very busy – so I was left to my own devices. My assistants and I ended up unpacking and hanging their clothes in the newly made wardrobes, arranging their shoes on racks, even making the

beds. When the whole place was ready they just walked in – a sort of latchkey arrangement.

It was a huge learning curve for me, coping with the staff of the apartment block, trying to get round people to let you do things that were forbidden! I'm sure being English helped a lot. One big problem was how to get furniture up to the second floor, and particularly things such as sofas that would not fit into the lift. To this day I'm not quite sure how we managed it, but I was allowed to put the sofa on the top of the lift and move the lift up to the second floor where we took it off. Incredibly, we also got the local authority to close their section of the road one Sunday to allow us to lift furniture through the front windows of the apartment with a crane.

When it was finished I felt I knew some of the difficulties of decorating in New York and if other problems cropped up I could somehow cope with them. As it happens they did crop up, because a friend of the Bershads, Steve Schwarzman, visited the apartment with his wife and she was keen on English country house decoration – our sort of look.[2] They had just got a new fifteen-room apartment in Park Avenue, and wanted me to see it. I went to look and as fifteen rooms was rather a large space to fill I asked what furniture they had. 'Oh no, we're not going to take any of our old furniture,' came the reply. I thought it might be helpful to see their existing apartment to get some idea of their taste. It was all beige and brown with modern paintings, unfortunately the sort I really didn't like, perhaps six feet wide and two feet high and consisting of red streaks of paint. 'Abstract painting' would not tie in with an English country house look in their Park Avenue apartment. I had to tell them their artwork wouldn't work, so he decided to sell it, probably for a profit, and buy things that were more suitable.

The only thing he really wanted was a library, as he had seen and admired Stephen's I suppose, but he didn't actually have any books! 'It shouldn't be a problem, you could buy them,' so I ended up buying books by the yard. Everything was designed in London, and a lot of things made in England and shipped over. The best upholstered furniture I looked at in New York was so expensive it seemed more sensible to make our best upholstered furniture in London and ship it over. It still worked out cheaper for the client

OPPOSITE The Schwarzman apartment.
CLOCKWISE FROM TOP LEFT The master bedroom: setting up the bed corona and the completed room; the red lacquer library; starting work in the circular hall; the finished hall, with *trompe l'œil* murals by Gordon Davies.

The Schwarzman apartment: the drawing room, looking towards the dining room. The desk, which had belonged to Ellen's grandmother, was the only piece of furniture they brought with them.

It was stipulated that the girl had to have two four-poster beds in her room, one being for a visiting friend. It seemed a bit over the top to me, particularly as the daughter was rather a boyish sort of girl and it was not really what she wanted herself.

An unusual feature of the apartment was a small circular hall. I suggested putting down a marble floor and produced a design and an estimate. Gordon Davies painted four murals to go on the walls.[3] A disastrous moment arrived when I returned to New York and they uncovered the newly laid floor. They pulled back the tarpaulin and I saw that the people who had laid the marble had reversed two of the coloured marbles (the sienna with the black), completely altering the design. It was one of those awful moments you get in decorating. I didn't know what to do and whether to admit this to the client, which would have meant ripping up the floor, and God knows what sort of wrangle would have ensued with the marble merchants. So I decided to keep mum and didn't breathe a word to the client, and it's there to this day. Actually no one has ever noticed the mistake!

Our clients were very amenable. My work was done with Ellen Schwarzman. Her husband didn't get involved at all: he only said he wanted firm estimates and an unbreakable finishing date. By the luck of the gods we just about achieved this. On the day they moved in we made the beds, and I put some freesias in little vases on the tables in the drawing room. There were glasses in the drinks cupboard and everything was ready to go. I can only think that when they arrived the rather sumptuous and exotic new decoration must have been a revelation to him after the beige, brown and modern art of the previous apartment.

The marriage later broke up and she remarried, but she still lives in the same apartment. Pierre and I redid the drawing room to give a change, but she couldn't bear to change her bedroom, which remains just as I did it all those years ago. He also remarried and he went on to amazing dizzy heights. The next I heard was years later when his company, Blackstone Group, had bought the London Eye to add to Madame Tussauds and Alton Towers, which they already owned.

The Schwarzmans also employed me to do a house for them in Jamaica. They had bought a cottage in a gated community with a clubhouse, large swimming pool and a beach. I went with my team to see this cottage, which, as I remember, had two bedrooms and was in a lovely position overlooking gardens in front of the sea. Mark painted the

and it was of better quality. We were also able to make loose covers, which the Americans didn't have, and I arranged for the curtain makers to come over and measure the windows, and then every curtain was made in England.

We went shopping for furniture and carpets in New York and also when Ellen Schwarzman came to London. It was a really big project since often a certain amount of alteration had to be done and that is very difficult in New York apartments. To put in a new window is almost impossible when you are nine floors up. You have to do it from the inside, with some sort of cradling on the outside. We did put an extra window in a family room at the back and completely ripped out, altered and enlarged the kitchen. We also installed a chic cocktail bar, which is something I had not done before, all granite slabs, mirrors and lots of light. They had two children, a boy and a girl.

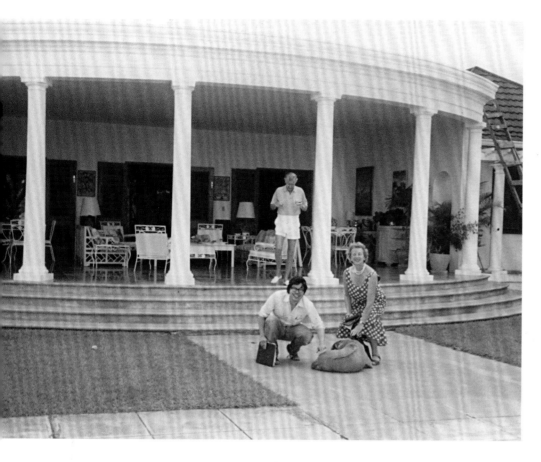

Mark Uriu and I outside the Schwarzman cottage in Jamaica.

Mark and Beverley Uriu painting
light switches for the cottage.

floor and we put in simple rustic furniture. During the week we were there we stayed in another of the cottages looked after by two lovely Jamaican ladies, a cook and housekeeper, and felt very spoiled. When the goods arrived from England, it was difficult getting things through customs and we had to pay quite high duty. All the local boys who were helping to unpack things were high on marijuana! I was nervous things would disappear, but they didn't. These boys didn't want to throw anything away: all the cardboard, paper, string and plastic were carefully packed up and disappeared. The owners gave some of the staff the pieces of furniture that had been in the cottage, and they were delighted.

Over the years I made many visits to New York, usually with assistants to help and nanny me, but occasionally alone. On one such occasion I stupidly left my bag, containing all my papers, estimates and, worst of all, my itinerary of places I should be going to and the telephone numbers, in a taxi. I got out of the taxi at the Mayfair Hotel, where I usually stayed. By the time I realized how stupid I had been, the taxi was halfway down Manhattan. I asked the concierge what I should do and he gave me a number to ring, but warned me the driver probably wouldn't hand it until he came off duty. No word all evening, so I went to bed. I was woken by the telephone at about two o'clock in the morning: a gentleman's voice said, 'Are you the owner of a tartan bag? I found it in a taxi. I must have been the next occupant.' I couldn't believe my luck but was curious how he knew where to ring and he said, 'Well, I looked at your itinerary. I see you're an awfully busy lady, and I saw you were staying at the Mayfair Hotel.' I was so delighted I asked if he could come to breakfast the following morning, but then it occurred to me I wouldn't know what he looked like – 'Oh yes you will. I'll be carrying a tartan bag!' He came to breakfast and we had a good laugh about it, but I was grateful to meet such a wonderfully honest man.

13

A COLLECTOR, CONNOISSEUR AND PATRON: FRED KREHBIEL

It was quite by chance that I met Fred Krehbiel.[1] While he set up the European side of his business he was living in a rented flat in Elizabeth Street in Belgravia which he found very depressing, so his wife suggested he come into the shop and see if we could jolly the place up. Just as he was explaining to the receptionist that he wanted some advice and some work doing, I happened to walk down the stairs. He said, 'It's a rented flat, so I don't want to spend a fortune, but I do want it to be made a bit more cheerful – I can't cope with the brown sofas and the gloom. Can you do anything? Here's a cheque – that should cover it. By the way, I'm going to Tokyo tomorrow. I'll be back in six weeks.' I was flabbergasted. He had met me just two minutes ago and here he was handing me a cheque for a considerable sum of money. I did remonstrate, saying I might do something he would hate, but he quickly swatted that away saying, 'Oh my wife tells me it's a very good firm. Just cheer it up. It's awful. Do something. I'm sure it will be lovely. Goodbye.' And with that he was gone. No contact details, no telephone number, merely a piece of paper with an address, a set of keys and a large cheque.

I rushed round next morning and panicked. The flat was indeed very depressing. It was typical 1970s decoration: cream walls and a brown dralon three-piece suite, even a brown carpet. The whole thing screamed cream and brown, Six weeks wasn't actually much time, because everyone I worked with was very busy, but I had the walls in the sitting room painted yellow, and some natural linen curtains made and trimmed, and found a

'Auricula', a mid-nineteenth-century design, probably English. The original pattern was in reds and greens, but we recoloured it in pastel shades.

needlepoint rug for the floor. I covered the dreaded brown dralon sofa and chairs with loose covers, put cushions on them, changed the lamps, put in the inevitable skirted table and hung a few pictures. Nothing too expensive. He duly came back after six weeks and walked into the shop – I was really dreading it because I had no idea what his tastes were, but he was delighted with the result. I thought he might not be too delighted with the final bill since I had spent more than he gave me. I explained that I had not been able to estimate the job and had to pay a premium to have work done quickly. He was very understanding and immediately wrote a cheque for the difference. He soon said to me he was considering buying a house in Ireland, as his wife was from the south-west of Ireland and had a lot of relatives there, and would I be interested in helping them with it? It was to be a holiday home for his wife and sons. But in the end nothing seemed to come of it.

He disappeared from my life for about two years, but then he suddenly reappeared. I enquired about the Irish house, thinking he must have given the job to someone else. In fact, it transpired that the house he had been interested in belonged to two brothers who could not agree on sale terms, so he gave up. He now wanted my help because he had recently bought an Aubusson carpet from C. John, the carpet dealers in South Audley Street. This carpet had been sent to Chicago but unfortunately it looked rather strange in the room. He was flying back the following day and wanted me to go with him to see what could be done with the carpet.

I agreed and off we went, first class on TWA, and we talked for most of the eight and a half hour flight, getting to know each other. I learned he was a Chicago businessman, one of two sons whose father had founded an electronics business. He had always wanted to travel, but his father insisted that both brothers should go into the business. However, he did give Fred the chance of setting up a European division – hence the Belgravia flat. I suppose he was about forty at the time, well versed in business, but perhaps just beginning on an aesthetic education. He wanted to know about me, my life, my interests.

I remember being driven out to Hinsdale, in the suburbs of Chicago, to a large house with (unusually for that part of the world) quite a substantial garden. The drawing room was a long, low, panelled room. The Aubusson was beautiful, but the central motif did not align with the fireplace. Plucking up courage – he had after all flown me over at some cost – I said that I was truly sorry but I couldn't do the room around the carpet. It wasn't the fault of either the carpet or the room – they just didn't marry.

He was unconcerned and thought of trying it upstairs in the bedroom where, needless to say, it didn't work either being far too big, and with the central motif under the four poster bed. 'Never mind we'll roll it up and use it later somewhere else.' He simply told me to do the

drawing room as I thought fit. I used an English chintz from about 1860, added needlepoint carpets, bought some furniture to augment the few nice pieces he already had and arranged some pictures and lamps. They liked the result, although I'm somewhat horrified when I look back at pictures of the room today. It was done in 1982 and now seems rather dated, being too chintzy and not entirely interesting. (We redecorated the drawing room in the 1990s.) He then commissioned me to do the rest of the house and that is how our extraordinary working relationship and friendship began.

A few years later, in 1988, Fred bought a house almost on Lake Michigan. It was actually one of the famous 'Seven Houses on Lake Shore Drive', a group of houses in various styles amid all the skyscrapers. Fred's was a neo-Georgian ten-room house, which looked like a large doll's house.

Built in 1911 and designed by Holabird & Roche for Lawrence Rockwell, it fronts on to Goethe Street (straddling the block between Lake Shore Drive and Stone Street) and is at right angles to the lake.

OPPOSITE The drawing room at the Hinsdale house after I had redecorated it in the 1990s.

LEFT The dining room, with painted decoration done by George Oakes.
BELOW The drawing room alcove as done in the 1990s.

The Hinsdale house.
OPPOSITE
ABOVE The entrance hall, which runs through the house. We decorated it as a reception room complete with grand piano.
BELOW The panelled library.

RIGHT
TOP The garden room, overlooking the rose garden.
MIDDLE The trellis sun porch, inspired by the trellis pavilion at Bagatelle in Paris.
BOTTOM The swimming pool loggia with delft tiles painted by Lucinda Oakes.

LEFT The Lake Shore Drive entry parlour. This was inspired by my visit to Sweden.
BELOW The dining room, decorated with a Mauny wallpaper and a very beautiful and unusual chandelier.

OPPOSITE The library, with faux panelling. This was one of my best rooms.

Although it looks huge it is actually only one room deep. When Fred bought the house it was in such a bad state of repair that it had to be completely gutted, leaving only the staircase. The builder, Barry Sylvester, was someone Fred knew from his yachting days, when he had been part of his crew. He was skilled at traditional construction techniques, so was just the man to renovate this house, A major drawback was that less than twenty yards away was an eight-lane motorway running along the lake shore, but once the house had been soundproofed and triple glazed you wouldn't know there was all that traffic.

By the time Fred and I began to decorate the house we had moved on from the 'brown furniture look'. I had been to Sweden on an architectural trip and seen some lovely painted rooms and quite enchanting houses. Fred indulged me and allowed me to do a Swedish-style entrance hall with a painted floor and painted panelled walls. It was a restrained sort of Gustavian look, which continued into the breakfast room and small kitchen. That was the theme

on the ground floor. As Fred was collecting rather grand furniture by then, including quite a bit of French furniture, the remainder of the house was rather sophisticated. The dining room, for instance, had French hand-blocked paper, a Directoire Aubusson and an English chandelier – I suppose a classic Colefax mix in a way.

Personally, my favourite room in the house was a small library on the second floor. I remember when I first saw this room it had neither floor nor ceiling – it was just a space. I had to conjure up the whole concept in my mind before I could start. I wanted the room to be intimate and cosy so I decided to faux panel the walls to resemble maple wood.

For the principal bedroom I had a large four-poster bed made. We painted it and hung it with a beautiful French taffeta. The taffeta is unusual because it is 'warp-printed', meaning the design is printed on the warp before the weft is woven through it, which gives it a slightly watered effect, actually rather impressionist. We used this taffeta throughout the room. It was expensive and very beautiful,

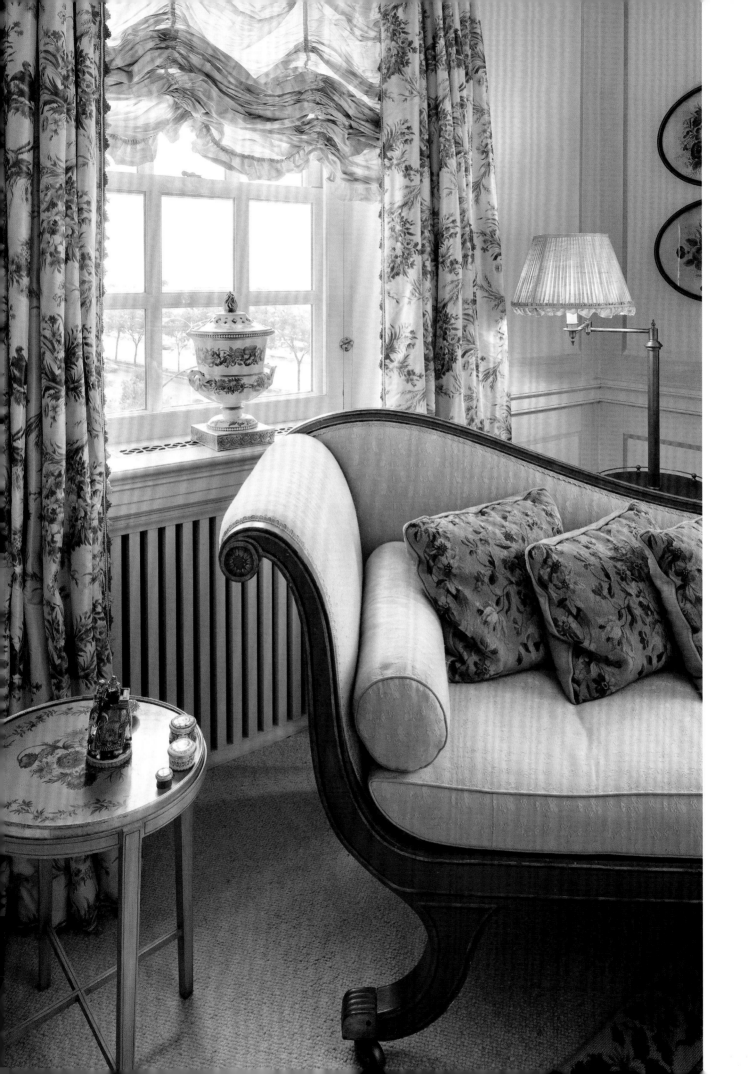

and made for a very pretty room because the design married well with Fred's ever-expanding furniture collection.

Fred was so amenable and flexible, but this wonderful house certainly stretched me because it is difficult to do a house which lacks floors and ceilings and any furniture. If you have nothing to begin with, just a hole, you have no reference point and you are forced to use your imagination to create a series of rooms that form a coherent whole. They enjoyed the house for the next twenty years before selling it in November 2010 to his nephew. The furniture was recycled, with some going to their son's apartment, while the bed with the warp-printed taffeta was moved to Palm Beach. Fred does spend a great deal of money on his houses, but nothing is ever wasted, merely recycled or stored until it can be used once more.

In 1984 Fred and Kay finally bought their holiday home in south-west Ireland. Churchill House was to become an absorbing project. As funds allowed, Fred gradually increased the acreage, enlarged the gardens and the park, and built a library and pavilions. One pavilion was built to hold their collection of Chippendale furniture, with another for their collection of Irish paintings, and yet another for antique farm implements. A bungalow was converted into a guest cottage and a farmhouse was turned into a modern picture gallery. Fred also built a *cottage orné*, a charming little house, as a present for Kay.

However, when I started working on Churchill House my initial brief was that as it was simply to be a holiday home we weren't going to spend much money on it. It was in moderate condition, but once the structural problems had been addressed I began to decorate it. I tried to upgrade it a little, correcting the obvious defects. Fred wasn't all that concerned about pipes in the dining room, but I was! I wanted to make it into a print room and they would get in the way. Gradually Fred began buying pretty things for the house and got more ambitious about it, and over the years as he acquired different and better things, we upgraded the house.

OPPOSITE A corner of the master bedroom at Lake Shore Drive. We used a warp-printed fabric which gives a rather impressionist effect.

BELOW LEFT The front door of Churchill House.
BELOW RIGHT The entrance hall, which I painted an intense yellow.

LEFT Tea in the dining room at Churchill House. From the left: John O'Connor, Pierre Serrurier, Gordon Davies, Mavis Long (who decorated the dining room), Lucinda Oakes, George Oakes and Andrew Christy. BELOW The print dining room.

OPPOSITE The conservatory.

I was surprised one day when Fred told me he had bought a wonderful suite of Chippendale furniture from an antique dealer in London. This suite had once belonged to the actor David Garrick and had been used in his house on the Thames at Twickenham. I remembered it well: it was in the French taste and painted blue. It had latterly belonged to Lord Rothermere and had been used by John Fowler in the salon at Daylesford in Gloucestershire. It was a large suite with two *canapés*, four *bergères* and six *fauteuils*, but curiously there now seemed to be only one *canapé*. It turned out that the antique dealer had retained one for his own use, but Fred persuaded him to reunite the suite. It needed a certain amount of restoration, and it's a

difficult suite in a way because of its unusual colouring. Part of it is in a sort of turquoise blue and part of it is in a more mauve blue. But all of it needed recovering, and of course he had nowhere to put it, so he decided to build a pavilion on the estate to house it.

He found an architect in Dublin, John O'Connor, who was fanatical about early nineteenth-century architecture, and John designed a pavilion in a sort of late Regency style. It's at the bottom of a slope, overlooking the sea and the mountains – a beautiful position. As the land rose at the back of the pavilion it was decided to create a cascade and to make it appear as though it ran under the building into a large circular pool beyond.

ABOVE Kay's *cottage orné* under construction.
BELOW The bedroom of the *cottage orné*.

OPPOSITE Looking down the cascade towards
the pavilion, at dusk.

The pavilion has a salon forty feet long, built above an undercroft containing a bedroom suite, a tiny kitchen and a bathroom. Naturally Fred wanted to know what I would suggest for the decoration of the salon, and with this very French-flavoured Chippendale furniture I thought of chinoiserie, which was popular in the mid-eighteenth century and during the Regency. I wondered if George Oakes, possibly with the help of his clever daughter Lucinda, could paint a modern version of a Chinese wallpaper. Fred agreed.

George was pleased to be given the commission, and he set to work designing a paper which was really a series of Chinese follies. It took many months to complete, but the final effect of the room, with its magnificent proportions, the bold plasterwork, the Irish Bossi chimneypiece and George's beautiful paper, plus the extraordinary views in all directions, is wonderful.[2] It is indeed a worthy home for the superb Chippendale furniture.

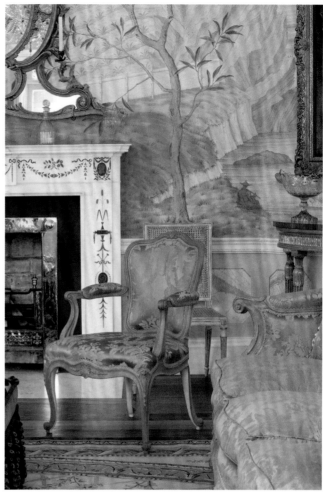

Beneath this reception room, which is used for parties, is a bedroom with two anterooms: one leading to a bathroom and the other to the kitchen. Fred had been shopping again and had bought a suite of early nineteenth-century painted Viennese salon furniture. Large and heavy, it was difficult to use in a bedroom. Fred soon realized I was having problems with this furniture so he suggested a day trip to see where it had originally come from.

We were in Paris, so a couple of planes were organized to take us to Vienna. John O'Connor, who was already

LEFT The salon of the pavilion, with the Chippendale furniture that once belonged to David Garrick.
ABOVE A detail of the salon, showing the Chippendale furniture set against the Bossi chimneypiece and George Oakes's wonderful chinoiserie wallpaper.

there, was delegated to organize a large exotic picnic, which he bought at Demel, the very best Viennese patisserie shop. We were to meet in the gardens outside a little museum.

Unfortunately, almost immediately after we took off Fred's plane developed engine trouble, so had to return to Paris. Another plane had to be hastily found. The rest of us enjoyed the picnic in the sunshine, and went around the museum, whiling away the time until Fred arrived, when we all set off for this beautiful schloss. It had been occupied by the Germans and subsequently by the Russians, so had suffered badly, but the family were still living in part of the house, making ends meet by renting the place out for wedding receptions. We went

RIGHT The bedroom, its early nineteenth-century painted Viennese salon furniture reupholstered in a damask I had woven in Lyon, and the walls hung with yellow silk.

OPPOSITE An alcove in one of the shell rooms Gordon Davies created in the Viennese suite.

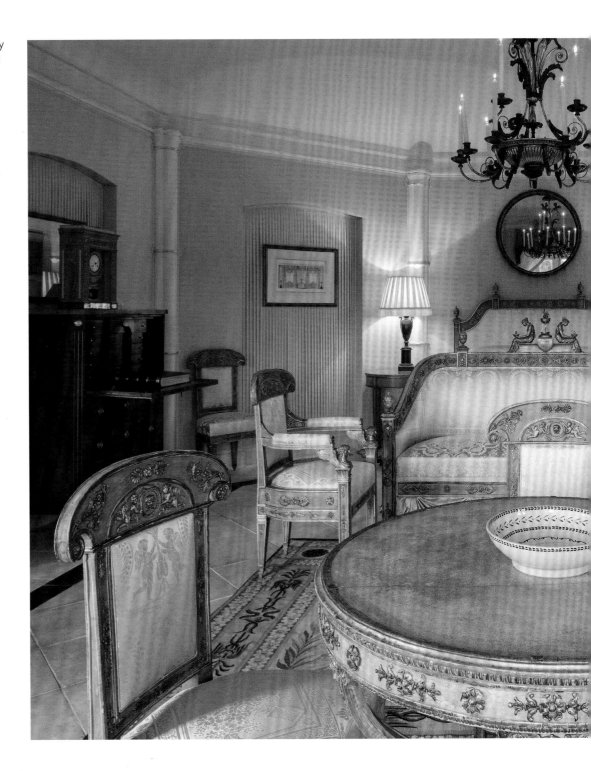

up on to the first floor, passing through an enfilade of rooms, all of which were bare, and finally to the room where this furniture had originally stood. The curtains were still hanging at the windows, although in shreds, but there was nothing else in the room. I had to sort of reinstate it in my mind to give a flavour of what I could do in this bedroom. Aside from a quick walk around

the Schönbrunn Palace gardens before we returned to Paris, that was destined to be my one and only glimpse of Vienna.

The result of that trip was that the walls of the pavilion bedroom were hung in yellow silk, broken by a series of lovely pilasters; in the alcoves that John O'Connor had designed we pleated the silk in knife pleating. The furniture needed a little restoration and it was really difficult to cover because nothing readily available looked right. However, eventually I found a damask document that was very suitable, so I had this damask design copied in Lyon. As it was salon furniture we didn't have a bed, so I had one made by Richard Philips and painted to match. It had carved pineapples on the finials, a bedhead to match and a very, very elaborate bedspread. We actually had a bedspread embroidered in Paris. It is in itself was a work of art and I have to say cost a fortune. In all the years I worked for Fred the cost of this bedspread was the only thing he ever complained about!

In the two anterooms at each side I commissioned my friend Gordon Davies to do two shell rooms. These shell rooms proved to be quite a headache because although London used to have a couple of shops selling nothing but shells, both had long since closed. Eventually we found people in the Philippines who sold shells and asked them to send some samples. When they arrived, in neat little boxes, they were all tiny, tiny shells and of course no good for wall covering. So we wrote back and asked if they could send some bigger shells. This amused them; however, they did produce an amazing quantity of scallop shells, which Gordon could use. Plywood panels were made in Ireland to fit the walls of the two little rooms and on all these panels Gordon fixed a lovely shell design. He made a pair of shell chandeliers and sea urchin shells were used as wall lights. The two anterooms were identical, so when you stood in the middle of the bedroom you could see both shell rooms, the vista terminated at each end by a round alcove in which stood a pair of Viennese marble pedestals with elaborate candelabra. The effect was absolutely ravishing.

We finished setting up the bedroom, with its beautiful silk walls, and the following morning, feeling rather pleased with ourselves, we all trooped down to look. It was a horrendous sight. All the walling had turned into what looked like corrugated cardboard – it was hanging in ripples all down the wall. My poor upholsterer, John Mason, and I looked at it and we didn't know what to think. Of course, the building is against the hillside, so inevitably it would be damp, but it couldn't be so damp it would cause this. When we called the builder, in his inimitable Irish way he said 'Oh my Lord! I think I made a mistake! I thought you said you wanted a humidifier, not a dehumidifier.' He'd been steaming the room all night as opposed to drawing out any damp. A couple of blow dryers were hastily installed, and like a miracle the silk stretched back to the right tension again. During the course of my career I've had many moments of drama when unforeseen things have gone wrong, but I never foresaw such a dramatic happening merely because of a simple misunderstanding.

As Fred became more successful, and I suppose richer, he was able to indulge his hobbies of collecting and doing up houses. He bought more land in and around Churchill House, and he got more interested in the history of Ireland. He started to seriously collect Irish paintings, which eventually required a gallery to house them. The only way this could be done was to convert and extend the old stable block. Inevitably it's a simple building, fairly close to the house, but when you go inside you are in a completely different world, a sophisticated eighteenth-century room with good plasterwork and lovely doors and windows. There are half a dozen rooms, all of them different sizes, each one holding a collection of Irish paintings through the centuries, starting with the eighteenth century. There are carpets, chandeliers, wall furniture and chairs, but the

OPPOSITE The entrance to the Churchill gallery, with faux stone decoration.

RIGHT One of the gallery rooms, hung with Irish paintings from the Krehbiel collection.

A corner of the colonnade at the Palm Beach house.

rooms are not furnished as sitting rooms, just like galleries such as you might find in a grand country house. I had to think about the pictures (I had a clutch of photographs of them to work from) to choose a colour that would be the right background for them, and in the end I did a series of glazed colours, including a faux stone room, painted a natural stone colour to give a *trompe l'œil* effect.

This is a very fine collection, second, I believe, only to that of the National Gallery of Ireland. It has expanded over the years, so much so that it has now moved on into the twentieth and twenty-first centuries, which required a separate gallery. This has been built in what was an old adjacent farmhouse, which has now been converted into a modern gallery in a sort of Shaker style. Of course, there is a huge element of surprise because who would think this farm building could possibly contain such a collection?

Over the years we have also altered Churchill House itself. Perhaps the most successful improvement we have made is adding a garden room on to the fairly moderate kitchen. This charming room is much used because it not only has wonderful views over the landscape but also leads into the walled garden. It's a sort of cross between a conservatory and an orangery, with plants, a water feature and lovely comfortable seating. The extension has actually enlarged the house by quite a bit because it also contains

cloakrooms and a sort of separate hallway. It was a very practical addition and makes the house work better.

I suppose it must have been in 1992 that Fred and Kay decided to buy a place in Palm Beach in Florida. It was to be a weekend house and a holiday home for the boys, as well as somewhere friends could come. Nothing very extravagant, indeed fairly modest by Palm Beach standards. Eventually he found a house he wanted. It was bigger and more expensive than he had originally planned, but I remember when he phoned he said, 'It's bad news for you Imo, because it's been decorated beautifully by the present owners.' However, I knew Fred! When Pierre and I went to look at it we made a few gentle suggestions as to how it could be improved. Needless to say, after he bought it we completely redid the place (with the exception of the kitchen, although even that was slightly improved). Of course, he then had a reason to buy furniture, which he loved doing, but it was quite different and more exotic than he might have bought for Chicago or Ireland. The house was a typical Spanish Colonial design built around a courtyard and pool. Inside it had walls panelled in 'pecky' cypress, painted beams in the dining and drawing rooms, and in the hall a beautiful old chequerboard marble floor, which had come from a monastery in southern California.

The house is not actually on the ocean, but on a side street just off the ocean. It was nicely designed, if not particularly pretty on the outside. Inside, the previous owners had wanted big walk-in cupboards, and had ruined a room to install them. We put back the rooms to their original shapes, and restored a fireplace where it had been taken out. The grounds were not huge, but then they never are in Palm Beach, with even the grand Addison Mizner houses built on rather modest plots.

Palm Beach was a house that was real fun to do, because you could be a little bit exotic. Fred was a stimulating client and, as he was a collector, objects he acquired — sometimes things I didn't even know he had — might give us a theme. I remember the panelling in one bedroom was rather French so I thought we could go with the French idea — 'Yes, but I've got these wallpaper screens I bought and I don't know what to do with them, could we make those our theme?' And that is what we did.

At the time Fred was particularly keen on Venice, so he wanted another bedroom to have a Venetian theme, which we did using some northern Italian painted furniture. For their own bedroom we used a Fortuny fabric we bought in Venice, and I had a white four-poster bed made and hung in broderie anglaise fabric, which we also used for curtains.

The main saloon at the Palm Beach house, with its painted ceiling and 'pecky' cypress panelling.

ABOVE The dressing room/bathroom of Kay's bedroom.
The walls are hung with fabric. This room overlooks the
pool and has a grapefruit tree outside the window, so that
you can reach out and pick your breakfast!
RIGHT Kay's bedroom. The bed was made to my design
by Richard Philipps and was hung with the same unlined
Danish broderie anglaise as the curtains. The floor was
painted by Mark Uriu and his team. We bought the
Fortuny cotton on the walls and chaise at a wonderful shop
in Venice. (In fact we bought up the entire stock, as we
didn't know how much we would need.)

LEFT The Italian bedroom, decorated around the *armadio*. We made the matching pair to conceal the doors to the dressing room. BELOW The French bedroom, with a pretty painted floor inspired by a French screen.

OPPOSITE The dining room with a wonderful chandelier we found in a Parisian antique shop. The carpet and the Italian chairs came from Ditchley and had been Nancy Lancaster's.

On one of his furniture-buying expeditions Fred had bought at Marietta Tree's sale in New York a Portuguese rug that Nancy Lancaster had had made.[3] It was a copy of an Empire Aubusson owned by Nancy that had fallen to pieces, and was made by the famous Lady Ellis (see page 87). He also bought a set of Italian chairs that had belonged to Nancy and had been in the saloon at Ditchley. He installed all of this in the dining room. To complement the rug and chairs he bought a rock crystal chandelier in Paris in the form of apples and pears. The chandelier was in a small antique shop and was so huge it almost touched the floor of the shop, but I was certain it was the right proportions for the room. We then found

a very temperamental Polish gentleman to paint panels to look like eighteenth-century painting between the cypress wood panelling, which he did beautifully. Apparently, he had restored churches in Czechoslovakia and Poland and had a feel for this sort of dry painted work. We also created a painted breakfast room, inspired by the Villa Monte Mario in Rome and done by Mark Uriu and his team from New York.

One of Fred's ambitions was to create a hotel like no other. His whole working life had been spent flying around the world, so he had a lot of knowledge of international hotels. Whether they were in Tokyo, Berlin or Bangkok, they were all much the same. He came up

with the idea of buying a house in Ireland and converting it into a hotel. After a considerable search in 2000 he found a house called Slevoir in County Tipperary. Pierre and I went over to view it, and we realized that though it was in a rather attractive area, with a river inlet from the sea, it had its limitations. Unfortunately, if we only used the house it would be too small to make a viable hotel, so an annexe would have to be built. We worked on this for many months, even to the point of getting permissions for the annexe that had been designed. We were surprised when in 2002 Fred said he'd been asked to look at a house which was very important, one of the top five houses in Ireland. I think Desmond FitzGerald, the last Knight of Glin, and Desmond Guinness had encouraged him to go and look at it. Ballyfin was owned by the Patrician Brothers, who ran it as a boys' school. They were a dwindling group and all getting old, so they had decided to sell the house and build a new school in a nearby village.

It was a great big nineteenth-century classical house and not really suitable for a school, so they had built an annexe for classrooms. Although it would take the Brothers five years to vacate the property, as they had first to build the new school, Fred bought it. Slevoir was no longer required and we were very upset having spent so much time on it. Pierre and I went to see Ballyfin on a grey Irish day, and it impressed us, but we found it depressing. The very austere exterior belied the richness within. The plasterwork was exquisite, but in a terrible state in some parts because of water damage. Rain was coming through the roof and there were buckets under bedroom ceilings where the poor monks lived in freezing conditions because there was no heating. The boys were more comfortably housed in the annexe and were only allowed into the house on special occasions, which actually meant that it had not suffered as much as might have been the case. The monks were also careful to pick up the pieces that fell off the plasterwork and any veneers that came off the inlaid floors, all of which they kept in cardboard boxes.

I foresaw that the restoration would take five years (it actually took nine!) and I would be over eighty and retired, 'if I was spared' as John Fowler use to say. It wasn't practical for me to take on such a major project. Fred asked me who I would recommend and the only person I could think of who I could trust to produce a classical interpretation of an Irish country house, an Anglo-Irish country house really, would be

Colin Orchard, who had worked with me for a number of years.[4] He had left and set up on his own with a small office in the King's Road, Chelsea. Of course Fred knew him, but he didn't know his capabilities. He was asked to do a small bedroom under the library pavilion at Churchill just as a trial run to see that he could carry out the work, on time and to estimate. Fred liked what he did and offered him the Ballyfin job.

Colin accepted, on condition that I would lend a hand with the principal rooms. But I was a really just a consultant. He would come down to Kent and show me samples and we would select things from that. I went over and did colour mixing with Nick Jewel, who was employed to do some of the painting work, mainly in the reception rooms. Some of these rooms were enormous. At eighty feet long the main library was a major challenge. It was quite difficult to get it right.

When it came to the saloon I realized that the appliqués on the wall had never been original to the room, and eventually we were allowed to remove them. The ceiling looked in a good state, except for one corner, which had to be repaired. Rather than repaint I thought it would be possible to just wash it and 'touch it up' as they say, and indeed that's what happened. The plasterwork was so crisp because it didn't have the layers of paint like most plaster, which loses its detail and definition over the years as it is repainted. I chose the damask fabric which was used to cover the walls, and I made them tone down the colours of the new Savonnerie carpet. It really was my last contribution to the world of decoration. My contribution was quite minor, but I enjoyed it very much because I watched Ballyfin grow from a painfully sad house to an absolute jewel in the middle of Ireland. It is quite unlike any other hotel in the world.

Fred and I have sort of grown together over the time we have been working with one another. He has given me an opportunity to do things a little differently and unusually, and also to expand my imagination. He has been interested in every detail. And it isn't just Fred, because behind all this is Kay, who has put up with the constant works and has always been very much part of it all. I suppose doing up houses and collecting have been Fred's hobby and passion. But for a decorator this has been a unique partnership.

He is also an exceptionally generous man and there have been a great number of 'treats'. Perhaps the treat of treats was the party at Versailles. Over the years the American

ABOVE Me, Fred, Kay, Julian Serrurier and his father, Pierre, in the garden at Kiftsgate Court in Gloucestershire, late 1980s.

Friends of Versailles in Chicago have raised considerable funds, which have been used to restore various things (principally the fountains) at the palace. It was arranged to give a Bal de Versailles in their honour and Pierre and I were included in Fred's party. We were all dressed up (at least the whole of the American contingent were dressed up in their very best with their jewellery) and dropped at the gates of Versailles, so we walked up the great courtyard escarpment in front of the palace in ball dresses and dinner jackets. It almost looked like a scene from the eighteenth century with these people going up into the entrance. The highlight for me was seeing the Hall of Mirrors entirely lit by candles and looking as it must have done in the seventeenth and eighteenth centuries. There was dancing and there were fireworks, and we enjoyed supper in the orangery with the fountains playing in the background. Returning to the Ritz, where I was staying, I could not help but think how John Fowler would have loved it all.

I've now known Kay and Fred for over thirty years, so I have redecorated their Chicago house more than

once when things wear out or tastes change. I have seen Fred's tastes change enormously since I first met him, from the sort of safety of brown English furniture, to rather more exotic, unusual and wonderful things, which he has gradually acquired from all over the world. He never sells anything. Sometimes he gives things away, but mostly he keeps them because he thinks he is going to do another project. It was not unusual for him to say, 'Let's do this room again because I would like to have better mirrors and I would like a better carpet' or perhaps he had bought something in a sale he wished to use, so the drawing room would be redone and upgraded. He was one of the few clients who consistently wanted more than ordinary conventional English or American style, wishing to create something unique and more individual. What has been so special about our relationship has been how we have changed, developed and educated each other's taste. And it was all by chance, because I happened to walk down the staircase at Brook Street one afternoon.

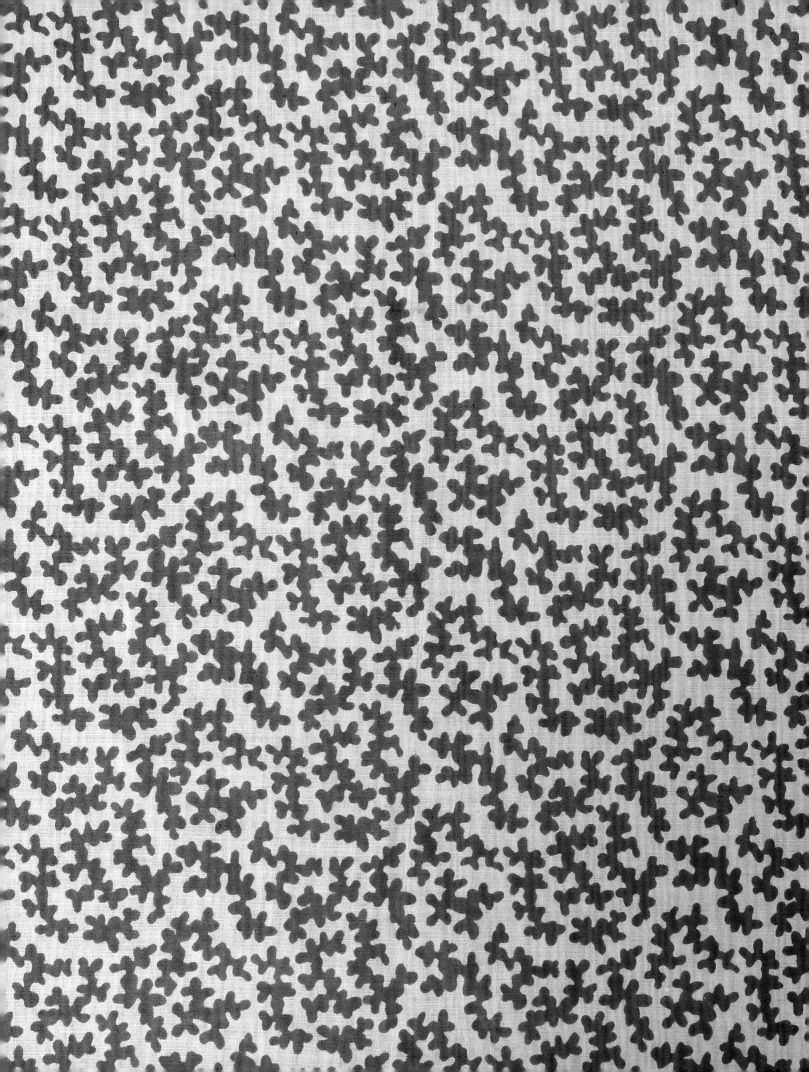

14

OFF THE FRINGE
– A LIFE BEYOND

My career, with all its diverse parts, has been the backbone of my life. It has given me so many openings for travel and for appreciating art and architecture and meeting people of all races and professions. Behind this, always, have been my personal interests and loves, which have also brought me great happiness and continue to do so.

I was born with a love of nature, which to some extent was frustrated by a busy career based in London. Now I have time for every season of the year, and every change, the different flowers, birds, bees and butterflies give me pleasure and I learn about nature all the time. Animals, all animals, enthral me and I've had loving relations with the dogs in my life and the birds I've tamed and cared for – all have been my great companions. I always think that if I had not been a decorator, I might have been a a botanist or a zoologist or run a home for unwanted dogs (or cats, or lions or elephants!).

My parents both loved the theatre, and went as often as they could. As I grew up they often took me with them, and I saw all the great stars – Sybil Thorndike, Peggy Ashcroft, Edith Evans, Ralph Richardson, Laurence Olivier, Paul Schofield and John Gielgud. Cinema and radio were in their infancy then and were less important, but my love of radio was formed in childhood, listening to Children's Hour and with my mother listening to Dylan Thomas reading his own poetry in his unforgettable voice. My love of ballet developed in my twenties, after the war, when I first went to Covent Garden to sit in the gods for half a crown. I saw all the great dancers in that post-war revival – Helpmann, Massine, Fonteyn stand out particularly in my memory. As the years went by I gradually descended from the gods to seats which

allow you to see all the stage. In those days people dressed up, and part of the pleasure was seeing the audience, particularly in the stalls, dressed and bejewelled. How times have changed, but the quality of the performances is just as high, and possibly even higher.

I was lucky enough to be taken to the opera by generous clients, and so my eyes and ears were opened to some magnificent performances. Sir Leon and Lady Bagrit and Sir Emmanuel and Lady Kaye treated me to superb evenings of opera.[1] Music was always part of my life, largely because of my father's love of classical music and opera. Popular music has passed me by and I know nothing about pop music or musicians. This is a failure in me; I wish I did understand it.

One very special treat from the Kayes was a trip to the Salzburg Festival in August 1990. We stayed in a lovely guesthouse and our fellow guests turned out to be Sir Isaiah and Lady Berlin.[2] At dinner I sat next to Sir Isaiah. I was anxious because I couldn't think what I could talk about. I wasn't very knowledgeable about music, much less philosophy, and certainly couldn't talk about anything on his level. I needn't have worried, as for some reason we got on like a house on fire. Apparently he said very nice things about me afterwards. The next day, we were at a concert with Alfred Brendel playing Beethoven superbly. We met Brendel over lunch the following day with Georg and Valerie Solti.

Without my passion for architecture I couldn't have done my job. Even as a child I was interested in buildings and when I first visited Paris in 1947 the architecture and culture had an enormous impact on me. Nearly all the travel I have done has centred on buildings. When I was young I only had two weeks holiday a year, and practically no money, so my travel was limited, but I went to France and Italy with friends and with my parents. The memory of those trips during the 1950s and 1960s is very vivid.

'Seaweed', an English pattern from the first half of the nineteenth century.

In particular I will never forget the magic of seeing Florence for the first time, visiting the Uffizi and standing alone in front of the Botticellis.

One of my most wonderful holidays was with two very good friends, David Vicary and Colin Anson.[3] David was a great influence on me in the 1960s, as he was hugely knowledgeable and enthusiastic about architecture and gardens. He had a list of gardens that we must see on a trip through France, Italy and as far as Rome and back. All this in his very dilapidated car that seemed to use more oil than petrol, and left a trail of pollution behind as we drove. Georgina Masson had published *Italian Villas and Palaces* in 1959 and *Italian Villas and Gardens* in 1961, and these books were our inspiration. Many of the properties were still rather dilapidated and unkempt, but they had a magic about them because of their formal design and use of water and topiary. Where the properties were not open to the public, David did not hesitate to drive up to the villas and ask if we could see the gardens. This was embarrassing but extremely profitable, since on several occasions we were invited in to have tea with the contessa. In the case of Villa Lante the owner saw our interest in his newly restored murals, and invited us to an evening of early Italian music played under moonlight at the top of those wonderful gardens, with the scent of orange and lemon blossom.

Of all the sixteenth-century Italian gardens, perhaps Villa d'Este at Tivoli is the most thrilling because of its use of water and the baroque. But the most fantastic of all was probably the Villa Bomarzo in Viterbo. It was uncared for and completely wild, and we had to climb fences to get in. I shall never forget the sight of a vast stone elephant and a giant tortoise, and 'the mouth of hell' surrounded by undergrowth and creating a paradise for birds. We met a workman on the road outside who said he had found Etruscan remains while digging the gulleys. We went back with him to his little square house in the middle of nowhere, and he opened up a big chest to reveal amazing finds. Although some were broken there were some entire Etruscan amphorae and bowls.

Over the years my love of Italy has increased. The more I have seen of it, the more I want to see. And over the years I have managed to see almost all of Italy. My parents' golden wedding anniversary was in May 1973, and I suggested we all go to Italy for a holiday. We flew to Pisa, hired a car and drove to Lucca where we spent a night before driving on up into the hills to Barga, which is now famous for its music festival. We were enchanted by the landscape and the

David Vicary and Jonathan Vickers examining fowls in the Paris bird market, in the early 1960s.

Carrara mountains above Lucca. We turned south, driving via places like Orvieto and Perugia all the way down to Rome and visiting many hill villages as we ambled south. The hill villages attracted all three of us because of their (to our minds) perfect way of living. Rome in May was very warm, but we found a charming hotel in the centre and were able to walk around the city, enjoying the numerous sites and treasures. In those days the Sistine Chapel was virtually empty of people and you could sit in the Piazza Navona and enjoy the fountains, or travel to Tivoli to see the water gardens.

Barga in particular made a great impression on me. To such an extent that I later went back determined to look for a house to buy. I must have been out of my mind, because

I had no money and when would I ever go there? I found a small run-down farmhouse on a tiny plot of land in the most beautiful setting. I saw it in the spring, surrounded by wild flowers, with the sound of birdsong and, of course, I was captivated. It was on the market for the equivalent of five thousand pounds, and I did seriously consider buying it, but luckily I came to my senses fairly quickly.

Another holiday which lingers in my memory is of a visit I made with David Laws, Stephen Long and Mark Heine in August 1986 to a villa which had been lent to us by the Gibson family, for whom David was working at the time.[4] It was a charming eighteenth-century villa overlooking the plains of the Veneto just outside the village of Asolo. We drove through Germany, Austria and the Dolomites to Italy and arrived at the charming house in the hills. I knew of the village from reading Freya Stark's travel books and knew she lived in this little town. Happily, Freya Stark knew we were coming from the Gibsons (they were friends), and she rang to offer the use of her pool.[5]

I was fascinated to meet this little dumpy elderly lady with her hat over one side of her head to hide her damaged ear. She was very welcoming and charming to us. As we swam she sat in a chair and talked to us. Later she asked, 'Would you like to come and see my wardrobe?' It seemed a strange invitation, but I accepted and we went to her bedroom, where there was a large wall of cupboards. She opened the door to reveal an amazing collection of Arab robes. They were all beautifully embroidered and very colourful. I had a vision of her in these exotic garments at some desert encampment, and it was rather thrilling to hear her account, and to be shown her specially made oval desk where she wrote her books.

She was then very old (ninety-three) and the house was getting rather too much for her, and she wondered if I knew anyone who could sell it for her. I wasn't in that world, but I thought Hamptons might possibly be the people as they dealt in overseas properties. Some correspondence flowed from that conversation and she did indeed sell the house and went to live in Asolo in a flat near the Hotel Cipriani, where she went for lunch each day. She was a fascinating character with fascinating conversation. I remember her talking about Pen Browning, the artist and only son of Elizabeth Barrett and Robert Browning and who had also lived in Asolo and whom she had known well.[6]

Those many visits to Italy inspired my decorating, not for the interiors themselves or the way Italians lived in their houses. In fact Palladian houses are very uncomfortable

for living and very difficult to furnish because of their size and height. They are really only summer houses. I found inspiration in the paintings, the landscape – the same landscape you saw both in the paintings and from the windows, looking exactly like the background of a Renaissance painting. More practically, I derived great inspiration from the colours of the houses, the earth colours, the siennas, the ochres and the venetian reds, all the colours John had taught me about. There they were all around me because they were derived from the very earth I was standing on.

I've always had a feeling for colour, natural colours connected to real minerals from the earth as opposed to chemicals. I was luckier than John because he was a non-traveller and only made one visit to Italy with the Georgian group in September 1955 to view the Palladian villas. He was glad he made the trip, which began and ended in Padua, and though he never went to Italy again it did not deter him from being an absolute authority on Italian buildings, paintings and colours – as indeed he was on French buildings, paintings and colours. He gained his knowledge by reading, studying and visiting museums, whereas I was very grateful for the privilege of being able to travel and see things at first hand.

Food also has always interested me – partly perhaps because we were denied so much during the war and for at least five years after, when rations were even stricter. The great influence on me and my friends was Elizabeth David, who published her book *Mediterranean Food* in 1950. This, along with *Italian Food* and *French Provincial Cooking*, which followed, became compulsory reading for the way they conjured the blissful world of cooks and food in lands we all longed to visit. I once met Elizabeth David with David Vicary when we went to have a drink in her Chelsea house. I was amazed to find her a somewhat austere and rather distant person, with a basement kitchen which was anything but modern. It had an old-fashioned pine dresser and scrubbed wooden table and was generally rather run-down. We sat at the kitchen table and had a drink (I seem to remember madeira) and though I worshipped her for her books she was not easy to talk to and I felt painfully shy. Later she opened a shop selling cooking utensils from all over Europe and we all went there to buy our mandolins, garlic presses, Provençal dishes and anything else we could afford.

David Vicary and Jonathan Vickers and I subsequently spent some enjoyable evenings at classes in the Cordon Bleu School in Marylebone, taking home the results of our cookery for supper together. As we could barely afford decent food – Jonathan at that time lived off kippers cooked in boiling water from a kettle in his bedsit – this was a great treat. Later the three of us went to Paris together and ate in cheap little cafés and had picnics bought from the beautiful markets, which we ate at the then unrestored Désert de Retz – another architectural excitement discovered by David.

When, in the mid-1960s, my friend the antique dealer Andrée Bessire, who lived in Paultons Square in London, decided to retire and sell her lovely house and collection of late eighteenth-century and early nineteenth-century French furniture, she went off to find a house in Provence.[7] She was Swiss by birth, but had a great feeling for the South of France and had always liked the idea of going to live there. She disappeared for close on two years, living in L'Isle-sur-la-Sorgue in a small hotel while looking for a property she could convert. Being a very determined lady who knew exactly what she wanted, she did all this on her own. It took time, but eventually she found a house near Oppède, a ruined village near Cavaillon in the south-west of Provence. It was an old farmhouse with an arcaded courtyard, a little gate lodge and a bit of land behind. It was the perfect house for her, with good, tall, well proportioned rooms, a magnificent carved stone staircase and two beautiful chimneypieces with big carved stone overmantels.

She started work on the house with the help of a few local artisans – scraping the floors to reveal beautiful tiles, and searching for the right furniture. She planned meticulously. Having sold all her smart London furniture she started to collect suitable Provençal country furniture instead. L'Isle-sur-la-Sorgue was a centre for antiquarians and a good source of armoires and Provençal commodes and tables and chairs.

By the time I was invited to go and see her she had it up and running using old French toiles and lovely pieces of furniture. I thought it was absolute heaven because it was fulfilling a dream of my own. I really liked, as John did, to mix French and English furniture, combining the comfort of the English sofa and chair and the discomfort but style of French furniture. She used a few English pieces, probably less than I would have done, but it made a comfortable house. She was working hard on the garden and the courtyard was cleared and cleaned, and for this she had a gatekeeper who helped her. Shearo and I were lucky enough to be invited there, and I fell in love with the whole idea of Provence.

Later on I had the odd experience of getting there by train for a lovely weekend only to be thwarted on my return journey because of the general strike of 1968 when all the students in Paris rose up on the Sunday and the whole of working France came to a standstill. We went to the butcher's to get our Sunday *gigot* only to be told, 'Haven't you heard? There's an all-out strike.' Nothing was working, so I couldn't ring anyone to explain what was happening. The banks were closed, which meant there was no money, and consequently shops emptied of goods immediately. Everybody bought everything, stripping the shelves – all that was left was salt, pepper and mustard! Almost the only people allowed to have petrol during that period were the flour mills, who were allowed to deliver flour to bakers. People had to sustain themselves on whatever they could. This seemed all the sadder because the fruit had just ripened in Provence, and all the cherries stacked in boxes on the trains were oozing in the sidings.

The only information available was from the brief radio announcements when de Gaulle spoke to the people. And now and then there would be an item about how foreigners could get out of the country if they were stuck. For example, there might be a coach going to Brussels from the Place Vendôme in Paris at five p.m., or something else going to Switzerland at eight a.m. the next morning. In deepest Provence we had no communications whatsoever. This situation lasted for three and a half weeks, by which time, although I personally was enjoying what I was doing, the situation generally wasn't a happy one because of the torment in France. I began to feel a burden to my poor friend, although we were living in strange luxury on asparagus, cherries, strawberries and bread. You can certainly enjoy such living, but even that gets a bit monotonous eventually.

I often walked up into Ménerbes (later made famous by Peter Mayle) and I developed a love for that particular hill village. However, my aim was to get out of France. I had little money and Andrée only had the equivalent of about thirty pounds and no way of getting any more. A French friend in a nearby village had friends staying who were professors from Mexico City and equally anxious to get home. The French lady had a Mercedes with some petrol; so together we set off through the Camargue towards the Spanish border – only to find that the Mercedes guzzled up all the petrol long before we got to the border. It was already running out of petrol when we reached Nîmes. I remember going up to the prefecture in Nîmes, all blocked off as it was by rifle-carrying gendarmes, and saying to them, 'We are *étrangers* and we need to get home.' My friends had a

Jean Monro in Provence in 1993.

I remember in July 1981 a very dear friend, the violinist Iona Brown, said she was giving a festival concert in Aix-en-Provence with the St Martin-in-the Fields orchestra, with Rostropovich as the cellist.[8] Shearo, her husband, Frank, and I decided to go to the festival to hear them. We stayed in a lovely hotel in Aix and in the morning went to hear the orchestra rehearse with Rostropovich, who was sitting on the platform in the courtyard of a monastery with his cello and a small pet dog on his lap. The evening performance, with Iona conducting from the violin, was sublime. Afterwards we drove on to Jean's house, north of Aix, on the day that happened to be that of Charles and Diana's wedding, and arrived just in time to watch it on the little square television in Jean's sitting room.

It is funny how the various circles of friends develop and overlap. I met Iona indirectly through Nina Robinson. I suppose it was in the early 1960s that John Fowler decorated Nina's country house. I remember that we did a very glamorous bedroom for her with a blue silk four-poster bed.[9] Nina was Polish – and a descendant of Tchaikovsky – and had managed to escape from Poland following the German invasion in 1939. When she arrived in London she got a job at the BBC foreign service broadcasting to Poland. Through her I met Jan Andrzej Sapieha and his wife, Maria, who lived next door to Lady Diana Cooper in Little Venice. Jan dealt in high-quality prints, which we were buying for clients – we used a lot of prints in our work.[10] Another member of this group of emergency Poles was Henryk Szeryng, the violinist and composer, who had been a liaison officer for General Wladyslaw Sikorski, Prime Minister of the Polish

paper from a previous year when they had come over to a conference in Paris so we changed the date and they said they had to get to the conference, at which of course the gendarmes laughed! After a lot of banter we did actually get coupons for thirty litres of petrol, which enabled us to fill up the car and get to the frontier. I spent that night in a little hotel sharing a room with the French lady.

It was a very inferior hotel with a dripping water tap and nothing much else beyond a modest meal. I spent some of my little remaining money to get to Barcelona, but when I arrived at the airport there was absolutely no possibility of getting a plane for several days. I stayed in the cheapest possible room in the cheapest hotel in the centre of Barcelona, living on melon and bread, and spent the time walking around admiring the Gaudí buildings. When I finally got back to London and went into the office John said, 'Where have you been, girl? Why the hell didn't you ring up?' The fact I had no money to phone and there were no phones anyway was a minor consideration.

This experience did not put me off Provence – quite the contrary. A few years later I got to know Jean Monro (the famous decorator Mrs Monro). She had a house near Andrée, in the village of Les Martins, and often invited me to stay.

Lunch at Jean Monro's house in Provence. Shearo, her husband Frank Stone, Iona Brown and viola player Tony Jenkins.

With Andrée Bessire in Switzerland.

01 626 7848

MANSION HOUSE PLACE
LONDON,
EC4N 8BL

HGAR/AMP   22nd October, 1973.

Miss I. Taylor,
Sybil Colefax and John Fowler,
39, Brook Street,
London, W.1.

                                            RECEIVED
                                            23 OCT 1973

Naughty mackerel,

        I am distressed at your infidelity although I do realise
that you are one of the busiest bees in the business.   Now that
things have settled down a bit at Carlos Place and a cooking lady
has come from wildest Ireland, perhaps you would care to lunch
or dine with me one day, or even pop in for a drink?

        There are one or two things that I think I might need and
your advice about them would be quite invaluable, although I know
that you will exact payment through my nose! I want some firebacks
and I know that these can be obtained from that shop in the Soho area
off Tottenham Court Road, whose name escapes me at the moment.
I am a little worried about going in there myself with some homemade
measurements in case I make a mistake.   I was wondering if you
could suggest what I could get, and help me to choose one for the
drawing-room and for the red room.

        I am awfully pleased with everything you have done and
many times your ears must have been burning for the compliments
that have been made.   True to my word though, I have told them
that the whole thing was entirely you.   I never made any suggestions,
looked at any patterns or asked for anything.   They all think I was
very lucky, or perhaps very shrewd, to put myself in your hands.

        I hope young Foxy is behaving herself and that perhaps
I might run into her one of these days.   I would like to browse
round your emporium but it is not open when I motor past on my
way to the City and by the time I get back, all the birds have flown!
Don't bother to write about this, give me a telephone call when
you have time.

                    Yours with deep sincerity
                    A Satisfied Customer!

A letter from Hugh Ross.

government in exile.[11] I remember going backstage to congratulate Henryk after a concert, and among the group of people surrounding him was a young blonde girl whom he embraced and called 'my lovely princess'. This was Iona Brown, who was to become my great friend.

Lady Diana Cooper was a close friend of Nancy Lancaster's. I knew her only slightly, in her old age, but she made an impression on me, as she did on everyone who met her. A great beauty, she was aways exquisitely dressed with her face rather white and plastered with make-up. I remember visiting her one morning and the interview took place from her bed, which was covered in papers and Pekingese dogs, but even in such circumstances she was a glamorous figure.[12]

In 1973 a client of mine, Mrs Thornton, introduced me to a bachelor friend called Hugh Ross. He had a very nice flat in Chandos Place, just off Berkeley Square, and I went round to see him. He had never had any decoration done professionally, and was a bit wary of this lady from Colefax, but I warmed to him immediately. Hugh had some nice pieces of furniture (he obviously had an eye for good things) and a library of books. I learnt from Mrs Thornton that he'd had a terrible war, having been a prisoner of war after being captured by the Japanese. Anyone who'd been through that and who survived was inevitably damaged physically and probably mentally.

Hugh was very charming and amusing, and once he'd got over his initial reservations we got on well. I produced some schemes for him, which he considered rather daring, but nevertheless accepted. We purchased a few extra pieces of furniture and made some chairs and sofas, and gradually over several years I did the whole flat. Hugh was unique. I have done so many of this type of London apartment, and there was nothing particularly special about this one, but Hugh had a keen sense of humour and would write me the most delightful letters. He addressed his letters to 'dearest mackerel', because he said I flitted about the world like a mackerel, he never knew where I was. Certainly then I was pretty busy. Many years later, he retired from his stepfather's investment company to Monte Carlo, where he had bought a modern apartment. We always kept in touch, and his letters were full of life in Monaco. When I was in Provence staying with Andrée he would drive down the coast to meet me for lunch in Aix-en-Provence, looking every inch a 'South of France' character in his white open tourer. Lunch was full of jokes and reminiscences of people we had both known. Sadly, he died a few years later in Monte Carlo, but he remains a treasured memory.

Sybil Connolly and her friend the Irish gardener Jim Reynolds.

Swiss Cottage, Kilcommon, County Tipperary. A *cottage orné*, probably originally designed by John Nash, which Sybil restored and decorated. This was the inspiration for the cottage Fred Krehbiel built for his wife (see page 142).

I travelled to Provence a lot, often staying with Andrée or Jean, and the more I got to know the area the fonder I became of it. It seemed so cheap in those days – very difficult to imagine now that Provence was ever cheap, but it was – and I actually put in an offer for a piece of land in Ménerbes, with the intention of building a small house. I got to the solicitor's stage with it, but came to my senses before signing anything because I realized it was going to be impossible to spend time there. Subsequently, as Provence has become so popular, I'm glad I didn't actually go there to live. But, of course, the influences remain and I do have one or two Provençal pieces in my very typical French house in Burgundy.

Later in my life I was lucky enough to get to know Sybil Connolly, who then still had her dress design business in Dublin.[13] She had become famous for her use of Irish fabrics, particularly tweeds and linens, which gained her an international following. She was popular with rich Americans like Jackie Onassis. She was always interested in decoration and used to come into Brook Street from time to time, which was how I met her. We talked and we got on rather well, so she invited me to supper at the Connaught, where she always stayed. She was a very elegant woman, always immaculately dressed. But she was also full of fun, laughter and wit. Over the years she would always look me up whenever she came to London on business and so I had many a happy evening with

her. The culmination of that was when she asked me to go to see her when we both happened to be in New York.

At the time she was working for Tiffany's, selling Irish products to the American market. She was staying with her great friend Eleanor Lambert, who had an apartment facing Central Park.[14] This extraordinary apartment was full of wonderful artefacts collected over the years in a very eclectic mix, and had a marvellous view over the Reservoir, which looks like a lake in the middle of New York. Not exactly a Colefax & Fowler look – more of a collector's apartment – but extremely appealing. It had an old-fashioned kitchen with an old-fashioned dresser, which was funny when you think of the New York style and modern apartments. Hers had a lovely feeling of quality and antiquity and charm.

Subsequently, Sybil asked me if I would like to go and see Ireland, which I didn't know at all well at that time. I had been working at Churchill House for Fred, but I hadn't really discovered any other bits of Ireland. She wanted to show me where Irish artefacts were made. She also asked George and Judith Oakes, Nicola and Richard Woodhead and Pierre Serrurier, and with huge generosity she insisted on paying for us all. We went over in July 1996 for a few days. Pierre and I stayed in the mews behind her Merrion Square house. I remember going to see these craft potters she knew and to Waterford to see the glassworks. I also recall she showed us this wonderful *cottage orné* that she'd restored, and another that had been restored by the owner of the pottery. She had by then retired, but I remember being shown the couture business salon below her apartment. I was able to see how she pleated linen with very fine knife pleats, an original idea of hers. She used to make beautiful clothing from fine tweeds in pretty colours, which couldn't be more different from the normal 'tweed suiting'.

I remember sitting in the Carlyle Hotel in New York with Sybil, Eleanor Lambert and Colin Orchard, who was my assistant at the time.[14] We were all sitting having drinks when Hubert de Givenchy walked by! There was a great welcoming, kissing and hugging of this enormously tall, elegant gentleman whom they obviously knew very well. To me he was only a name (a brand name to be exact) and I had to pinch myself at that moment and say 'Am I really here?'

Trudi Ballard (the press officer at Colefax) and I enjoying an elephant ride in Jaipur.

Now I've retired I have come to enjoy my gardens – both the one here in England and the rather small garden I have in France. My parents had both loved gardening and worked on our garden well into their late eighties, even though my mother sometimes toppled over into the rose bushes on unsteady feet. Alas, I now do exactly the same! It wasn't until I retired in my seventies that I could grow any plants and my skills are not very professional, but I love propagating from seeds and cuttings and get great pleasure from the results. Old French roses were introduced to me by John Fowler, who had a wonderful collection although they were not particularly popular at that time. John would reel off names such as 'Madame Alfred Carrière', 'Cardinal de Richelieu', 'Zéphirine Drouhin', 'Fantin-Latour', and he taught me to love these roses. A love of flowers and plants opens up so much and develops a need to care, with feeding and watering not to mention visits to endless gardens both grand and humble. You never visit a garden without learning something. My own house (or even a hotel room where I am staying) is never without flowers.

Since I was a child I have enjoyed maps and the geography of the world and been interested in different races of mankind. Because of this I am also fascinated by world affairs and never miss a day without knowing what is going on in the world. I have a particular horror of cruelty, whether physical or mental, to children. This has led me to sponsor several children in India, and now also in Georgia, which has opened up a new world to me. One of 'my girls' (as I call them) was found on Madras (Chennai) Railway Station by an orphanage worker. She had had her arms and legs cut to provoke pity and then had been abandoned by her mother when she was aged about three. I went to India with my friend Sally Houseman to see her when she was six in the S.O.S. Children's Village outside Chennai. It was Christmas time and we planned to travel through southern India after visiting the children. I will always remember seeing two little girls, Kavitha, my sponsee, and her little sister, running towards me with open arms. They were dressed in their party clothes, with ribbons in their hair, and I burst into tears! We had Christmas dinner with them, eating curries off banana leaves, distributing presents and enjoying meeting the house mother and her orphan children of all ages, boys and girls. My child grew up and was educated at secondary school and took an extramural university course, gaining a BA. She is married and both she and her husband have jobs.

I went to the wedding of another of my girls – Sharada – in Delhi. It was a three-day affair, and enthralling. Sharada

Kavitha, aged six, in Chennai.

After a seven-year training in a dance school near Chennai, Sharada became a classical Indian dancer.

had trained as a classical Indian dancer and I even saw her dance in northern Italy, where an Italian friend arranged for her and another girl to give dance performances.

Although I am not a political person – I suppose I would be best described as a small 'c' conservative or a liberal-conservative – I have in recent years supported the fight to make Iran a democratic and secular state. I vividly remember the day the Shah left Iran in 1979, with a soldier falling to his knees to kiss the Shah's hand as he walked to his plane, and the appalling terror that the ayatollahs unleashed soon afterwards. One day I happened to be making my way back to the office down South Molton Street when I fell into conversation with a young man from the Iran Liberty Association.[15] Appalled by the plight of the orphaned children of dissidents in Iran, I gave them a cheque for £250.

That was almost thirty years ago and they have become good friends; and one of the children I helped now counts me as a surrogate grandmother.

I suppose it all stems from my basic philosophy of life, which is one of tolerance. I have lived my life tolerating people's differences, which has given rise to much interest and the enjoyment of many varieties of people of all races and classes. In my career I was usually dealing with privileged wealthy people, but also with tradespeople, the artists and craftsmen who enabled me to carry out the work. We were creating dream homes for people, but it was a fulfilling and creative task. I never envied my clients: it was the end product of a beautiful room or home that pleased me. As long as the client and I were both happy that was all that mattered.

15

FULL THROTTLE

Inevitably some clients make more of an impression than others, and some become friends, as did Miranda, Countess of Iveagh.[1] I think she was introduced to Colefax by Mrs Hourigan, who had worked for the Iveagh family at Farmleigh House on the edge of Phoenix Park in Dublin, a house which they later sold to the Irish state. Miranda had a house in Cottesmore Gardens, Kensington – a large double-fronted house with what was by London standards a big garden at the back. At the time she had four young children, so it was a family house, and because of her connections she had some lovely furniture and pictures, which provided a good palette.

We got off to a good start because Alan Gore, an old friend of John's, was working on the kitchen, and we had amusing site meetings.[2] Miranda seemed to know everybody, including most of our old clients, and was such fun to be with, and it was a stimulating job because she had interesting ideas. I remember she wanted to use as a theme the musical instruments in her main sitting room – a harpsichord and an Irish harp among other things. There was a formal dining room with a Mauny wallpaper and we created a red library. She was into all the things that were fashionable at the time – the 1970s – such as

OPPOSITE 'Camellia', an English design from the mid-nineteenth century. Sibyl Colefax produced chintz with this design in the 1930s, and we revived it later.

RIGHT Miranda Iveagh's drawing room at Cottesmore Gardens.

LEFT ABOVE
The red library
at Cottesmore
Gardens. The green
cabinet to the left
was made to hide
the television. The
curtains are in 'Tree
Poppy' chintz.
LEFT BELOW
The elaborately
dressed bay window
in the drawing room,
with swag and tail
curtains and
festoon blinds.

OPPOSITE The main
bedroom, done
with a blue
Mauny wallpaper.

pattern on pattern, flowery chintzes, patterned carpets and wallpapers, all of which contributed to the look of that period and now looks rather dated.

Some years later in 1984, she introduced me to her boyfriend Tony Ryan, who founded Ryanair.[3] He had bought an estate in Tipperary (Kilboy House near Nenagh) and Miranda and I were flown over by Ryanair and driven to Tipperary to see it. On the way we stopped to have light refreshments at one of the local pubs – the light refreshments being champagne and oysters. I'm allergic to oysters (and probably drank a little too much champagne). When we arrived at the house I got out of the car, somewhat unsteady on my feet, and looked at an enormous flight of steps up to what should have been a house, only there was no house! I didn't know whether I was hallucinating or being teased. In fact, the original house had burnt down in 1922 but had been rebuilt by the

then owner, Lord Dunalley, only for it to be reduced to a single-storey house in the 1950s. What Tony had bought was a one-storey 'bungalow' mansion, but because of the steep steps I couldn't see it from where I was standing. Of course, I was ragged about this for many years to come. Subsequently, there was a fire in 2005, which gutted most of the house, so Tony's son Shane has rebuilt the original house from 1780.

Decorating the bungalow we created a lovely grand bedroom using Mauny paper and a four-poster bed, and designed an interesting red lacquer dining room, which was really a library entirely surrounded by bookcases. I enjoyed doing this because dining rooms are often quite boring spaces and here you had the feeling of eating in a library. The house had been built on top of the original basement, which was huge, and Tony had his offices down there and turned some of the space over to form an art gallery.

He then asked if I would help him and Miranda design the interiors for a fleet of leasehold planes which he was buying from McDonnell Douglas (later Boeing) in Los Angeles. The interiors had to be suitable for leasing to airlines in countries as different as Mexico and Finland. We travelled to a factory in Los Angeles to learn what you could and couldn't do inside an aeroplane. There were the problems of fireproofing and limitations as to what materials you could use for carpets, upholstery and even the antimacassars on the chair heads. There was the cutlery and the china to consider, and the colour of the walls. Because of the different countries they would be leased to we had to think of something that would appeal to all. In other words they had to be neutral, which is actually rather difficult to achieve. We designed a sort of herringbone carpet – which we had specially woven – and upholstery fabrics for the seating. All the colours were neutral and calm. It was an interesting project, but a boring design.

By coincidence, at the same time I was approached by a friend to put together an exhibition on the English country house in his local library. This friend, a famous antique dealer called Gep Duremburger, had a shop in San Juan Capistrano, south of Los Angeles.[4] Tony Ryan, Miranda Iveagh and I flew over. We stayed at the Beverly Hills Hotel, which was lovely. Around the hotel was a series of little cottages, each with a bedroom suite, which you walked through the garden to reach. I was mesmerized by the elegant comfort of the place – the vases of flowers

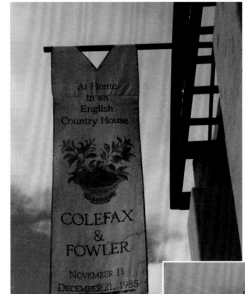

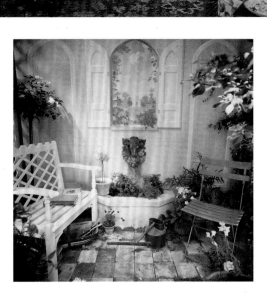

CLOCKWISE FROM TOP LEFT Gep Duremburger and me at
the English Country House exhibition at San Juan Capistrano;
the exhibition banner; me in my apron, assembling the
four-poster bed; the sitting-room fireplace complete with
flower fire screen; the garden arbour with *trompe l'œil* alcove
created especially for the exhibition; a wider view of the
exhibition sitting room.

and bowls of fruit on the table, and every sort of lavish thing laid out for your use. After working on the plane project for a few days I asked if I could catch the San Diego train down to San Juan Capistrano and they looked to me in a horrified way: no woman would ever travel alone on a train. It seemed the only way to get there was to hire a car.

My small exhibition, staged in the autumn of 1985, was intended to promote what English decorators were doing at that time, but it was very out of sync with Californian living. San Juan Capistrano is a little town with, by their standards, a long history, dating from the time when Spanish Catholic missionaries built a monastery there in 1776. A new library had just been built by Michael Graves, and a more unsuitable place for an English Country House exhibition could not be imagined. The rooms were soaring high. I had to think of a way of presenting my English rooms within those spaces, and decided to build a sort of capsule. The exhibition included a sitting room, a garden room and a bedroom, all. opening off an octagonal hall. This gave me a way to present three different types of English room. Aside from good painted walls, good painted floors and all sorts of gimmicks, I had to find people who would lend English furniture for the exhibition out of their own homes, or if they were antique dealers out of their own shops, and for a considerable period of time. People were wonderfully helpful and generous with their time and with what they could lend. I had a four-poster bed made in England, hung with Colefax chintz, and shipped over – there was even a breakfast tray with a copy of *The Times*. It was theatre really: people stood in the octagonal hall and looked into the rooms. I took a team to set it up and spent the night before the opening up a ladder painting the walls myself, and trying to hang pictures on cardboard walls – I had specified hardboard, but this had been misunderstood to mean cardboard!

I also had to give a lecture both there and in Santa Barbara. That was my first lecture and was shared with Mario Buatta as the main speaker with me as his warm-up act, a sort of stooge – he was extremely amusing and sent me up, as was his wont, and everyone laughed.[5] Lectures and exhibition were well attended, but they didn't bring me any work. There were masses of American designers, and the English country house was not really a Californian look. So ultimately it wasn't very successful as a public relations exercise for Colefax & Fowler.

However, from my point of view it was very enjoyable, and Gep and I remained good friends.

Very occasionally you get a client whose ideas are so impossible, or at least so at variance with what one would normally do, that it becomes hopeless to try and work for them. This happened with Barbara Cartland.[6] She asked if I would go down to see her house, Camfield Place, near Hatfield in Hertfordshire. It was quite a nice stucco Regency house. She came out to greet me dressed head to foot in bright pink Harris tweed, with a white Pekingese under each arm and her white hair neatly coiffed. She wanted me to decorate her drawing room, which was a large room, and she was adamant – 'I want strong red silk curtains and I want white walls.' That wasn't the sort of a country house feel we would normally aim for. I said to her 'that sounds a bit alarming to me,' and offered to produce some sort of scheme around soft reds and off-whites. 'Not too soft,' she snapped, and she took me upstairs to see her bedroom. It had a large four-poster bed in which, apparently, she did most of her writing. The bed was made up of carved and gilded Italian *baldacchino* posts (with a barley sugar twist), and was hung with scarlet taffeta. Now I was more than alarmed, because I saw what she meant about the drawing room – she really meant violent pillar box red.

We went back downstairs and she said, 'We'll have some tea.' She was into the health properties of honey, and a poor, rather sad-looking maid brought in tea. Somehow everyone in her house had this poor run-down look, I suppose to make her feel better about herself. We sat down to the honey tea – honey cake, of course, honey scones, etc. I was forced to confess that I had never read any of her books. 'Oh! We can soon remedy that. I can give you some of my books.' We went into her library, which was quite sizeable and entirely filled, floor to ceiling, with her own books in twenty different languages or however many it was that they were printed in. I went away with a pot of honey and three books, one of which was an autobiography, which I did attempt to read. But every sentence started with 'I', which made it rather heavy going. I remember she said, 'You know I always make happy endings, there is no explicit sex. it's all romance and I think people like it because of that.'

I went back to think out what scheme I could do. I thought of a sort of soft rose-crimson damask with off-white walls and put together a scheme based on this and took it to her. She turned it down immediately.

'Not bright enough,' she said. 'I don't want off-white – I want white. And I want some gilding.' I did try to remonstrate, pointing out that she had a very nice Regency house, which didn't want to be quite so harsh and jazzed up. Much good that did me – 'But I want it that way, go away and think about it.'

I did think about it and I produced another scheme in which I tried to heighten the colours and add something more vibrant, but it was really an impossible task. Eventually, I wrote and said we were on completely different wavelengths. I was used to doing the shabby chic country house look and the style she wanted was alien to me. I must say, she took rejection rather well. She wrote to me to say, 'What a brave girl you are to turn me down. I do admire you for your honesty.'

If trying to work for Barbara Cartland was a dismal failure, working for Barbara Goalen proved to be a great success. Barbara Goalen was the most sought-after fashion model of the immediate post-war era.[7] A very beautiful woman, elegant in every way, she was a great favourite with Dior and Balenciaga. After the austerity of the war, people were thrilled with the New Look of voluptuous full skirts and big hats. And she could carry off that look beautifully. She modelled for everybody, and she seemed to be on every page of *Vogue*.

Later, in the early 1970s, she asked me to do her house in Chester Square. This was the first house where I used the 'double mirror' effect which was to become fashionable. The entrance halls in those Chester Square houses are comparatively small and narrow, but using mirror on the walls, right down to the floor (and that's the important thing) makes the room appear to continue into infinity. It gives an extraordinary effect. You can hang things on the mirror if you want to, another mirror for example. But above all it is a way of playing with space.

'I'm not mad about getting older,' Barbara Goalen once said. She tried very hard to fight age. She had plastic surgery, which caused an awful problem because after that she found it very difficult to close her eyes at night. This was the first time I had to completely black out a room, because she would be woken by the slightest light at dawn. It's extremely hard to quell light. I had special blackout blinds put behind triple-lined blackout curtains, which were in turn pinned down at the edge so that no crack would show.

As a decorator you get used to people's foibles and eccentricities. I doubt there is a more eccentric race than the English. I remember being asked to Yorkshire to see the Halifaxes.[8] We all know that Lord Halifax was a very prominent figure in the 1930s, and was with Neville Chamberlain at the beginning of the Second World War trying to placate Hitler, which turned out to be a rather futile occupation. His daughter married Lord Feversham and John had worked for them at Helmsley. It was Anne Feversham who recommended me to her brother, who succeeded to the earldom in 1959. The Halifaxes lived at Garrowby Park, a large country estate near York. They commissioned Francis Johnson to add a library to hold his father's books and papers and some wonderful Stubbs paintings.[9] They were entirely typical of the English aristocracy in that their lives revolved around country pursuits – hunting, shooting and fishing. Lady Halifax was really a countrywoman, and in that regard she was very much like the Queen. I remember going up to discuss the work and we had lunch in the large dining room. We sat around a spacious table with me in the middle and them at either end. Under the furniture and all around the room were dogs of all shapes and sizes, large and small, eleven of them in all. The butler served lunch and we chatted about the house, but I was rather mesmerized by these very good, placid animals. Coffee was brought in and on the tray was a large bowl of brown, crystal coffee sugar, which Lady Halifax threw all around the carpet using a large silver spoon. Out came eleven dogs in a flash to consume the sugar for which they had waited so patiently. Apparently, they did this every day. A particularly English form of eccentricity.

I began working for John Goodwin when he was a bachelor and was buying good antiques and paintings. His taste was perhaos more restrained than I was used to at the time, with less clutter. He subsequently married and had two children, so the house had a different atmosphere but, unusually, the main rooms remained as they were done during his bachelor days.

Over my career I have done so much work, yet little has survived. Decorating is an ephemeral thing. People move houses, or change husbands, or just die. You soon learn that what you do may only last a short time – sometimes rather shorter than you had bargained for. I remember working for Duncan Sandys MP. His first wife was Churchill's daughter Diana, but they divorced in 1960, and when I knew him he was married to an adorable French lady called Marie-Claire.[10] They lived

The drawing room and master bedroom of John Goodwin's Knightsbridge house, which we decorated in 1985. The drawing room, especially, is a good example of our work of this period.

within the division bell in a nice house in Vincent Square. I had just finished helping her with the drawing room when there was an almighty fire overnight and part of the house was burned out. I was called next morning to see what could be salvaged – not much, was the answer. I had to do the work again, which was amazingly difficult. It is never easy to redo something.

By an odd quirk of fate a similar disaster had happened to me once before. I was working for Virginia Thesiger, (née Graham), who was married to Tony Thesiger.[11] Virginia was a great friend of Joyce Grenfell, and a collection of their letters spanning fifty years has subsequently been published. She was a lovely, intelligent woman, and she had a second-floor apartment in Hyde Park Gardens, which we did together. We had just hung the last curtain when one morning I had a telephone call with a strong voice: 'We're all right, but we had a terrible night.' Virginia and her husband had gone to bed, but during the night heard sudden cracks and thuds and thought someone had broken in. Virginia got up and opened the door to the drawing room, but was thrown back by the blast of the heat. Opening the door had let air

in and the house almost exploded. They were very lucky not to have been seriously injured or worse.

When I went round the firemen were still damping down. It was a desperate scene: the whole of the drawing room floor – including the grand piano – had fallen into the apartment below. Ironically, the only thing left intact was the fireplace, with the coal still in the grate. The rest of the apartment was very badly damaged by the terrible effects of smoke, which left a sort of brown treacle on the walls. And of course everything was soaking wet. The only good thing was that the flat below was not occupied and nobody was hurt, with the Thesigers escaping in their nightclothes.

I hasten to say that fires have not been common on my jobs!

16

KEEPING IT IN THE FAMILY

When a client engages a decorator there has to be some rapport, or the relationship simply won't work. As a decorator it helps to be interested both in your client and in their house. Initially Gordon and Margaret Richardson came to see John about a house in Chelsea Square, one of a modern development just behind John's house on the King's Road. John wasn't particularly keen on the house and must have shown it, but we had a meeting at Brook Street and we all visited the house. They weren't very taken with John, but they had been told he was the best decorator there was, and at that time Gordon Richardson was climbing the ladder of success in the banking world. Eventually they came to see me at Brook Street and said they felt John didn't want to do the job. They were quite right, but I tactfully explained he wasn't very well, which they understood. They then asked if I could help them, which of course I had to tactfully explain to John.

I did the whole house with them, even the buying of the furniture. It was an interesting relationship and they became good friends as well as clients. Gordon Richardson came from Nottinghamshire and had married Margaret (Peggy), who was the daughter of Canon Dick Shepherd.[1] The house in Chelsea Square was a success and they lived there with their teenage children for many years. Then they decided they wanted a country house. They told me they had found a house which was in a wonderful position, but unfortunately rather ugly. They wouldn't buy it until I had seen it and considered if anything could be done to make it better. Duntisbourne House was old, but it had been radically altered in the 1930s and little of the original building was left. The then owners had made lots of small rooms, putting up partition walls, and it had a sort of 1930s entrance. But the position was indeed magical, on an escarpment on the top of a hill near Cirencester.

OPPOSITE 'Tree Poppy', a mid-nineteenth-century design, possibly French but designed for the English market.

LEFT Duntisbourne House in Gloucestershire.
I added the extension to the right.

I suggested they could make an addition at one end of the house. This would centre the house on the terrace and at the same time allow them to enlarge the main living room and have a better bedroom and bathroom above. I had recently been using a very good builder called Thomas Williams, who had wonderful stonemasons. I thought we could extend the house without its looking as if any addition had been made. With this advice they bought the house. I then got cold feet because of the major structural alteration and asked Philip Jebb if he would give his opinion. He came down and confirmed the extension would be a good thing to do, since after so much drastic alteration it would return the house to its original intended design. It became a very interesting project and from an unpromising start it made a very easy house to live in, with decent-sized rooms on three floors, nice bedrooms and bathrooms, a stable yard, a swimming pool, a tennis court, lovely views and a charming garden. In fact when it was sold, after Peggy's death, I think the asking price was £4 million but it went for £8 million, rather proving what a desirable property it had become.

At the beginning they hadn't any furniture for the house so it was a complete revamp. The budget wasn't enormous, but was sufficient in those days to buy pretty country furniture. We bought a lot of French things, including some French stone fireplaces. One of Gordon Richardson's recreations was antiques and he would come and look at our showrooms, while other things came from O.F. Wilson in the Fulham Road.

We also went to Lisbon, to visit the Fundação Ricardo do Espírito Santo Silva, which was based in the Azurara Palace. This foundation produced reproduction painted furniture, good metal lanterns and lovely gilded bindings for books with tooling. They also made traditional carpets with designs taken from documents, often French sourced.

We chose a Portuguese needlepoint carpet for their drawing room, which was a low squarish room. The Portuguese rug, French stone fireplace and French Mauny wallpaper combined in an eclectic mix to make a lovely room where they liked to sit in the evening with a big roaring fire.

This was actually the first time I'd had an empty house which had to be furnished from scratch, and I was lucky enough to be doing it with people who liked participating and were easy to deal with. They were quite different characters. Gordon was surprisingly hesitant, which I found strange in someone who was to become Governor of the Bank of England. I would have expected him to be very decisive – as indeed he probably was in his own area – but he found it difficult to visualize things. Peggy was like me and would decide almost straight away. We kept up our relationship for the rest of their lives, and I added to the house over the years, converting and enlarging the lodge while they improved the gardens.

They could only use Duntisbourne at weekends. When they moved from Chelsea Square they bought a little house in St Anselm's Place, a mews at the back of Brook Street, which was very handy, and they lived there for the rest of their lives. It was a gem of a house, partly because it had an unusually large garden with some huge trees. We turned the garage into a dining room, with French doors to the garden. We painted the dining room red, which was perhaps rather bold, but the rest of the house was sort of country cottage style, with plenty of colour. It would probably today be regarded as rather cluttered. There was an elegant curved staircase and a tiny hall, and we added some architectural details to play up the spaces and chose a Mauny wallpaper for the hall and stairs. Upstairs there were two small bedroom suites, and for their bedroom we used a blue and white theme with quite a strong blue 'Middlehurst' chintz from Warner's. There was a lot of painted and lacquer furniture throughout the house, and I remember they bought a very pretty set of Regency hanging shelves from us for which my father made the pair. It was always a source of pleasure to them that my father had made it. Lady Richardson died first and Sir Gordon lived on in the house until his own death in 2010.

Quite often when you work for a family you are passed on to the children too, and this happened with the Richardsons. Their daughter Sarah, whom I had known since she was a schoolgirl, married Sir John Riddell in

OPPOSITE FAR LEFT The drawing room at Duntisbourne, with a charming French chimneypiece we found in London.
OPPOSITE LEFT The library-sitting room.

ABOVE LEFT The master bedroom, with faux panelling.
ABOVE RIGHT The Richardsons (right) with Lord and Lady Franks.

1969.[2] Sir John worked in banking, like his father-in-law, but in 1985 became Private Secretary to the Prince and Princess of Wales. They first approached me to help them with their nice house in Camden Square, but as funds were limited we did only a small amount of work there. Shortly after that he was appointed Private Secretary to the Prince, and with the job came a grace and favour house in Kensington Palace. It was called Wren House but it was really a cottage, with small rooms and a garden.

I've no idea when it had last been occupied, but it was rather run-down and needed everything doing, including rewiring and plumbing, a new kitchen and a new bathroom, as well as painting and furnishing throughout. They had some furniture of their own, but needed new covers and curtains. We were working with the ministry, so every single item had to be approved, which all seemed to take for ever because you had to go through several layers of people before arriving at the person who could pass it. It was very frustrating and the whole job took far longer than it need have done. It wasn't an exceptional piece of work, just pretty cottagey interiors and fresh colours.

I worked again at Kensington Palace when Michael Peat became Treasurer to the Queen in 1996.[3] His father, Sir Gerrard Peat, had previously been auditor of the Queen's Privy Purse. Along with the job came a grace and favour apartment within the palace. This had previously belonged to the old Princess Royal, and hadn't been lived in for many years. Kensington Palace is a very chopped up building and in this case the chopping made for a rather awkward flat. The kitchen was on the floor below the

dining room, and there were attic bedrooms. It did have a magnificent reception room and an excellent dining room, which they needed for entertaining, so perhaps the attic bedrooms for the boys and the rather ropey kitchen were a small price to pay.

As with Wren House, the ministry was responsible for the fabric of the building and the occupants were supposed to provide the furnishings. But as the Peats didn't have many suitable pieces of furniture – the furniture from their Clapham house wasn't really suitable for these large rooms with their high lofty ceilings and plasterwork – we were allowed to visit the storage rooms

The drawing room of the Peats' Knightsbridge house. Lady Peat loved bright, strong colours.

at Windsor Castle, where they kept leftover and spare furniture from various royal palaces. This wasn't long after the disastrous fire at Windsor and the rooms were full of pieces that had been salvaged. It was very sad to see wonderful pieces of fine furniture and chandeliers badly damaged, although fortunately in time they were magnificently restored. We did find some pieces that would be suitable for the Peats to use in their home. There were lots of chairs and tables, but everything needed repair. There was a large commode which I thought would look wonderful on their landing, but it needed hundreds of pounds spending on it because the metalwork was

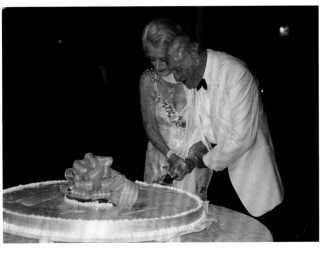

Sir Gerrard and Lady Peat at their golden wedding party in Tuscany.

The breakfast room of the Peats' Knightsbridge house.

lifting and the veneers were coming off. In fact, we had to limit what pieces we chose simply because of the costs of restoration. We did take a side table, the commode, and a few lamps, all of which needed repairing and new shades. We had to buy a lot of chairs and sofas, and of course all the curtains were new. They had a small library and with the large drawing room and dining room it worked very well for them. I can understand why Diana, Princess of Wales once remarked it was 'a grander house' than hers!

Although I only worked once for Michael Peat I did a lot of work for his parents – five houses in all.[4] The relationship was long, over many, many years – similar to my relationship with the Richardsons in that I became part of their lives, and as they moved through life and had different requirements – from a large house in Kent when the family were growing up, to a smaller house in Walton Place, behind Harrods, when the children had left home – I always seemed to be there. I had a lovely time with Lady Peat because she enjoyed doing the decorations. Sir Gerrard was not really interested, so she and I did all the work together with his final approval.

I also worked for several members of the Kleinwort family.[5] Over the years John had worked at Sezincote for the Kleinworts, doing the great salon on the first floor, which was one of his most magnificent rooms. After John died I became involved with the decoration of the small dining room underneath the salon, which was an apse-ended room. It was here that George Oakes painted probably his finest murals in the Indian vernacular, very

Sezincote from the garden. It is probably
the most exotic house in England.

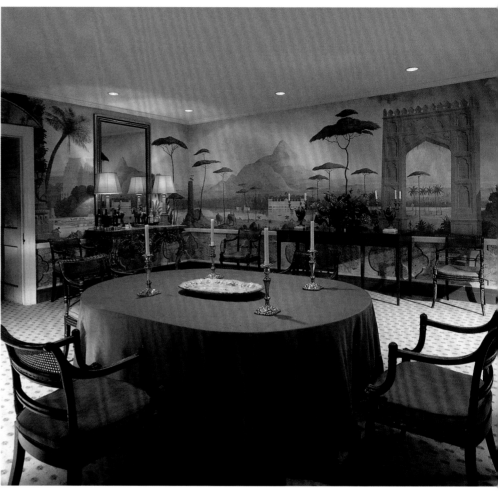

The dining room at Sezincote, with George's wonderful 'Indian' mural.

much in the style of Thomas and William Daniell. As
it was a Mughal-inspired house, designed by Samuel
Cockerell, who also designed Daylesford for Warren
Hastings, the theme was eminently suitable.

I also did the whole of their house in Cheyne Walk,
Chelsea, which was a lovely eighteenth-century house
on the river with a garden behind. I do remember
when things were a bit tough economically in England
– something that has happened many times during
my lifetime – Lady Kleinwort said, 'We're trying to
economize, imagine that! I don't know what I'm going to
do, but I think I'll stop the newspaper. I'll read the cook's
Daily Mail when she's finished with it. That will save a bit.'
I love the economies of the rich.

When Lady Kleinwort was widowed she moved out of
Sezincote to the dower house, Eyford House, a beautiful

house near Stow-in-the-Wold. It was a pastiche of an
eighteenth-century house, designed by the architect Sir Guy
Dawber in 1911. This was a fun job because she had lots of
pretty things, some brought from her London home, and
she liked colour so it was quite a colourful house. It was
also an eminently liveable house. I was very pleased when
years later *Country Life* readers voted it the English house
they would most like to live in. Lady Kleinwort was also a
great gardener and she made a lovely garden to complement
the house. Her daughter Charlotte (who had worked at
Colefax & Fowler) inherited it from her mother and lived
there happily for many years, subsequently passing it on
to her own daughter. Previously I had sort of emulated
John by assisting entirely by post with the decoration of
Charlotte's house in Melbourne, Australia. It was done
with the help of photographs, and although I saw final

photographs of it when finished I never went there to see it in person, as it were.

Being passed between different generations of a family is one thing, but being employed by three sisters was another! I had the pleasure of decorating for three beautiful young women who were the daughters of Lady Mancroft.[6] The three of them had very different lives. Victoria married Prince Friedrich, the son of the Prinz von Preussen, a grandson of the Kaiser. For her I did a house in the west country. I already knew Victoria's half-sister, Venetia Barker, because she had married Captain Fred Barker, for whom John had decorated Lushill in Wiltshire. I suppose she introduced me to Victoria, who subsequently introduced me to the third sister, Miranda, who was married to Peter Sellers.

In 1972 Miranda asked if I would go down to Anstey, in Wiltshire, where she'd seen a little house she wanted to buy. She invited Peter Sellers to come with us (he was, after

BELOW Eyford House. Although it looks like an eighteenth-century house, it was actually built in 1911.
RIGHT, TOP TO BOTTOM The drawing room; the dining room; the master bedroom.

all, going to pay for it), and he did indeed come, but he seemed totally uninterested. His main obsession seemed to be anything new that had to do with recording. It was the beginning of the era when everybody went around with Walkmans, which were then very clumsy things with great big headphones. He turned up plugged in to his Walkman and during the journey down to Wiltshire he never said a word.

I had seen his films and enjoyed them, but in person, especially wearing these great big headphones, he seemed extremely unfunny. When we were discussing with the builder what turned out to be a fairly unimportant but pretty country house, I did my usual decorating spiel of trying to rationalize the house for them, but it was rather difficult with this very morose gentleman walking around. Miranda was enthusiastic and we chatted away about what could be done. When we got on the train to come back I expected another boring journey, but in fact Peter had been watching the builder and all of us during this period. He was a fantastic mimic, and we were treated to a one-man show with him mimicking the builder's Wiltshire accent and mannerisms, and those of everyone else who had been there. He'd taken it all in. Sadly, his acting ability seemed to be the only thing that was attractive about him.

I did further work for Miranda when, again with Peter's reluctant approval, she purchased a lease on a stable block at Carton House in Maynooth outside Dublin. The stable needed a lot of work to make it liveable as a home. Again he took no interest in the project at all; it was purely for her. I presume, in fact, that by this point the marriage was already breaking up – they divorced a year later. Miranda was very keen on dogs, particularly small Pekingese, and on parrots, and when we eventually finished the decoration they all moved in; the dogs and the parrots took over and between them they pretty well destroyed it almost immediately.

I met Miranda again later, when she was married to Sir Nicholas Nuttall. They lived at Lowesby Hall in Leicestershire, where we did some work, and they also had a flat at Eaton Place in Belgravia. Lowesby had been slightly remodelled by Edwin Lutyens for the Brassey family, who were tenants in the early years of the twentieth century. Sadly, a fire in 1980 destroyed a beautiful baroque ceiling by Antonio Verrio, which had been superbly restored twenty years before, and some of the Lutyens rooms. By then Sir Nicholas had sold the house and retired to a villa at Lyford Cay in the Bahamas.

Sadly, Fred and Venetia Barker's marriage also broke up. Venetia later married Lord Wimborne. They bought a house in the centre of Paris – the 16th arrondissement – which was very exciting for me because it was a chance to work in France, and on a lovely nineteenth-century Passy house with a garden and tall, elegant architectural rooms with beautiful parquet floors. In the dining room I was able to use something I much admired, which dated back to the days of the East India Company. The French had copied the Indian Tree of Life on to great cotton toile panels with a stylized tree and birds, in a limited palette of reds, blacks and greens. These panels were stretched from the skirting to the cornice, and together they formed a room of toile, almost like a painted room, with a Tree of Life design. It might not find favour today, as tastes have changed, but Venetia and I liked it and it gave a lovely ambience. Opening on to the garden, with a parquet floor, mirrors on the wall and lit by candlelight, it made a very good dining room. Dining rooms are difficult because they're not used except for eating and then usually at night, and so most of the time they're rather dead. This room was pretty to walk through, and if you looked through from the salon it was a fun treatment.

This was the only house I ever did in Paris, but in 1975 Tom Parr decided we should open a retail shop there. It was a daring move, not least because French fabrics are renowned – and we used a lot of them in our work – but we were trying to take English chintzes to the French. The French are not particularly receptive to English style, but Tom reckoned it was worth a chance because we were doing well in England with our fabrics. He eventually found an adorable shop on the corner of the place de Furstenberg. This beautiful little French square, where Delacroix had his studio, had a small garden at its centre. I remember one lunchtime seeing the local circus come and sit in the square. They were all in their make-up and clown costumes, ready for the afternoon performance in *Pierrot*. It could have been a painting by Renoir.

The shop had a pretty facade, which we painted black, with the little shop all on one floor. There was a flat above and I begged Tom to lease that at the same time so we could go over and stay, but that wasn't financially possible. We were able to make a balcony area at the back of the shop to give a little extra space and this was decorated with racks of toiles. The shop was purely to sell fabrics, and we employed a very chic French woman to run it. I remember the opening. The British ambassador and his wife graciously attended, and I invited the 'baby' I had looked after when I first went to Paris in 1947 (who was rather surprised by

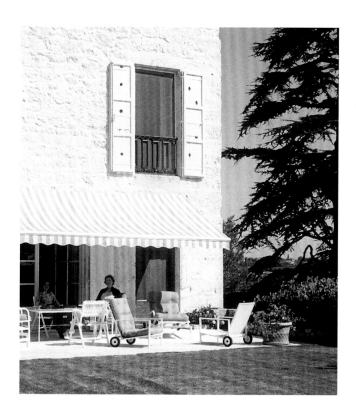

The Château de St Pierre in the Lot-et-Garonne, the French home of Vincent and Jackie Paravicini.

the invitation since she hardly remembered me as I left when she was only two). I rather splashed out and had a dress made for the occasion by my dressmaker, Georgette, copied from one I had seen worn by Queen Soraya of Iran – leopard-printed silk with knife-pleated frills!

It was at around this time that I worked for Vincent and Jackie Paravicini.[7] They were old and rather favoured clients of John's. He loved them dearly and had done very nice work for them at Nutley Manor in Hampshire, a lovely eighteenth-century house where they had brought up their family. By the time I inherited them, after John's retirement, they had downsized and were living in a flat in Burton Court, overlooking the Royal Hospital in Chelsea. At the same time they decided to buy a house in France: the Château de St Pierre in the Lot-et-Garonne area of France.

I flew over to Toulouse to be met by a car which they thoughtfully sent. The French chauffeur (he was actually just the handyman) was the most appalling driver I've ever experienced, either driving far too close to the next car, or recklessly overtaking and then almost stopping in front of the car he had just passed. I was white and shaky by the time I arrived at the house and had to be revived with a gin and tonic. (Within months the poor man had killed himself on the same road.)

FROM LEFT TO RIGHT The red sitting room; another sitting room, the windows dressed in 'Berkeley Sprig' fabric; the through hall.

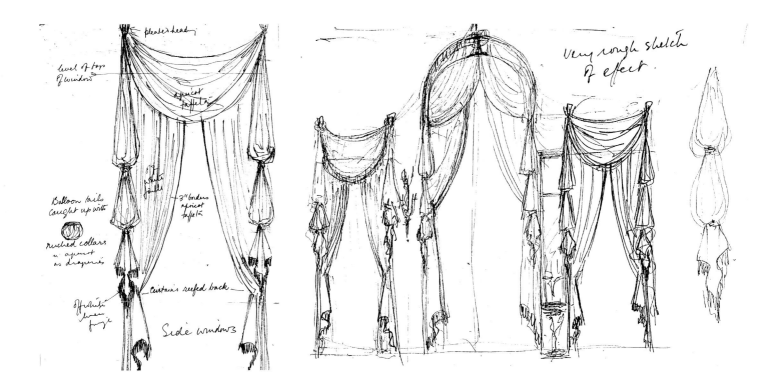

It was an interesting project because they had some pretty things brought over from their past life, and they understood the principles of English country house style. The château as we designed it was a subtle melange of French and English, which was enjoyable for me, as I particularly love French provincial furniture (not the grand, elaborate, inlaid furniture of the Versailles school). This Anglo-French style, with a lot of pattern, old carpets and a mixture of European furniture and porcelains worked very well.

Over the years, both with John and on my own, I worked on many grand stately homes, but as the years passed that sort of work gradually declined and I suppose Sandbeck in South Yorkshire was the last grand country house that I was asked to help with. After the war it became so difficult to run a house like Sandbeck, because of changes in taxation and death duties, which destroyed a family's wealth – once you had to sell bits of the estate you fatally undermined the whole economics upon which the house rested. It is part of the change I have seen over my lifetime in the social structure of England.

The Earl and Countess of Scarborough asked me to come and help with the ballroom.[8] The house was divided in half by this huge empty ballroom on the first floor, which one had to walk through to get to rooms on either side of the house. Enterprisingly, they had decided to turn the room into a huge drawing room. It was very long front to back, going

ABOVE My drawings for the curtains in the ballroom turned drawing room at Sandbeck Park.
RIGHT The finished drawing room.

right through the house, with a beautiful eighteenth-century ceiling and Venetian windows at either end. I immediately thought of Bellamy's of York, with whom John and I had worked: I knew they had the necessary skills to repair and paint the wonderful ceiling. This meant a great deal of scaffolding and a great deal of repair, and was a costly project. There wasn't a lot of money left over to buy furnishings, but Lord Scarborough mentioned a large carpet rolled up in the cellar. We had it dragged up to the ballroom and unrolled, and after a good cleaning it actually furnished the main part of the room. From this carpet I then drew the colour palette. The Venetian windows were the biggest problem because they are the most difficult windows to curtain, but I devised a way to do it. I used an oyster-coloured silk, which looked beautiful with the apricot walls, but was very impractical as the sun cracks the filaments of the silk, which then rots, so the curtains had to be replaced twenty years later. However, it was a major transformation for the house and brought it back to life. I suppose that is what all my work has been about: bringing life to houses and making them comfortable and beautiful so people could live in them with pleasure.

17
AT HOME

In 1944 our house in Banstead was requisitioned for victims of the Blitz, and we moved to a modern detached leasehold house outside Croydon. When we reclaimed the Banstead house after the war we found it had been left in a ghastly state. For many months my father and I cycled to Banstead each weekend to repair and redecorate it before moving back. By law, if a house had been requisitioned you had to live in it for a year in order to reclaim it. Having lived in it for the necessary year, we sold it and returned to the Croydon house.

Father retired from the Civil Service in 1957, when he was sixty. After a three-week holiday in Italy he then needed something to keep him occupied. My parents had always longed to have a country house. We saw an advertisement for a cottage called Gun Green Farm near Hawkhurst in Kent, which was being sold at auction. We went to view it and discovered it was absolutely derelict. It was a Tudor cottage with earth floors that were soaking wet. The people who lived in it previously had looked after blind people in disused railway carriages in the garden. We were told these people were happier than if they had been in a blind home, so maybe it wasn't as bad as we imagined. My mother was opposed to the idea, feeling it wasn't viable, but my Father made some excuse on the day of the auction and bid for it and got it. He came home and announced, 'I've bought it for £1,300 and I'm going to go and camp in it.'

At the time I lived in a small rented flat in London during the week and went home at weekends. Once my father had bought Gun Green Farm I would come back from London on Friday night and we would all go down to work on it. We did this for about a year. We had a caravan in the garden to make our stay a bit more comfortable. We borrowed £3,500 to build on a wing, which would enlarge the kitchen and allow

My flat in Redcliffe Gardens. The windows were very large, so I was lucky to be able to buy some 'Blue Fuchsia' chintz cheaply from the firm. John left me the circular table.

for a bedroom and bathroom above for me. In those days there was no need for planning permission and you could do whatever you liked. Builders then were in a parlous state as there was no work about, so basically the builder did the job at cost to keep the men on. My father laid wooden floors, made the staircase and put in twenty-six windows which he bought from a junkyard in Hove. A Tudor house had been demolished near the town and by a miracle the windows fitted our house. It was a huge job for a man of sixty, but he did it and a little later we went to live there. I would come down to Tonbridge station on Fridays, change to the branch line, which still had a steam engine, and be met off the train by my father. By the time of the move the house was still

OPPOSITE 'Blue Fuchsia', an early nineteenth-century English design.

The Old Vicarage in spring 2016. CLOCKWISE FROM TOP The main façade;
looking through from the hall into the main sitting room; the magnolias just in bloom.

rather primitive and it remained a bit like camping, with us cooking sausages on top of one of those black, round primus stoves for our first meal in the house.

Sadly, two years later a financial crisis arose and all the banks foreclosed, so any loans had to be paid off in six months. We had no means for this as my father was on a low pension, while I earned virtually nothing. The only way was to sell the cottage and miraculously some Americans came to see it and loved it. They wanted a holiday cottage and as it was so typically English they adored it, but they wanted it fully furnished so they could just walk in. We agreed to furnish it down to the spoons, linen and all for £7,500, which would be enough to pay off the loan with a bit left over to buy another house. We took some of our furniture with us, but anything we didn't particularly like was left behind. This included some of the things I'd grown up with, for which I was rather grateful since I had got used to Colefax by then. We went around junk shops buying things for two pounds, or even just ten shillings; luckily my father was good at repairing things.

Finding a house with the remaining limited amount of money was really hard, partly because we wanted an old house. We started driving around, but it was rather an expensive area. We then went a little bit farther out in Kent, which is how we found the Old Vicarage at Egerton. My mother wasn't so keen on this part of Kent as it is very flat agricultural land – the Weald of Kent. We went up the hill opposite, and in those days I could see across (you can't now because the trees have grown) to a little square facade with a sign saying 'For Sale'. It was a pretty facade and I thought it was really nice, so we walked up the garden path and knocked at the front door. It was going for £4,500, but as we didn't have £4,500 it was negotiated down to £4,100. It had water and electricity, and had been divided into two flats. We bought it and moved in upstairs. My father worked on it for five years, while we lived upstairs. To eke out his small pension I got him the job of making the column lamps, bamboo tables and side tables that we sold at Colefax. They were John's designs and Father would be sent a model to copy. He made them for years, even roping in a friend who had a lathe so he could go in for mass production – twelve column lamps or twelve bamboo tables. Things were usually bought by the dozen and painted up in the studio. It was a way of making a bit of money, but they were only a few pounds each.

We worked on the house as a sort of trio, with me, needless to say, bringing home ideas for decoration. They had to be things that didn't cost much, such as a wallpaper, or *trompe l'œil* panelling we could do ourselves. It was a sort of cottage industry. Father also made all the curtains in the house, some chairs and a beautiful mahogany wine table. All I seemed to do was help with the painting and the supply of things. A blue and white fabric George designed, which is the curtaining in the large sitting room, was from a collection that George and I jointly owned. It was printed on very good quality cotton, but eventually we were forced to wind up the business, with each of us making about £180, which paid for the carpet in my London flat! I did buy a chimneypiece from a house being demolished in the same terrace as John Fowler's house on the King's Road. All the architectural bits and pieces went to the G.L.C. dump in the East End, where I went with Jonathan Vickers to choose. It was just the right period and the right size. Everything in those days was always hand to mouth and such a contrast from working as I did for the rich. But we managed to keep up a style of living that was comfortable and hopefully looked pretty, though it was all done on nothing.

By 1966 we were able to come downstairs and enjoy the whole house. My father loved the village and became part of village life, but my mother was shy rather than gregarious, and never quite integrated into the village as my father did. They had a few friends locally, but I would bring home her amusement, all the news, which was what she liked. They made the garden and spent the rest of their lives there. My father died in December 1986, five years before my mother, who died in September 1991. They were five difficult years because mother was frail, and I was still working. I began to work only four days a week and when I wasn't abroad I would stay with my mother and commute to London daily. Trips had to be as short as possible and I had someone sleeping at the house when I was away. My mother coped amazingly well and was always interested in all I did, but wished that I would retire. However, that wasn't possible for many reasons, not least because my life as a decorator just seemed to be taking off.

After she died I considered selling the house and buying something in the Cotswolds or wherever. However, I stayed. In many ways it was sentimentality. My father had done most of the work on the house; he had laid the floors and put in the windows; and ultimately I couldn't bear to leave it. I began to integrate into the village and then George and Judith Oakes moved to a nearby village and not long after Donald Church also arrived, so I had the company of old friends and other sympathetic people.[1]

LEFT The small sitting room at the Old Vicarage. BELOW The main sitting room, with the *trompe l'œil* panelling my parents and I painted fifty years ago. The chimneypiece came from a demolished house in the King's Road, Chelsea.

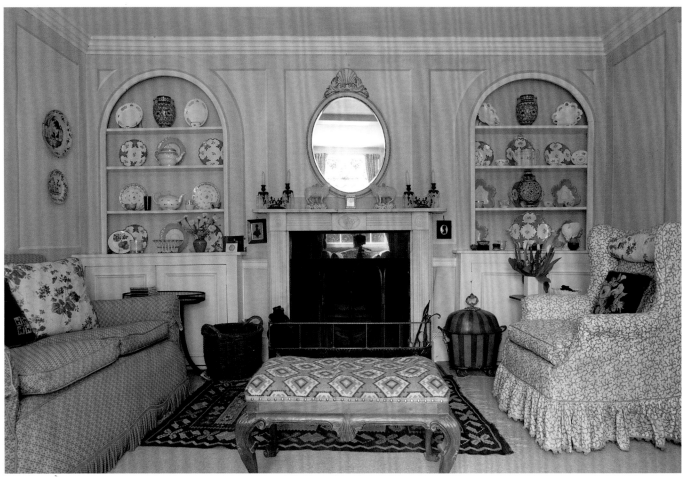

RIGHT The guest bedroom, done in raspberry *toile de Jouy*.

BELOW The dining room. My father made the table from wood that came from a bombed Tudor house in Norwich.

LEFT The Château de Bussy-Rabutin. It was the memory of this château that drew me to Burgundy.

OPPOSITE Daisy, my border terrier, in the grounds of the Château de Bussy-Rabutin. She was never really at home in France.

After I retired from Colefax & Fowler in 1999 I realized three of my dreams. First, I found a little border terrier. Daisy was born in October 1999 and came to me at Christmas. Also, I had never owned my own car as I'd always had company cars during my years with Colefax. It was a great excitement when, well into my seventies, I bought my first car, a Volkswagen Golf!

The third plan was the most ambitious. I decided to sell my London flat and use the money to buy a house in France. Frankly, it was a mad idea: I was seventy-six. France has been a passion in my life ever since I went to work in Paris just after the war. It has a lifestyle and a way of living that I like. I also like the architecture, the countryside and the towns and villages of France, which are enormously varied. And I love the sense of space you get in France. I love Italy too, but distance made that an even less practical proposition. I decided on somewhere in the middle of France, not more than a day's drive from my home in Kent. A day's drive will take you to the Loire or to Burgundy. I went first to the Loire, and I did find a house that belonged to people about ten years younger than me. They said they were going to live in the town as they found the upkeep of the house and garden too much. It was on a hillside with terraces, but as the house really was far too big for me I decided against it.

I then turned to Burgundy, of which I had outstandingly happy memories. In the 1960s, I had two very good friends,

David Vicary and Colin Anson, and we decided to do a tour of some of the Italian gardens mentioned in Georgina Masson's books (see page 160). On the way through France David (or maybe Colin) said, 'We must go and see Château de Bussy-Rabutin in Burgundy.' The Comte de Bussy-Rabutin had made the château over to the state before the war, and by that time it was in the dilapidated state we all appreciated. The parterres laid out in front particularly stand out in my memory. A mixture of old roses and vegetables all within perimeters of very low espalier apple trees, they had a magical quality. That valley with the château and the beautiful drive through Burgundy remained with me. I came again to Burgundy with my parents on a winter break. We sauntered through France, stopping to see the wonderful Basilica of St Mary Magdalene in Vézelay, which we all adored, and staying near Saint-Sauveur-en-Puisaye, the village where Colette had been brought up. This brought back memories of reading Colette, as well as all the smells, sights and sounds of Burgundy.

Now, in 2002, I discovered in Burgundy a town called Semur-en-Auxois, which I found magical because of its medieval qualities. The town is walled and turreted, surrounded by a river and largely unspoiled, with lots of medieval houses, as well as houses of the seventeenth, eighteenth and nineteenth centuries. It was a bit run-down, not on the tourist map, and very much to my taste. I returned

for another week's holiday with two friends, Lynette and Hugh Maclennan, renting a cottage together not far from Semur. We started to search, giving ourselves a week to find a house. I didn't want to spend years looking and we went to the usual sources.

The estate agents were extremely offhand, and all the places they sent me to were totally unsuitable. Eventually someone recommended I go to a *notaire* to see if any of his clients had a house to sell. I went to see a *notaire* in Venarey-les-Laumes. The staircase was narrow and made narrower still by piles of files on every step. We were greeted by the *notaire* himself, who was sitting at a desk in a little room at the top and was rather agitated to find I had turned up unannounced. He said, 'You should have made an appointment,' but I explained I had merely been passing. Did he have any houses on his books? He was rather grumpy, but told his assistant to show me the so-and-so house tomorrow. It turned out to be the most unsuitable place: an enormous farmhouse, very dilapidated but with a certain grandeur. Huge barns, and more than 10 acres of land: not ideal for a single lady aged seventy-six. We mused about how I could develop it and make it into a home, but in reality it was totally absurd. I had spent the whole week looking at unsuitable houses, and by Thursday afternoon was in near despair, as we were leaving on the Saturday.

We went to visit another house in a pretty village and, stopped at the gate of a charming mini-château with children playing in the garden. I asked them if their house was for sale. 'Oh, we'll have to ask Maman.' They called out Maman, who said, rather indignantly, 'Certainly not! It's not for sale. It's a family house.' Apologizing profusely I said we had been told the house at the end of the village was for sale – 'But it's the house at the other end of the village that's for sale.'

Disappointment lay in wait, for at the other end of the village we found a converted barn. It faced north, and had an ugly central fireplace which served two rooms. The garden was rented from the farmer. It transpired that another English couple had looked at the house and had similar reservations, but had found something that suited them better in the next village. We drove along to the next village and Lynette spotted a man she was certain was English – I must go and ask him. 'Oh, I am that. I come from Yorkshire and we moved in yesterday. Come and have a look.' They had come there because their daughter had married a Frenchman. I was intrigued to know how he had found the house and he told me it was through Madame Robin, of whom I had never heard. He explained how to find her, which was not easy. When we arrived at her door it was half past six, but she was still at her desk. She asked me what sort of house I wanted and I explained it had to be an old house, in or near a village, and not in too bad a state of repair. I wanted three bedrooms, a little garden, a good view and of course it must have charm. 'Argh, well, of course, that's the hardest thing.' She had in front of her a huge tome with 150 houses, all with photographs. I started looking through, turning the pages, and she would remark, 'Oh, that wouldn't be suitable because it's near the motorway,' or 'That one's got 50 acres. This one has two barns, and this one is in too much disrepair, and this one's near a pig farm.' She put me off thoroughly as I passed through the book, but I suddenly stopped at a photograph – a small white *presbytère*. 'Oh, that's very difficult because the people who own it won't allow me to show it unless they're there.' She did telephone, but there was no reply. I begged her to ring them in the morning and left her the telephone number of a house near where we were staying. The following morning someone came down from the house and said, 'There's been a phone call from the agent and you can go and view the house.'

We had to go a considerable distance, over the hills, and finally arrived at the white gates of the house. I walked up some very steep rather wobbly steps, and the minute I walked into the salon I turned to Lynette and said I would buy it. She thought I'd lost my marbles: 'Don't be silly, you haven't seen it yet.' But it felt right. With its stone floor and high room with lovely beams, it had the French atmosphere I sought. It was a single-storey house with two bedrooms, a bathroom, a rather small kitchen and two reception rooms. It had electricity, and the vendors had lived there for ten years, so I thought it must be sound. It was one of the few houses I had seen that actually had charm. The owners were a delightful elderly French couple who encouraged me, sensing, I suppose, that I was the right person for them. They'd previously had a German couple looking, but he had lived in Normandy as a child and remembered the German occupation and the British liberation! They were rather amazed I was prepared to sign that very morning. I was going home the following day so I did exactly that. In the end I bought the house in about five minutes flat.

It was near my favoured town, Semur, but needed more bedrooms and an additional bathroom, so that I wouldn't be too restricted in the number of people I could have to stay at the same time. I couldn't quite see how to adapt the house, but there was a granary above, in the roof, which might provide additional space. Anyway, I thought I would work it all out later. I was thrilled, although my friends were very apprehensive at the speed of my decision. In many ways it was a daft idea. Seventy-six is not generally regarded as a time to start changing your lifestyle. The money from my flat was going to buy the house, and I would have a little put aside to increase my pension. (Of course, when it came to it I spent the lot on the house.)

I came over and stayed with the nice French owners while we negotiated the sale of various small items, and I got to know them and the area rather better. Eventually the time came to sign the final papers and pay the remainder of the money. On the actual day we all went down to the *notaire* in Semur. His offices were in a nineteenth-century building. The waiting room was small and dilapidated, with peeling paint, plaster dropping off the ceiling and magazines to read that were at least six years old! The *notaire*'s office was just as dilapidated. There was quite a crowd of us — myself, the owners of the house and their solicitor from Switzerland (a charming young man), and the agent who'd sold it to me, looking extremely chic in her French couture. Needless to say the notaire kept us waiting for over an hour — he wasn't even there when we arrived. He handed me a great sheaf of papers and said, 'You must understand every word before you sign it,' which I didn't but I signed anyway, and then he wanted

The town of Semur

to know 'Where is the money?' It had, of course, been sent to his bank the previous week. It was there, thank goodness. An old *presbytère* in Burgundy was mine.

It was 21 December 2002 and I finally retired that week, after fifty-three years in the world of decorating. This was to be my retirement project and I asked a young colleague who'd worked for me, Piers Northam, to come in January to help me decide what to do. It had snowed the night before, so it was difficult to get out of Egerton, but with some help from the garage and some grit we managed. It didn't augur well for the journey through France, which is some 360 miles, and by the time we got to the house it was minus 12°C. We came laden with food and bedding so we could stay in the house, and called at the local supermarket for extra food and a bottle of champagne, which we chilled in the snow!

The house was reasonably warm (the central heating was on low) and in the salon the fire was lit, flanked by two deckchairs, a little garden table covered with a tablecloth and a bunch of marigolds put there by the farmer's daughter,

Florence. For the next two days we tried to decide how to make it a viable house. The agent recommended a local architect who was used to old buildings, and I persuaded him to come and meet us. We climbed up into the granary, which was completely unused and in a terrible state, and we tried to think how we could incorporate a staircase. The beams in the granary were large and elaborate because the original building had a stone roof, which had now been replaced by pantiles. The space cried out to be bedrooms, but there was no obvious means to access it from downstairs.

When the architect came he said he needed time to think about the problem; but he was enthusiastic. The following morning he appeared with a plan, but no solution to the problem of the staircase. Eventually, he had a flash of inspiration. If a slice was cut from the chimney it would give extra room to get up into the granary. The staircase could then run up from where the kitchen was. My heart sank. This meant moving the kitchen to build the staircase, and involved putting in bathrooms at each end of the house where

My house in Burgundy. I added the dormer windows and restored the lime render.

ABOVE The kitchen.
LEFT The sitting room of my French home, which is very simply decorated.

the plumbing was difficult (in the end I had to put in separate plumbing in the furthest bathroom, with a separate septic tank). However, I realized this plan would give me two lovely en suite guest bedrooms, with my own bedroom and bathroom downstairs with a door into the garden.

The architect became the project manager and recommended the artisans, who were employed separately – a stonemason, a joiner, an electrician, a plumber and the carpentry shop. When I came over, I camped in the house at first and when that became impossible I rented a cottage not far away. Daisy and I arrived together in the middle of winter at this little cottage with its wood stove and large stock of wood. The whole thing took thirteen months, with six months prior planning. It was fun working with the Burgundian builders. They definitely worked to French timetables, with a break for a good lunch.

With George Oakes in my French home,
on my eightieth birthday.

sort of blue jeans colour, and emulated the colour as best I could for all the outside shutters. Luckily, there isn't much garden to keep, but there is a lovely weeping willow, which affords shade in the heat of summer, and when you look across from the house seems just right.

The building work cost more than I had hoped (it always does), so I had to decorate on a shoestring. I told the painters what I wanted and they understood immediately. When I said I wanted the walls lime-washed in earth colours, they brought a big vat of chalk lime and a *bidon* of water, as they called it, some big brushes and powder colour. We mixed the colours together, dried them on the wall with a hair dryer to test them and wiped them out if we didn't like them. I mixed very pale colours out of earth pigment, which they put on with a large brush leaving brush marks. The colour was broken and looked a bit like the dragged paintwork John had so often used. I had a *toile de Jouy* bedroom for myself because I had always wanted one and it's very French. The house is modestly

I was involved in every aspect of the project and made most of the decisions. The main salon windows were all renewed and the library windows reglazed, the pattern – rather square and with six parts – copied from the little house where the keeper of the hounds used to live at L'Abbaye de Fontenay. Five dormers were to be added, and I looked at dormers around the area all the time, thinking what to do because they're all shapes and sizes. Eventually, I ended up with the ones I have, which are limestone-faced and seem just right, as though they had always been there.

Lime rendering the whole of the outside was a big decision, because it meant removing the existing cement render, carrying every bit of it down the steps and down to the road to put into two enormous skips. The architect suggested leaving it as a stone house and just repointing it, but I really liked the idea of a lime-rendered house because it's somehow more cheerful, as well as characteristic of the area. I thought twice because it was so expensive to do, but in the end decided to go for it. It was given a rough first coat followed by a smooth coat, which was tinted. 'What colour?' they asked, and I decided to make it just a tone lighter than the church. They got the colour exactly right and to complement it I found an old door in Semur, which was a marvellous

The *bibliothèque*. My desk, originally John's at Brook Street, was a retirement present from David Green.

LEFT Another view of the sitting room. The French *bergère* chair was a gift from Dodo Peat, and the Friar's chair was originally John Fowler's.
BELOW The *bibliothèque*. I had the bookcases made for the room.

decorated and only the principal guest bedroom has any hint of my past, and that purely because Lady Kaye, that good client and friend, was emptying a flat and offered me the bed and its hangings.

I moved in in July 2004. George and Judith Oakes came with me to help. My furniture from the flat had been in store for over a year and I bought some extra things to add to the house. The furniture arrived at ten o'clock on the dot – together with a very elderly gentleman and a very young youth. They couldn't park their van near to the house, so parked under the tree in front of the church, and brought everything up the steep stone steps. They looked at them and grumbled a bit, as they had some heavy things to carry, but gradually the rooms filled up. George hung all the pictures, Judith helped me put in the books and sort out the kitchen, so by the evening the house was set up.

It is essentially a holiday house, although I hope it has never looked like one – I've always tried to make it seem

like a home. I couldn't afford to decorate in the style my clients had for their houses, but in any case I didn't want it to look like a decorated house: I wanted it to be an accumulation of things that I happen to have, arranged in a comfortable way. Strangely enough, the contents of my flat seemed to fit in very well. It's a mixture of English and continental furniture, some of which I inherited from John Fowler, to my everlasting gratitude. I did buy some French furniture, including various large armoires, *buffets* and the kitchen table, which is a *vendange* table, used for the celebratory meal after the grapes are harvested. The big salon, with its stone floor, high ceiling, beams and tall windows, looks very French and totally unlike my house in Kent, which is more English and Jane Austen.

Over the years since I bought my French house I've had a wonderful time entertaining friends, making new friends in the area, and exploring the countryside. Daisy never quite got my enthusiasm for France, always preferring her home in Kent, with its fields and woods – and only rather regretfully following me every time I packed a suitcase for France. But Daisy's successor, Benji, loves his French residence.

I had my eightieth birthday here and more than thirty friends came. We had three birthday party evenings – one in the house, one in a château and one in a hotel. Everybody remembers these with great pleasure. The people who came, from all over the world, were all my friends and had all heard of each other, but some of them had never met, as friends from different sides of one's life often don't. It has been a very nice part of my life. It was

rather late to start such a venture, but it has given me a huge amount of pleasure. What has been surprising is the number of new friends I have made in the area. They are mostly British, as it seems to be difficult to get to know French people in the same way. And that is perhaps my one regret: that I have not been able to bridge that divide and make more French friends.

OPPOSITE, CLOCKWISE FROM TOP LEFT
A corner of the landing which was created out of the old granary; the principal guest room, with a a beautiful majolica rabbit I bought years ago topping the chest of drawers; the bed corona, bedhead and bedspread in the main guest room were all gifts from Elizabeth Kaye.

BELOW LEFT My bedroom: I had always wanted a toile bedroom and this one works particularly well, as it opens on to the garden.
BELOW RIGHT Two beautiful glass vases turned into lamps decorate the early eighteenth-century commode in my bedroom.

18

TAKING STOCK

In 1999 I had been at Colefax & Fowler for an incredible fifty years, having started in November 1949. I was doing a short four-day week in the office with my team being managed by Pierre Serrurier. Work wasn't that prolific, so I thought my decorating years were drawing to a close and perhaps it was time I retired, but I really dreaded it. George Oakes, although younger than me, had retired in June 1993 and I missed him very much. Luckily, in his retirement Judith and he came to live a few miles from me in Kent and they remain some of my closest friends.

Pierre had worked with me for a long time, initially on my first Saudi Arabian job when I shared him with David Laws. In 1982 he returned to South Africa with his wife and children and set up his own decorating business (in a shop that coincidentally had once belonged to Stanley Falconer, a Colefax partner).[1] Later he moved to Italy, where he started another business with a Peruvian designer friend, printing collections of fabrics to sell to designers.

He came back to work with me in 1989 – I say 'work with' because although I was technically the boss it was more of a partnership. We would decide on design details and colours together. We each had our strengths. He was always better at the paperwork than me and he was very good at planning and design, but I was more in tune with the painting and designing of curtains, all the traditional things I'd learned from John.

Pierre left Colefax in July 1999 and in my state of semi-retirement he encouraged me to join him in a little design studio we could set up together. He would do the managing and I would just be a consultant. We met someone who had an upstairs room above her decorating business in Bourne Street. David Green kindly gave me the mahogany pillar desk I had sat at for the last thirty years and that had

Pierre and I at my party to celebrate 'fifty years in decorating' on 16 June 2000.

previously been John's desk, and with this, a borrowed table, a couple of chairs and an early model mobile phone, we were in business. We had a small staff, which consisted of Piers Northam, who had been working with me at Colefax, and lovely Joanna Harper, an ex-Colefax girl who later sadly died of cancer. Some of our clients found us, including my Kuwaitis and Fred Krehbiel, who kindly paid some fees in advance so we had capital to start. We were doing a lot of work in Kuwait, plus Maria Davila's Madrid flat, and we were working for Marcus and Kate Agius both in the country and in London.

Marcus Agius was then chairman of Lazard's, and he later became chairman of Barclays Bank.[2] They commissioned us to do a house on the Exbury estate for

OPPOSITE 'Lisbon', a design copied from a tablecloth I bought in Portugal and subsequently screen-printed by hand.

At last I have decided that the time has come to retire, which as you can imagine has proved to be a very difficult decision after all my happy years in the world of decoration.

I have bought a little house in Burgundy for Daisy and me in order to spend some holidays and entertain my friends in a beautiful place. This project will keep me busy and I intend also to start on my book.

Pierre will continue the business and for very special clients and friends, like yourselves, I will be there to lend a hand as a consultant.

As you know, working with you has always been the greatest fun and pleasure and our times together will always remain a very happy memory.

Announcing my retirement – at last!

them. Famous for its rhododendrons and azaleas, Exbury is owned by Mrs Agius's father, Edmund de Rothschild. The house the Agiuses were renovating was rather ramshackle. Pierre and I were asked to go down and help them with it. It was in a lovely position in the New Forest. Mrs Agius liked quite heavy colours and big bold patterns and we did a rich, colourful drawing room for her. The rest of the house was very much in the Colefax style, pretty bedrooms using colour and chintz, with good bathrooms. This led to us doing their house in Alexandra Square in London. It had a typical L-shaped drawing room to which a veranda had been added at some point. I got Lucinda Oakes to do a very pretty painted leafy mural, which transformed the space.[3] They used grander furniture, more upmarket carpets and wall covering fabrics than at Exbury, so it was a very dressy little house. Subsequently when I actually retired, leaving Pierre on his own, he did another house for them in Chelsea Square.

Maria Davila was an old client (see page 109). Her tastes were very different from mine – she seemed to love everything I loathed! She came originally from northern Spain, but she always kept an apartment in Madrid. It was in an Art Nouveau block, and she wanted an apartment in that sort of style. I'm sorry to say that Art Nouveau – along with with *cloisonné*, jade, and Fornasetti furniture – was something I've never understood or enjoyed. I suppose it must have been Maria's idea to give the main sitting room a leather floor. We actually had cowhide cut into large two-foot squares, so it resembled big carpet tiles, but in shiny black leather. It was polished, but not like patent leather, just like an ordinary black leather shoe. We found Art Nouveau fabrics and bought a few pieces of furniture of the period.

She also wanted a mosaic bathroom in the Art Nouveau style, and as we had been to the mosaic works in Vicenza and seen how it was made, we were able to produce a glamorous feminine bathroom. I remember she bought a fancy Swiss lavatory-bidet, which was a headache to the plumbers. Maria liked exotic and pretty things and she loved jewellery – she was a passionate collector. Naturally she wanted to keep some of her best jewellery at the apartment, but it had to be safe. We created a hidden jewel cabinet with drawers lined with beige suede leather, which had different compartments for necklaces, rings and brooches, etc. I had never done anything like it before, but these leather-lined drawers were just like a jeweller's shop.

Our business flourished for the first two years, but thereafter work generally began to peter out. In the decorating business you're always living on the edge: you either have too much work or too little, so it is hardly surprising that decorators are notoriously apt to go bankrupt. I was working three days a week, living in London and commuting for long weekends to the Old Vicarage in Kent. I found the travel rather wearing, so in 2002, when I was seventy-six, I decided it really was time to retire completely. Pierre (he was sixty-two) had a viable business, which he moved to near Chelsea Harbour, and continued for a few years. Unfortunately, his health began to deteriorate and in 2005 he closed the business and retired to South Africa.

Most of us do not think about old age until it arrives, and with it all the complications of bodily decline. Social and medical advances have given us, if we're lucky, many extra years. I have been one of the lucky ones, but even so I'm severely handicapped with arthritis and deafness and a handful of other boring complications. The great sadness of old age is losing so many of one's friends and family, but happy memories are a great support. And there is a bonus in

A doll's house made to raise money for the Leukaemia Research Fund at Great Ormond Street Hospital. Seven decorators each did a room in Ormond House, a thirty-inch-high recreation of an 1840 town house. My contribution on behalf of Colefax & Fowler was the night nursery.

that you do gain a certain confidence. The shyness of youth goes, and you don't give a damn. I have got through into late old age enjoying life to the full. I have a philosophy of life which sustains me. The core of this is a belief in tolerance. Most religions teach love, generosity and peace, and of course all these would be marvellous in a perfect world but, alas, the world is not perfect.

Nearly fifteen years have passed since I bought my *presbytère* in Burgundy and this has given me much happiness and hopefully provided some fun for my friends who have come to stay. My neighbour, Monique, was an elderly, rather simple lady, with a painful past. She had had her first illegitimate daughter at the age of sixteen; this child was adopted by her parents. She subsequently had two husbands who died early and fourteen more children. Two of the children died and all the rest were taken into care. She was now living, with an old man and two rescue dogs, in this tiny dilapidated cottage at my gate. The cottage had no running water and no sanitation, though there was one electrical cable. When the chimney became blocked she just knocked a hole in it, with the result that the beams are black with soot. In 21st-century Europe all this hardly seems possible, but she was private and independent. I used

to see her carrying buckets of water from a spring nearby. She would sit on a plastic chair outside her cottage reading, and when I asked what she was reading she said, 'always romantic novels'. They found hundreds of them in the cottage when she died. She lived her life in an imaginary world of the sort Barbara Cartland created in her novels.

As the cottage abuts my own barn, I could not bear to see it deteriorate further, unlived in, unloved and crumbling. It belonged to a nephew who had never been inside and after two years of negotiations (the French prefer acquiring property to selling it) I bought it when I was eighty-eight. George pithily said, 'You're mad, woman!' Well, probably I am, and I suppose it will prove to be my last project. What I started at the age of six when my father made me a doll's house, which I adored and spent hours decorating and imagining the life of the dolls inside, will probably end with this last doll's house. I have enlarged it to give two bedrooms and two bathrooms, and with its new terrace, simple garden and rural views I hope it will be let to people who enjoy the French countryside as much as I do.

Looking back, as I now so often do, I realize that I have lived through a period of enormous changes, in my own small world of decorating as well as in the wider

The cottage from the garden in October 2015, before the dormer windows were added.

Benji at his French residence.
The successor to Daisy, he loves France!

The French cottage with new windows, in May 2016.

world beyond. After the Second World War people thought they could go back to the life of the late 1930s, picking up the threads again. But that way of life never really returned. In the houses that I was working on with John Fowler in the 1950s and 1960s the main difference was the lack of servants – after the freedoms afforded by the war in the armed forces and in the factories no one wanted to go back to serving others. Those who could clung on as long as possible to their privileged lifestyle, with their butlers, ladies' maids, cooks and gardeners. But heavy taxes, particularly death duties, forced many to cut down, sell up or bequeath their houses to the National Trust. After many years of austerity, with rationing even more severe immediately after the war than it had been during the war years, the country went through troubled times with strikes and unrest in major industries. During these dark days we sat in our overcoats and gloves in unheated and unlit offices trying to decorate as usual. With financial recovery we began to work for a different kind of clientele, those making money in industry and particularly in the City. Once I began to work in America, virtually all my clients were the new rich. They did not have inherited heirlooms and this gave me an empty canvas on which to work. It was a different kind of work really, more creating a backdrop against which people could live their lives, rather than rearranging and reordering as had once been the case.

I have seen the end of so many crafts, although a few valiantly struggle on. Skills have sadly been lost and this I much regret. Craftsmen who are able to make beautiful, elaborate and rich things such as trimmings, handwoven silks and velvets and handmade curtains are now very hard to find. This decline in craftsmanship has changed taste, and so the minimalist look has emerged, with every room pared down to the bare essentials. I have to say that I feel the life has gone out of houses. The sort of decoration I did for over half a century was harking back to the past, with antique furniture, pictures and objects, but included the comforts of the modern age with good lighting, heating and comfortable seating. I feel sad to see so much of this go and I hope there will be rebirth when people will once again enjoy pattern, colour and texture – rooms with personal character.

It has been a wonderful time to live in, despite the troubles of the world. I fear I do rather cling to the past, enjoying the beauties of the countryside, old buildings and

The Colefax & Fowler girls! Barbara Berryman (Heale, seated), Elizabeth Winn (middle) and me (right) in the Yellow Room at 39 Brook Street, at the party to celebrate the publication of *John Fowler: Prince of Decorators* in October 2007.

the arts of times gone by. I cannot imagine the future, as things move so fast these days. Still, I enjoy the possibilities of fast travel, good medicine and modern conveniences and I am always interested in the present and what is happening in the world, so perhaps I have the best of things. I have been, and am, so very lucky. If I had been a teacher, I would have tried hard to open the eyes of children to all the wonders of nature and the creations of man in order to encourage their imaginations and pleasure in visual things. History is all around us if only we have the eyes to see it. That is what I was taught by those who knew what matters. I am enormously grateful to them.

NOTES

1. MY FAMILY

1 My great-grandfather Harry Taylor (born c.1841) lived at 17 Sherbourne Street, Islington. He married Rosina Evelyne Lansdell of 337 Durant Street, Bethnal Green, on 24 July 1866 at Islington Parish Church and is described as being a 'widower', but a search for his first marriage has not yielded any results. His father, Robert Taylor, was described in the records as a 'Gentleman'. Harry and Rosina Taylor are recorded in the 1871 Census as living at 1 Vernon Rise, Clerkenwell.

2 My grandfather Harold (Harry) Howard Taylor (1867–1932) married Ada H. Weaver (1862–1892). After her death he married Rosina Webb (1874–1952) in 1894.

3 According to my mother, my other great-grandmother on my father's side was a Busoni and aunt of the famous composer Ferruccio Busoni (1866–1924). One Ferdinando Busoni was believed to have had emigrated from Corsica to Italy in the late eighteenth century, settling in Spicchio, a village near Empoli in Tuscany, where he established himself as a barge owner. He had three sons and they became prosperous felt hat makers. Ferruccio's father, also Ferdinando, was born in Empoli in 1834; he became a noted clarinetist and died in 1909. His only son, Ferruccio, married Gerda Sjostrand, daughter of a Swedish sculptor, and they settled in Berlin. For most of the First World War he lived in Bologna and Geneva, before returning after the war to Berlin, where he died.

4 My father, Edgar John Howard Taylor, was born in 1897 and died in 1986. My uncle Howard William Taylor was born in 1898. My aunt Cecily Rose was born in 1896; she married William Orpwood in 1921.

5 My maternal grandfather was Walter Joseph Snelling (1868–1921). He owned a coal merchant's business, H. J. Snelling & Co. of Crystal Palace and Honor Oak, which had a coal yard parallel to the railway at Crystal Palace. He died in 1921 leaving an estate of £5,388. The family lived at 10 High View Road, Upper Norwood, and latterly at 74 Central-Hill, Upper Norwood.

6 They had a large family: Walter Carbery Snelling (born 1890); Eric Ernest Snelling (born 1891); Edith Clara Snelling (born 1893); Warren Worsley Snelling (born 1894); Edna Alice Snelling (born 1896); Violet Margaret Snelling (born 1898); Herbert Charles Snelling (born 1900).

3. THE WIDE, WIDE WORLD

1 Philip Jones (1933–2008) was educated at Malvern College, where he was taught art by Harry Fabian-Ware. He went to the Slade School of Fine Art 1953–6 and subsequently became a leading contemporary artist.

4. A NEW JOB: COLEFAX & FOWLER

1 John Beresford Fowler (1906–1977) was born at Limpsfield in Surrey, where his father was clerk at the racecourse. After leaving school he eventually went to work for Thornton Smith, a firm of commercial decorators in Soho, in the paint studio. He left to work for Peter Jones Ltd, the Sloane Square department store, where he set up a studio painting furniture, etc. He left in 1934, taking with him most of the staff, and established John Beresford Fowler Ltd, which was run out of his flat in the King's Road, Chelsea. In 1938 he went to work for Sybil Colefax in Bruton Street, a business that became Sybil Colefax and John Fowler Ltd. The company was bought by Nancy Lancaster in 1948. He retired in September 1971 and devoted the rest of his life to working for the National Trust. He died in October 1977.

2 Joyce Maud Morant (1903–2000), later Joyce Stone, was the daughter of Maud and Alfred Shears. She was brought up at Munstead, in Surrey, a near neighbour of Gertrude Jekyll. She married Basil L. Morant in 1938, but he died later the same year. She worked for John Fowler as one of his assistants, retiring in the late 1960s. She had long been friends with Frank Stone, who, after working as a decorator in South Africa and in Melbourne, Australia, set up in business in Salisbury. Joyce and he were married in 1966 and they went to live at Ferry Cottage on the Radnor estate near Salisbury.

Gladys Muriel Hourigan (née Davies, 1906–1995) worked for George Trollope and Sons, a firm of decorators in West Halkin Street (the company was dissolved in 1931), and was subsequently a secretary at Prudential Assurance before she went to work for John Fowler when he set up on his own in 1934. After she left Colefax & Fowler she worked for Hammonds, and then set up in business on her own, sharing premises with Micky Raymond, who was an antique dealer. She married Daniel P. Hourigan, a

wood carver (1905–1982), in 1936, and Cyril Wopshott (1909–1998) in 1985 (see chapter 8, note 8).

Barbara Heale (1912–2009) was born and brought up in Buckinghamshire and married Leonard (Chris) Berryman in 1957. She went to work for Colefax following a recommendation from Lady Gunston, with whom she had run children's homes during the war. She left Colefax and set up in business on her own with John Fowler's blessing. He sent the children of his clients to her: she was never out of work for forty years.

Gwendoline Gervis (1904–1990) was born in Hampstead and worked with John Fowler at Peter Jones Ltd. In 1963 she married Alexander Ivanovich Bilibin (see chapter 5, note 2).

3 Nancy Lancaster (1898–1994) was born at Mirador, near Charlottesville in Virginia. She was brought up in the USA and married, first, Henry Field (1895–1917), who died six months later. She was married again in 1920 to Ronald Tree (1897–1976), who was Field's cousin. They divorced in 1947. She finally married Colonel Claude 'Jubie' Lancaster in 1948. They were divorced in 1954. She bought Colefax & Fowler in 1948 at the suggestion of her former husband. She was renowned for having 'the finest taste of anyone in the world'.

4 Frederick Caryll Cavendish, 7th Baron Waterpark (1926–2013), was educated at Eton and served in the Grenadier Guards during the war. He settled in Kenya where he farmed in the Kinankop Plateau (Subukia), high in the Aberdares of central Kenya. During the emergency he was Assistant District Commandant of the Kenya Police Reserve. He returned to England in 1959 where he had a number of business interests, usually related to aviation. He married Daniele Guirche in Paris in 1951.

5 Michael Raymond (1931–) was born in Manchester where his parents were appearing in the music hall – his father was a singer and his mother a dancer. He went to work for Peter Jones Ltd as a trainee, hoping to become a decorator. He then worked for Mrs Hourigan at Trollope & Sons, but when she left to form her own business in 1953 he followed her and opened an antique shop in the King's Road (with her running a decorating business above). He helped her to decorate with Belgium Suite at Buckingham Palace in preparation for the state visit of the Shah of Iran in 1959. After Tom Parr bought into Colefax & Fowler, Michael went to work for them as an assistant to John Fowler. After decorating an office for Legal and General in 1962, he established 'Colefax & Fowler Associates' in Hanover Square to do commercial and modern work. He retired to Tangier in Morocco in the early 1970s.

6 Jean Monro (1916–2013) ran the decorating firm 'Mrs Monro', founded in 1926 by her mother in Montpelier Street opposite Harrods. Jean shared John Fowler's passion for the eighteenth century, although she did not have his depth of knowledge. She enjoyed a long career and many prestigious commissions, including the British Embassy in Washington, DC, the Foreign Secretary's residence in Carlton House Terrace and Château de Sarans near Paris for the Champagne house Moët & Chandon. She also did some work for the National Trust.

7 Nancy ('Wissy'), Countess of Ancaster (1909–1975) was the daughter of William Waldorf Astor, 2nd Viscount Astor, and Nancy, Viscountess Astor. She married Gilbert Heathcote-Drumond-Willoughby, 3rd Earl of Ancaster, in 1933. She was Nancy Lancaster's cousin and was devoted to John Fowler, who redecorated Grimsthorpe Castle for her.

8 Joan Rosaline Dennis (née Clarkson, 1904–1982) had been a Cochran girl and was known as the 'English Rose'. In 1928 she married James William Mollison but they were divorced, and in 1942 she married Jack Dennis, whom she also eventually divorced. She had a long-running affair with Sir Harold Wernher of Luton Hoo, who showered her with gifts and gave her an allowance. It was Wernher who paid for the alterations and decoration of Hay's Mews, which was probably John Fowler's finest town house.

9 Laurence Olivier (1907–1989) and Vivien Leigh (1913–1967) were probably the most celebrated theatrical couple of the 1940s and 1950s. Olivier had seen Leigh in The Mask of Virtue and they began an affair while starring in Fire over England (1937). Olivier was then married to Jill Esmond, whom he divorced in 1940, and promptly married Leigh. The marriage was stormy, not helped by Leigh's poor health (she contracted tuberculosis during the war and suffered from bouts of depression), and they divorced in 1960, with Olivier marrying Joan Plowright soon after.

10 Nancy Graves (1899–1977) was the only daughter of the artists Sir William Nicholson and Mabel Pryde and the sister of sculptor Ben Nicholson and architect Christopher Nicholson. She married the poet Robert Graves in 1918, but eventually the marriage broke down and they were divorced in 1949. After the war she ran a textile business in Motcomb Street doing block printing on her kitchen table. She produced many of the early fabrics sold by Colefax ,such as 'dot and cross' chintz.

11 Keith Irving (1928–2011) was born at Nairn near Inverness, where his father worked in insurance. When he was eleven his father was appointed chairman of his company and the family moved to Richmond-upon-Thames. He went to Epsom College, where one of his friends was Stephen Long (see chapter 14, note 4), and went on to study at Kingston Art School and the Royal College of Art. He started work at Colefax & Fowler in 1955 and stayed at Colefax for four years before leaving to work for 'Sister' Parish in New York. Unfortunately, 'Sister' had completely forgotten she had offered him a job. They detested one another ever after. With Robin Roberts he established Clarence House, a textile company, while in 1967 he set up Irving & Fleming in partnership with Thomas Fleming. Noted for his acidic wit, when once asked what he associated with the term 'good taste', he replied, 'approach of a depressing fog'.

12 Charles Duncombe, 3rd Earl of Feversham (1906–1963), succeeded his father when he was nine. He followed a career in politics, serving under Ramsay Macdonald, Stanley Baldwin and Neville Chamberlain in various minor offices. He served in the 13th/18th Royal Hussars during the war and was awarded a DSO. He married Lady Anne Dorothy Wood, daughter of the 1st Earl of Halifax, in 1936.

13 Dorothy ('Dolly') Mathilde de Rothschild (née Pinto, 1895–1988) was born in London and married James de Rothschild (of the Paris branch of the family) in 1913 when she was seventeen and he was thirty-five. In 1922 he inherited Waddesdon Manor in Buckinghamshire, which he in turn bequeathed to the National Trust on his death in 1957. She moved to Eythrope, which she developed and subsequently left to her husband's great-nephew Jacob Rothschild, 4th Baron Rothschild. On her death in 1988 she left £94,117,964, then the largest probated estate in England and Wales.

14 Lieutenant Colonel Weetman John Churchill Pearson, 3rd Viscount Cowdray (1910–1995), was educated at Eton and served in the Second World War, losing his left arm at Dunkirk. He became chairman of S. Pearson & Son in 1954 and was president of Pearson PLC until his death. He was distantly related to Winston Churchill – his mother's grandfather was the 6th Duke of Marlborough.

5. 'JEKYLL & HYDE': JOHN FOWLER

1 Elizabeth Winn (1925–) is the daughter of Major Hon. Reginald Winn (1899–1985), younger son of the 2nd Baron St Oswald of Nostell Priory in Yorkshire, who in 1924 married Alice Perkins, Nancy Lancaster's sister. Elizabeth was the receptionist at Colefax from 1947 before leaving in 1953. She set up her own business in 1954.

2 Alexander Bilibin (1903–1973) was probably the son of Ivan Yakovlevich Bilibin (1876–1942), a prominent artist in Tsarist Russia. Ivan Bilibin is remembered for his monograph Folk Arts of the Russian North (1904), and for illustrating Alexander Pushkin's Fairytale of the Tsar Saltan (1905). Unlike his father, Alexander was an indifferent painter, as can be seen from paintings that occasionally come up for auction. Little is known of his life, save that he is thought to have been brought up by his Irish mother (Mary) in England, with his brother, Ivan Ivanovich (1908–1993), who worked for the BBC Russian monitoring service.

3 Thomas Simon Parr (1930–2011) was born in London. His father was seriously wounded in the First World War and died when Parr was a child. His mother, Vera, subsequently married Sir Antony Burney (1899–1988), who became managing director of the department store group Debenhams.

4 Michael Tree (1921–1999) was the elder son of Ronald and Nancy Tree. In 1949 he married Lady Anne Cavendish, daughter of the 10th Duke of Devonshire. He was a director of Christie's and a keen painter. He and Lady Anne lived for a number of years at Mereworth Castle, which he inherited from his uncle Peter Beatty, but subsequently they settled at Shute House in Dorset, where, working with garden designer Sir Geoffrey Jellicoe, Lady Anne created a fine garden.

5 George Oakes (1928–) was a freelance painter for seven years, occasionally doing work for John Fowler through the antique dealer Jack Wilson, before coming to work full time at Colefax in 1959. He set up and ran the design studio and was a pivotal figure in the development of the business. His colour sense and tastes underpin the business to this day.

6 David Brian Green (1946–) was born in Hampstead, the son of Cyril Green, a shirt manufacturer. With his brother Michael he founded the printing and direct mail firm Tangent Industries, which made them both millionaires in their early twenties. They went on to found Carleton Communications, which was listed on the London Stock Exchange in 1983. He became chief executive of Colefax & Fowler in 1986 and subsequently became chairman in 1999 when Tom Parr retired.

7 Pamela Harriman (1920–1997) was born in Hampshire, the daughter of the 11th Baron Digby. At the age of seventeen she went to a boarding school in Munich, where she was introduced to Adolf Hitler by Unity Mitford. In 1939 while working for the Foreign Office she met and married Randolph Churchill. They divorced in 1945; she subsequently married Leland Hayward and in 1971 W. Averell Harriman, the wealthy railroad heir. She became a prominent figure in Democratic Party politics and President Clinton appointed her United States Ambassador to France in 1993. She died of a cerebral hemorrhage while swimming at the Paris Ritz.

8 Winston Spencer-Churchill (1940–2010) was a grandson of Sir Winston. Educated at Eton and Christ Church, Oxford, he was a journalist, notably on Middle Eastern affairs, until elected to Parliament in 1970. He retired in 1997 when his seat was abolished in a boundary review.

9 James Lees-Milne (1908–1997) was born at Wickhamford Manor in Worcestershire to prosperous minor gentry who had made fortunes in industry. He was educated at Eton and at Magdalen College, Oxford. In 1936 he was appointed secretary to the newly formed Country House Committee of the National Trust, a job he acquired partly on the recommendation of Harold Nicolson. He became their architectural advisor after the war and was a key figure in the growth of the National Trust during the 1950s and 1960s. In 1951 he married Alvilde, Viscountess Chaplin, who died in 1994. He was a prolific writer of biographies and books on decorative art, but is perhaps more famous today for his many volumes of diaries, which have acquired a cult following. He was a great friend of John Fowler.

6. GRANDES DAMES: SIBYL COLEFAX AND NANCY LANCASTER

1 Sibyl, Lady Colefax (1874–1950) was born Sibyl Halsey in Wimbledon. Her uncle was the journalist and constitutional theorist Walter Bagehot. In 1901 she married Arthur Colefax, a rising star at the Bar who specialized in patent and trademark law. They lived at Onslow Gardens and in 1921 bought Argyll House on the King's Road in Chelsea, where she established herself as one of the leading hostesses of the period. She lost most of her capital in the Wall Street Crash of 1929, so turned her hand to decorating, taking over the decorating division of Stair & Andrew, a firm of Mayfair antique dealers in Bruton Street. John Fowler became her business partner in 1938; they moved the firm to Brook Street in 1944. Declining health prompted her to sell the business to Nancy Lancaster in 1948.

2 Ruby Hill (1898–1995) was the daughter of a diplomat and was born in the Baltic States. She became a personal secretary to the Viceroy of India, the 2nd Marquess of Linlithgow (1887–1952), who held office from 1936 to 1943. After his death she went to work for Nancy Lancaster as her secretary, a position she held into the 1960s. She and Nancy would speak on the telephone every day until Nancy died in 1994.

3 Haseley Court, Little Haseley, Oxfordshire, is an early fifteenth-century house which was redeveloped and rebuilt in 1710. It was bought by Nancy Lancaster in 1954 for £4,000. Though the house appears huge, it is mostly one-room deep. Behind the east end is a two-storey wing, which is the surviving part of the fifteenth-century house. Decorated by Nancy and John Fowler, this one house came to embody the Colefax & Fowler style and was widely written about and much celebrated. A fire in 1972 destroyed the saloon and after its repair Nancy moved to the adjacent Coach House, where she lived for the rest of her life.

4 Jonathan Vickers (1928–1997) was born and brought up in Lincolnshire. After National Service in the RAF he went to work for Strutt & Parker, the estate agents, in their Oxford office. The firm sold Haseley Court to Nancy, and he subsequently worked for her land agent, Kenneth Winterschladen. Fascinated by Nancy, he came to work for John Fowler, an arrangement that was not a success. After a spell at the London County Council he went into partnership with David Style in the antique dealers Arthur Brown on the Fulham Road, and was a familiar sight around London in his Rolls Royce, usually accompanied by a foul-mouthed parrot called Birt. He lived at the Old Vicarage, West Malling, where he created some eclectic interiors, enjoyed by many guests. The house was featured in World of Interiors in May 1998.

5 David Nightingale Hicks (1929–1998) was the son of a stockbroker and born at Coggeshall in Essex. After attending Charterhouse he went to the Central College of Art and subsequently worked for J. Walter Thompson (the advertising agency) designing cereal boxes. In 1954 House and Garden featured his London home at 22 South Eaton Place, which launched his career as an interior decorator. In 1958 he went into partnership with Tom Parr as 'Hicks and Parr' at Lowndes Place, off Belgrave Square. The partnership was dissolved in 1960 with Parr buying a minor share in Colefax & Fowler and Hicks going off to marry Lady Pamela Mountbatten. Hicks was for a time a lodger in John Fowler's home, where he was apparently rather shy at paying his rent, and as a consequence Fowler would not employ him. In style he could not have been more different from Fowler, with a predilection for strong colours and rather modern design.

6 Joyce Grenfell (1910–1979) was a comedian and actress perhaps best remembered today for her roles as Miss Gossage in The Happiest Days of Your Life and as Ruby Gates in the St Trinian's films. She was the daughter of Paul Phipps (1880–1953), who was an architect and former pupil of Lutyens, and Nora Langhorne (1889–1955), one of the legendary Langhorne sisters (who included Nancy Astor). Though she was famous as a comedian, when the family gathered at Cliveden every Christmas she was never allowed to join in charades: the family deemed she wasn't funny enough!

7 Deborah ('Debo'), Dowager Duchess of Devonshire (1920–2014) was the youngest daughter of Lord Redesdale, one of the six famous Mitford sisters. In 1941 she married Andrew Cavendish, younger son of the 10th Duke of Devonshire. His elder brother was killed in action in 1944 and in 1950 Andrew succeeded to the dukedom. Faced with crippling debts they set to work making the Chatsworth estate profitable. Her contribution to the success of this enterprise was considerable. She was a friend of John Fowler's and worked with him on the National Trust restoration of Sudbury House.

8 Wallis, Duchess of Windsor (1896–1986) was born Bessie Wallis Warfield in Pennsylvania. Her affair with the Prince of Wales led to the abdication crisis in 1936. She became Duchess of Windsor when she married the Duke (as Edward VIII became after he abdicated) the following year, and they settled in Paris.

7. ON MY OWN

1 Lady Manton (1906–1983) was the daughter of Major Philip Guy Reynolds; she first married John Player, heir to the Player tobacco fortune. The marriage was not a success and they divorced. She married secondly George Miles Watson, 2nd Baron Manton, in 1938; he died at Plumpton Place in 1968. Thirdly she married Peregrine Cust, 6th Baron Brownlow of Belton, in 1969; he died in 1978.

2 Susan Stirling (1916–1983) was the daughter of the Hon. Noel Gervase Bligh, younger son of the 8th Earl of Darnley; she married Lieutenant Colonel William Stirling in 1940.

3 George Baillie-Hamilton, 12th Earl of Haddington (1894–1986), married Sarah Cook (died 1995), daughter of George Cook of Quebec, Canada, in 1923. They divided their time between Tyninghame House and Mellerstain House. On the death of the 12th Earl his successor chose to retain Mellerstain, while Tyninghame was sold and turned into apartments.

4 Air Commodore Douglas Douglas-Hamilton, 14th Duke of Hamilton and 11th Duke of Brandon (1903–1973), was educated at Eton and Balliol College, Oxford. He succeeded his father as Duke and Keeper of Holyroodhouse in 1940. In 1937 he married Elizabeth Ivy Percy (1916–2008), daughter of the 8th Duke of Northumberland. He had attended the 1936 Berlin Olympics, where he met most of the leadership of the Nazis. In May 1941 Rudolf Hess parachuted into Scotland, supposedly to meet the Duke and arrange a peace treaty between Germany and the United Kingdom. Hess was arrested and soon found himself in the Tower.

5 Philip Vincent Belloc Jebb (1927–1995) was a grandson of the writer Hilaire Belloc. He went to King's College, Cambridge, where he read architecture. He practised from 1953, working as a freelance in London, New York and San Francisco in 1955–6, establishing his own practice in 1958. He was a very versatile architect, able to work both in contemporary and classical styles. He collaborated extensively with John Fowler and Colefax & Fowler.

6 Sir Emmanuel Kaye (1914–1999) was born in Russia; he came to England as a small child and was educated at Twickenham Technical College. In 1940 he founded J. E. Shay Ltd and in 1943 took over Lansing Bagnall, which he turned into the largest manufacturer of forklift trucks in Europe. He married Elizabeth Cutler (1925–2012) in 1946.

7 Harry Hyams (1928–2015) was born in Hendon, north London. His father ran an import business and was prosperous enough to send his son to private school. Initially, Hyams worked for an advertising agency, but soon left to work for an estate agent. He eventually became a property developer specializing in commercial buildings. He preferred to find a single blue-chip tenant who would take a repairing and full insuring lease, as was the norm. He was able to manage a large portfolio with a staff of just six. He attracted much adverse publicity after he built Centre Point, which remained unoccupied for many years because he was unable to find a single tenant for the 202,000 square feet of space. He married Kathleen ('Kay', 1920–2011) in 1954. He bought Ramsbury Manor in 1965 for £650,000, at the time the highest price ever paid for a house. The house had been decorated twice before by John Fowler and Hyams used his services yet again. He was a noted art collector and in 2006 the house was subject to a burglary by the notorious 'Johnson gang'. They were caught and received lengthy prison sentences, but some of the objects stolen were never recovered.

8 Henry (Jindrich Jaroslav) Melich (1924–1999) was born in Bohemia, Czechoslovakia, but moved to England in 1939 and became a British subject in 1948, when he was described as an 'architectural assistant'. He trained as an architect and specialized in ecclesiastical buildings, which were badly in need of repair after the ravages of the war. Together with Lord Mottistone and Paul Paget he worked on many London buildings, particularly St Paul's Cathedral, Lambeth Palace, City Temple and Windsor Castle. He subsequently settled in the Bahamas, where in 1954 he set up a private practice, becoming a leading architect.

9 John Aspinall (1926–2000) was born in Delhi, where his father, Robert Aspinall, an army surgeon, was stationed. During the 1950s and 1960s his activities as a gambling club host took him to the centre of British high society. In 1962 he founded the Clermont Club in Berkeley Square: the original members included five dukes, five marquesses and twenty earls. In 1957 he established a private zoo at Howletts in Kent and in 1973, in need of more space for his collection of animals, he bought Port Lympne in Kent, formerly the house of Sir Philip Sassoon.

10 Lady Osborne (1905–1987), born Mary Grace Horn, was the daughter of Clement Horn of Goring-by-Sea, but the family had been resident in India for four generations. Her first husband was Robert Aspinall. In 1938 she married George Francis Osborne, who became 16th Baronet in 1948. The Conservative politician George Osborne is her grandson.

11 John 'Jack' Profumo (1915–2006) was the son of Albert Profumo (4th Baron Profumo of the Kingdom of Sardinia) and educated at Harrow and Brasenose College, Oxford. He was elected to Parliament in 1940 for Kettering. He lost his seat in 1945, but was elected again in 1950 and was appointed Secretary of State for War in 1960. In 1954 he married the actress Valerie Hobson (1917–1998). He was at the centre of the scandalous Profumo affair in 1961. After his resignation from Parliament, he devoted his time to being a volunteer at Toynbee Hall in the East End of London and was seldom seen in public. Lady Thatcher invited him to her seventieth birthday party, where he sat next to the guest of honour: the Queen.

12 George Jellicoe, 2nd Earl Jellicoe (1918–2007), was the sixth and youngest child and only son of the 1st Earl, who was Commander-in-Chief of the Grand Fleet during the First World War. He succeeded to the earldom in 1939. He was briefly First Lord of the Admiralty, the last person to hold the post before the office of Lord High Admiral was restored, and Lord Privy Seal and Leader of the House of Lords from 1970 to 1973. He married twice: first, Patricia O'Kane (divorced 1966) and second, Philippa Dunne, daughter of Captain Philip Dunne of Gatley Park.

13 Sir Edward Heath (1916–2005) was Prime Minister from 1970 to 1974.

8. IN PRAISE OF CRAFTSMEN

1 Chamberlain & Mason: J. Sidney Mason Ltd was founded in 1879. John Mason senior joined in the early 1930s and went into partnership with Joe Chamberlain of Chamberlain's, combining at Mason's works in Fairfax Road, Hampstead, to form Chamberlain & Mason Ltd. Frank Chamberlain joined the business after the war and John Mason junior joined in 1959. Colefax & Fowler bought the business in 1975. John Mason subsequently established J & A Mason (Upholsterers) Ltd in 1977, from which he retired in 1998.

2 We became famous as a company for our window treatments. John was meticulous in ensuring that every detail was correct. We were noted for our 'swag and tail' draperies. The depth of the 'swag' was very precise as was the length of the tails; the fabric folded elegantly at either side, and was longer for a Victorian house than a Georgian one. We would use details such as choux (French for cabbage), scrunched up balls of fabric rather resembling a cos lettuce, which appeared to hold the drapery in place. On flat pelmets we also used 'bells', small additional tapered panels which were pleated, thus standing proud of the pelmet.

3 Howard & Sons was founded by John Howard in 1820, trading at 24 Lemon Street, London, as a cabinet manufacturer. In 1872 the company moved to Berners Street in Mayfair with workshops in Cleveland Street, but in the 1930s it was bought by Lenygon & Morant Ltd.

4   In America a 'P' arm is known as an English arm.

5   W. F. Atkins was founded in 1936. Walter Atkins died in 1966 and the company was taken over by his nephew, Peter Atkins. The company operated out of premises at 3 Portman Mews South. Peter Atkins closed the company in 1999 and retired. A number of John Mason and Peter Atkins workers established their own businesses: notably, Harty & Williams, Geoff Kent of Sadlers in Pimlico, and Andrew Christy, all of whom carried on traditional upholstery and curtain making.

6   B. A. Clark Ltd. No one knows when the business was founded, but it probably dated back to Edwardian times. The company occupied the top of a Victorian building in Little Britain, a street to the north of St Paul's Cathedral. Bernard Clark lost his sight and retired in 1970. For further information see 'The Art of the Trimmings Maker', Country Life, 10 December 1970, pp. 1109–12.

7   Mattei Spassov Radev (1927–2009) was born in Bulgaria; he was forced to flee the Communists in the early 1950s as his parents had opposed the regime. With difficulty he escaped to Istanbul and was able to stow away on a British freighter. In London he met Patrick Trevor-Roper (brother of Hugh), who helped with his entrée into London society. He met and had brief affairs with Eddy Sackville-West and Eardley Knollys, but in 1960 he met the novelist E. M. Forster, and despite the age difference of forty-six years, they fell in love and embarked on a secret affair. He learnt picture framing from Robert Savage in Chelsea, and then with help from Knollys he set up in business on his own in Fitzrovia. Vanessa Bell, Duncan Grant and Graham Sutherland all used his services, as did the Queen's Gallery at Buckingham Palace, so his business prospered. In 1991 Knollys bequeathed Radev his art collection, most of which he had himself inherited from Sackville-West.

8   Cyril Wopshott (1909–1998) was brought up in London; he was a painter at Haywood's, a painting contractor based in Hay's Mews, off Berkeley Square. He started his own business in 1954 and Barbara Heale gave him his first job. He married Muriel Hourigan in 1985.

9   The Marble Hall at Syon House was redecorated by John Fowler in the late 1960s for the Duke of Northumberland. The Hall is Robert Adam's finest Roman work. However, if painted in a single white, on many days of the year it would look dead. Fowler painted it in a more elaborate but very subtle manner, and because of the play of light it was difficult to work out exactly what had been done. In the main storey he used a warm white, which appeared a pinky or lilac white in differing lights. The upper storey was a cooler white. The ground of the main frieze, the rings of the columns, the frieze of the upper windows and the coffers was, despite appearances, the same blue-grey as the skirting. The apse has three whites and there are four blue-whites in the ceiling – grey-white for the main border echoing the dado, banded by the same warm white as in the main wall colour, which is also used on the cross-ribs.

10   When I met Mavis Long (1938–) at Squerryes Court in Kent in 1980 she had just started doing painting jobs to support her two children. Prior to this she had done some dressmaking (much against the wishes of her mother, who wanted her to do a Pitman course and become a secretary). I taught her many of the specialist painting techniques John had taught me. She has subsequently enjoyed an extensive career working in many large houses in Germany and Austria, in Greece (where she had a house), Egypt, Lebanon, Bermuda, Guatamala and all over the United States. Her daughter has followed in her footsteps and works for many London-based interior designers.

11   Mark Uriu (1956–) was born in Los Angeles, California; he studied painting and choreography at University of California, Santa Cruz, graduating in 1977. He travelled to Europe to experience the great works of art in situ, staying with future business partner Gordon Knox, who was studying social anthropology at Cambridge University. At Cambridge he was introduced to John Lister (also studying anthropology), who had recently formed the decorating company Colchester Lister Associates in London. He worked for Colchester Lister for a year and a half (between trips to the Continent). Then he returned to New York to pursue modern dance and choreography. Gordon Knox was working towards a PhD in social anthropology at the University of Chicago, and together they started a company to paint apartments to support their primary pursuits. Together we worked on a string of projects in New York, Chicago and Palm Beach, and the collaboration with Colefax & Fowler continued first through Knox-Uriu Inc., then Mark Uriu Inc. and now Uriu Nuance Inc.

12   John Crossley & Sons, a manufacturer of carpets based in Halifax, West Yorkshire, was founded in 1621. In the mid-nineteenth century they were the largest carpet manufacturer in the world. The company closed in 1989. A director founded Avina Carpets and bought many of the looms, pattern cards and documents from Crossley's.

13   Mauny was founded by André Mauny in 1933. He trained as a decorator, working for two years for Jansens before going into business with Robert Caillaed, who had founded a wallpaper business. Caillaed died but Mauny continued to print wallpapers. For further information see 'The Vitality of Papier Peint', Country Life, 11 July 1985, pp. 103–6.

10. GOING COMMERCIAL

1   See Chapter 16, note 1.

2   Stephen Bershad (1941–) was born and brought up in Southern California before going into the law and then investment banking. He was a managing director of Lehman Brothers from 1974, setting up the London operation for them. He left in 1986 to pursue other interests.

3   Thomas Daniell (1749–1840) was the son of the landlord of the Swan Inn at Chertsey, Surrey. He was apprenticed to a heraldic painter who worked for a coach painter in Queen Street, London. He went to the Royal Academy Schools, but found it difficult to establish himself as a landscape painter. He obtained permission from the East India Company to travel to Calcutta as an engraver, arriving in 1786. Together with his nephew William Daniell (1769–1837) he toured parts of India. They returned to England in 1794 and published six volumes of engravings between 1795 and 1808. He designed various garden buildings at Sezincote for Sir Charles Cockerell and painted views of the house.

11. GOING TO AMERICA

1   David K. E. Bruce (1898–1977) was born in Baltimore; his father was a lawyer and a politician. Bruce followed in his father's footsteps, being called to the Bar in Maryland. He became a diplomat and served as United States Ambassador to France, West Germany and (from 1961 to 1969) the United Kingdom. John Fowler redecorated the ambassadorial residence in Regent's Park. In 1926 David Bruce married Ailsa Mellon, daughter of Andrew Mellon and sister of Paul Mellon. They divorced in 1945 and he married Evangeline Bell (1914–1995). He purchased and restored Staunton Hill in Virginia, which had been the family's former estate.
For Bunny Mellon, see chapter 12, note 1.
John Hay 'Jock' Whitney (1904–1982) was born into one of the richest families in America. On the death of his father in 1926 he inherited a trust fund of twenty million dollars, but was to inherit four times that from his mother; and he also made a large fortune in business. He was a major supporter of Dwight D. Eisenhower and was appointed Ambassador to the United Kingdom, a post his grandfather had held sixty years previously. He married Mary 'Liz' Altemus, a Pennsylvania socialite, in 1930. They divorced in 1940, and in 1942 he married Betsey Cushing, who had previously been married to James Roosevelt, son of the president.

12. NEW YORK, NEW YORK!

1   Rachel Lowe 'Bunny' Mellon (1910–2014) was the eldest daughter of Gerard Lambert, president of Gillette Safety Razor Company. In 1932 she married Stacy Barcroft Lloyd, a banker from Philadelphia. They divorced in 1948 and she married the widower Paul Mellon (1907–1999), heir to one of America's greatest fortunes. She became a noted garden designer and was asked by President Kennedy to redesign the White House Rose Garden in 1961. Her principal home was Oak Spring Farm in Virginia, but she also had homes in Antigua, Nantucket, Paris and a town house in New York.

2   Steve Schwarzman (1947–) was born in Pennsylvania. After Yale and Harvard Business School he worked for Lehman Brothers and became head of mergers and acquisitions. In 1985 he left and with Peter Peterson founded Blackstone Group. He married Ellen Phillips in 1971 but they divorced in 1990. In 1995 he married Christine Mularchuk, former wife of Austin Hearst, grandson of Randolph Hearst.

3   Gordon Davies (1926–2007) lived at Hastingleigh near Ashford in Kent. He was an artist of considerable abilities and a regular exhibitor at the Royal Academy. He was particularly skilled at shell work and did a number of such projects for me.

13. A COLLECTOR, CONNOISSEUR AND PATRON: FRED KREHBIEL

1   Fred Krehbiel (1941–) was born in Chicago and educated at Lake Forest College, Georgetown University and the University of Leicester. In 1965 he joined Molex, a manufacturer of electronic components founded by his grandfather and namesake in 1938. Molex became a public company in 1972. He served as executive vice-president of Molex Inc. from 1975 to 1988, when he became chief executive officer. He was elected chairman in 1993 after the death of his father. Molex was acquired by Koch Industries in 2013 for 7.2 billion dollars.

2 The *stuccadore* Pietro Luigi Bossi (dates unknown) is thought to have been born in Italy (although it could have been Dresden). He came to work in Dublin, probably via London, in around 1785 and is known to have been active until 1798. He perfected the technique of inlaying marble chimneypieces with polychrome scagliola designs.

3 Marietta Peabody Tree (1917–1991) was the daughter of Rector Malcolm Peabody. In 1939 she married the New York lawyer Desmond FitzGerald. During the war she was part of the American delegation assisting the British Ministry of Information. Through her work she met Ronald Tree, Nancy Lancaster's second husband, and they began an affair. They married in 1947. The marriage was not a huge success, however. Ronald Tree spent more and more time at his house in Barbados, Heron Bay. He died in 1976. A tireless worker for the Democratic Party, Marietta Tree was described by Sir Isaiah Berlin as 'a progressive, liberal figure who was mixed up with a lot of naive left-wing sympathizers'.

4 Colin Orchard (1955–) was born and brought up in Edinburgh; after leaving school he did a four-year apprenticeship with a furnishing and fabric company, which was followed (at the insistence of his father) by a two-year business management course. He worked for the Edinburgh decorating firm A. F. Drysdale Ltd, which was the Scottish agent for Colefax & Fowler. He dealt with Colefax and sometimes helped oversee the company's projects in Scotland. Frequent visits to London meant he was a known character, so in 1982 he was approached to work in Brook Street. On joining he soon migrated to become one of my team. He left in 1989 to form his own company, and subsequently inherited some of my former clients.

14. OFF THE FRINGE – A LIFE BEYOND

1 Sir Leon Bagrit (1902–1979) was born in Kiev in Tsarist Russia; he and his parents came to England in 1914. He studied at Birkbeck College, University of London, before establishing his own company in 1935, which was taken over by Elliott Brothers two years later with Bagrit becoming managing director. The company developed automated control systems for industry and became part of the English Electric Company in 1967. He was a director of the Royal Opera House and founded the Friends of Covent Garden. He married Stella Bagrit (1906–2001) in 1926.

2 Sir Isaiah Berlin (1909–1997) was a political theorist, philosopher and historian who is considered to be one of the greatest scholars of his generation. Born in Riga, his family moved to St Petersburg, where he witnessed both the February and October Revolutions in 1917. As life deteriorated under the Bolsheviks, the family returned to Riga in 1920 before emigrating to the United Kingdom in 1921. Berlin was educated at St Paul's School and Corpus Christi, Oxford. He remained at Oxford (New College and then All Souls) for the rest of his life.

3 David Walter Vicary (1926–1995) trained as an architect. He is remembered especially today for his design of the Fountain Garden at Wilton House in Wiltshire. Vicary was a friend of John Fowler's and indeed seemed to know everyone involved in the country house world. He lived for many years at Kilvert's Parsonage, Langley Burrell, near Chippenham in Wiltshire. Towards the end of his life he became a tragic figure, gradually losing his mind. His death, as the result of a fire, was very sad.

4 Stephen Long (died 2011) began life as a schoolmaster, but soon gave that up to become an antique dealer. After a stint with Mayfair Oriental art dealer John Sparks, he took a stall at Portobello Market before moving to a shop at 348 Fulham Road, where he remained for the rest of his life. In the 1950s he met John Fowler and they became great friends. He was a regular guest at the Hunting Lodge. He wrote regularly for *World of Interiors*.

5 Freya Stark (1893–1993) was born in Paris. Her mother was Italian of Polish/German descent, while her father was an English painter from Devon. When she was nine she was given a copy of *One Thousand and One Nights*; this sparked her fascination with Arabia, which she was to explore extensively and chronicle. She was among the first Europeans to travel through the southern Arabian deserts. She lived at Asolo in northern Italy, where she died a few months after her 100th birthday.

6 Robert Wiedeman Barrett Browning (1849–1912), known as 'Pen', was the only child of the poets Robert Browning and Elizabeth Barrett Browning. He was born in Florence, where his parents had settled. He was educated at home, but his father was keen that he should attend university. His command of English left much to be desired, but he was accepted into Christ Church, Oxford, though he left before taking his degree. He studied painting and sculpture in Antwerp, where Auguste Rodin and John Singer Sargent were among his teachers. He married an American heiress and they restored Ca' Rezzonico, one of the grandest palazzos on the Grand Canal in Venice. The marriage gradually disintegrated and Ca' Rezzonico was sold in 1906. Browning subsequently dividing his time between his house in Asolo and Torre all' Antella near Florence.

7 Andrée Bessire (died 1998) was born in Switzerland. She came to live in England with her sister Babet, who was a great friend of the artist Augustus John. Andrée became an antique dealer with a taste for eighteenth-century things, usually quite 'dressy'. She was a great friend of Joyce Shears, which is how I got to know her.

8 Iona Brown (1941–2004) was born in Salisbury; both her parents were musicians, and she, her two brothers and her sister all became musicians. She played violin in the Philharmonic Orchestra before she joined the Academy of St Martin-in-the-Fields, eventually becoming leader, solo violinist and director in 1974. She was famous for her rendition of Vaughan Williams's 'The Lark Ascending'.

9 This four-poster bed subsequently came on the market with its hangings still intact and was bought by Miranda Iveagh. After a brief spell in Ireland it is now at Wilbury House.

10 Jan Andrzej Sapieha, Prince Sapieha-Rozanski (1910–1989), was the son of Eustachy Kajetan Wladislaw Sapieha (1881–1963) and Teresa Izabela Karolina Lubomirska (1888–1964). He was married to Maria Zdziechowska (1914–2009). After Poland gained its independence in 1918, Jan's father became Polish Ambassador to the United Kingdom and was subsequently Minister of Foreign Affairs.

11 Henryk Szeryng (1918–1988) was born in Zelazowa Wola in Poland into a wealthy Jewish family ('Szeryng' is a Polish translation of his Yiddish surname). He studied under Carl Flesch in Berlin and then under Jacques Thibaud at the Conservatory in Paris. When war broke out he was asked by General Sikorski to join his staff as a liaison officer and interpreter. On a visit to Mexico in 1943 he was so moved by the generous response of the Mexicans that he became a Mexican citizen in 1946. He lived mostly in Paris and later in Monaco, travelling on a Mexican diplomatic passport.

12 Lady Diana Cooper (1892–1986) was the younger daughter of the 8th Duke of Rutland and the former Violet Lindsay. Her real father was probably the writer the Hon. Henry Cust (of Belton). In 1919 she married Alfred Duff Cooper (although her parents had hoped she would marry the Prince of Wales). Duff Cooper was elected to Parliament in 1924 and in 1944 he became Ambassador to France. She was a great success as hostess at the beautiful embassy in Paris, and after Duff Cooper retired they continued to live in France at Chantilly. In the 1950s she published three volumes of memoirs which remain an interesting portrait of the period.

13 Sybil Connolly (1921–1998) was a Dublin-based fashion designer famous for her use of Irish linen in her collections. She was trained at Bradley & Co. in London, whose clients included Queen Mary. In 1940 she returned to live in Ireland, working for Richard Alan. She launched her eponymous fashion label in 1957 and acquired a great following, including Elizabeth Taylor and Jacqueline Kennedy.

14 Eleanor Lambert (1903–2003) was a major figure in American fashion and public relations. Born in Indiana, she studied fashion at the Chicago Art Institute. She was Press Director at the Whitney Museum of American Art in the 1930s and helped to found the Museum of Modern Art. She did much through her publicity agency to further the careers of many fashion designers, including Oscar de la Renta, Norman Norell and Bill Blass. In 1962 she founded the Council of Fashion Designers of America, which she ran for over a decade.

15 The International Liberty Association (formerly the Iran Liberty Association) was formed by Iranian exiles in the 1980s following the overthrow of the Shah of Iran in 1979. A group of intellectuals established a refugee camp, Camp Ashraf, in Iraq under the protection of the then Iraqi government. This has subsequently been relocated to Camp Liberty, the former US base near Baghdad.

15. FULL THROTTLE

1 Miranda, Countess of Iveagh (1940–2010) was the daughter of Major Charles Smiley; she married Arthur F. B. Guinness, Viscount Elveden, in 1963. In 1967 he succeeded his grandfather to become the 3rd Earl of Iveagh. They divorced in 1984 and she later had an affair with Tony Ryan (see note 3 below).

2 Alan Gore (1926–2006) was born in Drinkstone, Suffolk. His father had been a tea planter in Assam, but after the First World War he retired to Britain. Alan trained to be an architect at the Architectural Association, where he met his wife, Ann. They were married in 1953. He met and became a great friend of John Fowler, who inspired his love of the eighteenth century. This led to him persuading his mother to buy the Vicarage at Barnes, a beautiful eighteenth-century house, which they christened 'Strawberry House'. The family trustees resigned en masse in protest at this acquisition. He set up in practice as Gore, Gibberd & Saunders, which specialized in restoration. Gore also built new property and one example in Oxfordshire was so well done the editors of Pevsner's architectural guides were completely

fooled, much to his delight. Early on he pioneered modern kitchens and became known as 'the king of the kitchen'.

3 Thomas Anthony (Tony) Ryan (1936–2007) was born in Thurles, County Tipperary. In 1975 he founded Guinness Peat Aviation in a partnership with Guinness Peat and Aer Lingus. Together with Christopher Ryan and Liam Lonergan in 1984 he founded Ryanair, the budget airline, from which he derived considerable wealth.

4 Gephard 'Gep' R. Duremburger (1936–2015) was a noted antique dealer at San Juan Capistrano, California. He lived at Capo Beach in a cottage, built in 1929 for the oil magnate Edward L. Doheny probably as a beach house, with a large English-style garden. He started his business in 1967 and finally retired in 1995, moving back to Le Sueur, Minnesota, where he had been born. A number of noted interior designers worked for him over the years, including Michael S. Smith, who decorated the private apartments at the White House for President and Mrs Obama.

5 Mario Buatta (1935–) is an American decorator known as the 'Prince of Chintz'. He was born on Staten Island in New York and attended the Parsons School of Design. He was a friend of John Fowler and is a fixture of New York society. He is noted for his whacky sense of humour and love of practical jokes.

6 Dame Barbara Cartland (1901–2000) was the daughter of Major Bertram Cartland; she was born in Birmingham. After her father was killed in the First World War, her mother opened a dress shop in London. She wrote a phenomenal number of romantic novels (723 plus 160 unpublished manuscripts) and she ensured she had the longest entry in *Who's Who* by listing every title! She is said to have sold over a billion books.

7 Barbara Goalen (1921–2002) was the daughter of a rubber plantation owner in British Malaya. She was an ambulance driver in the war and became engaged at seventeen to an RAF pilot who was killed in action. She then married Ian Goalen, a commercial pilot who was killed in a plane crash in 1947. She began to model at the age of twenty-four, not because she needed the money but for 'for myself'. She gradually restricted the commissions she would accept and charged a fee four times the usual rate. Her wasp-waisted shape made her perfect for the post-war 'New Look'. In 1954 she married the Lloyd's underwriter Nigel Campbell (died 1995).

8 Charles Ingram C. Wood, 2nd Earl of Halifax (1912–1980), was educated at Eton and Christ Church, Oxford; after service in the Royal Horse Guards he entered Parliament in 1937, but lost his seat in 1945. In 1972 he became High Steward of York Minster. In 1936 he married Lady Ruth Alice Primrose (1916–1989), daughter of the Liberal politician and soldier Neil J. A. Primrose, son of the Earl of Rosebery.

9 Francis Johnson (1911–1995) was born in Bridlington, Yorkshire; he studied at the Leeds School of Architecture. He set up his own practice in 1937 and became renowned for his renovation of Georgian country houses and for creating new houses in the Georgian style. He also worked on many churches.

10 Edwin Duncan Sandys (1908–1987), the son of a Conservative MP, was educated at Eton and at Magdalen College, Oxford. He went into the diplomatic service, serving in the Foreign Office and in the embassy in Berlin. He was elected to Parliament in 1935. In that same year he married Diana Churchill, daughter of Winston Churchill. They were divorced in 1960. In 1962 he married Marie-Claire (née Schmitt), who had previously been married to Robert, 2nd Viscount Hudson.

11 Anthony Frederic Lewis Thesiger (1906–1969) was the son of the Hon. Percy Mansfield Thesiger; he married Virginia Margaret Graham in 1939. Wilfred Thesiger was his cousin. His wife was a great friend of Joyce Grenfell (see chapter 6, note 6) and a collection of their letters, *Joyce and Ginnie*, was published in 1997.

16. KEEPING IT IN THE FAMILY

1 Gordon W. H. Richardson (1915–2010) was educated at Nottingham High School and Caius College, Cambridge. In 1941 he married Margaret Sheppard (1916–2005), the daughter of the prominent Christian pacifist Canon 'Dick' Sheppard. After the Second World War he was called to the Bar. He became a director of J. Henry Schroder & Co. in 1957 and chairman in 1962. He was appointed Governor of the Bank of England in 1973. Not seeing eye to eye with Prime Minister Margaret Thatcher, he retired in 1983. He was made a peer and also a Knight Companion of the Order of the Garter.

2 Sir John Riddell, 13th Baronet Riddell (1934–2010), was educated at Eton and Christ Church, Oxford. Having trained as an accountant he worked for the International Bank for Reconstruction and Development and then as an associate director of First Boston Corp. He was appointed Private Secretary and Treasurer to the Prince of Wales in 1985, resigning in 1990. In 1969 he married Sarah Richardson, the daughter of Gordon Richardson (see above).

3 Sir Michael Peat (1949–) is a great-grandson of William Barclay Peat, who founded the accountancy firm Peat Marwick (now KPMG). He was educated at Eton and Trinity College, Oxford. Like his father (see note 4 below), he trained as an accountant, joining KPMG in 1972 and becoming a partner in 1985. In 1987 he was appointed Auditor to the Privy Purse and later became Director of Finances and Property Services of the Royal Household. In 1996 he was appointed Keeper of the Privy Purse and Treasurer to the Queen, and also Receiver General of the Duchy of Lancaster. In 2002 he was appointed Private Secretary to the Prince of Wales, a post from which he retired in 2011. He married Deborah Sage in 1976.

4 Sir Gerrard Charles Peat (1920–), son of Charles Peat, MP for Darlington and Parliamentary Private Secretary to Sir Winston Churchill during the Second World War. He was a partner in the accountancy firm KPMG from 1956 to 1987and was the third member of his family to be appointed Auditor to the Privy Purse (1980), for which he was knighted in 1988. His son succeeded him and held the post from 1987 to 1990. He married Margaret J. ('Dodo') Wylam-Walker in 1949.

5 Lieutenant-Commander Sir Cyril Hugh Kleinwort (1905–1980) married Elizabeth Forde in 1933. They had three daughters.

6 Diana Lloyd, daughter of Lieutenant Colonel Horace Lloyd, married Stormont Mancroft, 2nd Baron Mancroft (1914–1987), in 1951; she had previously been married to Richard B. St John Quarry (1912–2002), by whom she had a daughter, Miranda Elizabeth Quarry (1947–). Miranda married, first, the actor Peter Sellers (1925–1980) in 1970 (divorced 1974); second, Sir Nicholas Nuttall, 3rd Baronet, in 1975 (divorced 1983). She married Alexander Macmillan, 2nd Earl of Stockton, in 1995.

7 Lieutenant Colonel Vincent Paravicini (1914–1989) was the son of Charles Paravicini, Swiss Ambassador to the United Kingdom from 1920 to 1940. He married Elizabeth Maugham, daughter of the novelist W. Somerset Maugham and Syrie Maugham, the celebrated decorator (and a neighbour of John Fowler's), in 1937. They were divorced in 1948. He married Jacqueline Dyer, daughter of Sir John Dyer, 12th Baronet, in 1949.

8 Richard A. Lumley, 12th Earl of Scarborough (1932–2004), succeeded to the title in 1969 and the following year married Lady Elizabeth Anne Ramsay (1941–), eldest daughter of the 16th Earl of Dalhousie. Lord Scarborough had considerable knowledge of architecture, pictures and furniture and was an honorary member of the RIBA. He was also a trustee of Leeds Castle in Kent.

17. AT HOME

1 Donald Church (1938–) was born in Halling near Rochester in Kent; he was educated at Medway and Maidstone Art Colleges. From 1960 he worked for many London design companies, including Taylor-Grigg, Dudley Poplak, Mrs Monro Ltd, and from 1965 to 1973 for Mary Fox Linton. He was recommended to John Fowler by David Hicks and became his personal assistant. In 1974 he became a freelance artist and designer producing working drawings and colour perspectives for many interior decorators.

18. TAKING STOCK

1 Stanley Falconer (1930–2010) was born in Edinburgh and brought up in Cape Town, South Africa. He initially worked as a cost clerk at a paper bag company, but left to start his own antique shop in Johannesburg. This led on to decorating and he built a successful business. He returned to the United Kingdom and initially worked for Trollope & Sons before helping to establish Colefax & Fowler Associates in Hanover Square. Subsequently, he became a partner in Colefax & Fowler. His own house, Tughill in Gloucestershire, was featured in a number of magazines.

2 Marcus Agius (1946–) was educated at Trinity Hall, Cambridge, and Harvard Business School. He went to work for Lazard's in 1972, becoming chairman of the London branch in 2001 and deputy chairman of the whole group the following year. He joined the board of Barclays Bank in 2006, becoming chairman in 2007. He resigned in 2012. He married Katherine de Rothschild, daughter of Edmund de Rothschild of Exbury House, in 1971.

3 Lucinda Oakes (1966–) is the youngest daughter of George and Judith Oakes. She has followed in her father's footsteps and is a decorative painter.

LIST OF COMMISSIONS

This commissions list, though by no means complete, gives an indication of the scope and extent of Imogen Taylor's work.
The following books have been used and references to properties are taken from these sources. References are also given to *Country Life*
drawn from the magazine's standard published index. Other magazine articles have been referenced where these are known.
John Cornforth, *The Inspiration of the Past: Country House Taste in the Twentieth Century* (Viking, London, 1985)
John Fowler and John Cornforth, *English Decoration in the 18th Century*, 2nd edn (Barrie & Jenkins, London, 1986)
Chester Jones, *Colefax & Fowler: The Best in English Interior Decoration* (Barrie & Jenkins, London, 1989)

Abbots Ripton Hall, Huntingdon, Cambridgeshire
Client: Lord and Lady de Ramsey

81 Abbotsbury Road, London, W14
Client: Mrs Douglas Wilson

Abu Dhabi Embassy, Princes Gate, London, SW7

Aitken, Mr and Mrs Maxwell

Albany, Piccadilly, London, SW1 (Set A10)
Client: Lady Margaret and J. Walker

Albany, Piccadilly, London, SW1
Client: Mr Haber

Albany, Piccadilly, London, SW1
Client: Lord and Lady de Ramsey

Alexander Square, Knightsbridge, London, SW3
Client: Mr and Mrs Marcus Agius

Arundel Park, Arundel, Sussex
Client: Lavinia, Dowager Duchess of Norfolk
With John Fowler
Country Life, 20 June 1996, pp. 60–65
Inspiration of the Past, pp. 127, 181

Ascot Place, Ascot, Berkshire
Client: Sir Leon and Lady Bagrit

Ascot Place, Ascot, Berkshire
Client: Mrs Drew Heinz

Ashby St Ledgers Manor, Northamptonshire
Client: Mrs Sandra Billington

Atlanta, Georgia, USA
Client: Mr Richard Lewis

Melbourne, Australia
Client: Charlotte Gwyne (née Kleinwort)

Avenue Road, St John's Wood, London, NW8
Client: The Hon. Mrs Thomas Davies

Bahamas
Client: Mr and Mrs D. Rolle

Bank of England, Threadneedle Street, London, EC2
Client: Gordon Richardson (Governor's flat)

Barry Farm
Client: Mrs Peter Kirwin Taylor

Beaufort Castle, Scotland
Client: Mr and Mrs Simon Fraser
Note: George Oakes did a mural in Mrs Fraser's
bedroom

Bedford, New York State, USA
Client: Mr and Mrs Wyser-Pratte

Beeleigh Abbey, Malden, Essex
Client: Christina Foyle
Country Life, vol. 52, pp. 406–12

Belton House, Grantham, Lincolnshire
Client: Lady Brownlow (formerly Lady Manton, see
Plumpton Place)

Bentley, Halland, Sussex
Client: Mrs Gerald Askew
Country Life, vol. 88, pp. 368, 390; vol. 101, p. 47; vol.
153, pp. 524–5; vol. 176, p. 694

Blithfield, Rugeley, Staffordshire
Client: Lady Bagot
With John Fowler, then on own
Country Life, vol. 116, pp. 1488, 1576, 1664
Inspiration of the Past, pp. 159, 164, 165, 183

Bourne Street, London, SW1
Client: Mrs V. (Jackie) Paravicini

Bowood, Calne, Wiltshire
Client: Marchioness of Landsdowne
Country Life, vol. 7, pp. 432–6; vol. 15, p. 738; vol. 17,
pp. 126–36; vol. 34, pp. 324–31; vol. 127, p. 159;
vol. 151, pp. 1448–51, 1610; vol. 152, pp. 546–9;
vol. 159, p. 964; vol. 166, p. 273
English Decoration in the 18th Century, pp. 79, 205
Inspiration of the Past, pp. 183, 190

Broad Chalke, Wiltshire
Client: Iona Brown

Broadway, Worcestershire
Client: Mr and Mrs Herrick

Brompton Bryan Hall, Bucknell, Shropshire
Client: Mrs C. Harley

Bruern Abbey, Oxfordshire
Client: Mrs Michael Astor (later Lady Ward)

Burton Court, Chelsea, London, SW3
Client: Mr and Mrs Vincent Paravicini

Buscot Park, Faringdon, Oxfordshire
Client: Lord and Lady Faringdon

Bywell Hall, Bywell, Northumberland
Client: The Hon. Wentworth Beaumont, 4th
Viscount Allendale

16 Cadogan Square, Belgravia, London, SW1
Client: Mrs P. Miller-Mundy

Calgary Castle, Tobermoray, Isle of Mull, Scotland
Client: Philip Profumo (Peter Watkins)

Cameley House, Temple Cloud, Bristol, Avon
Client: Colonel and Mrs J. Mardon

Campden Hill Gardens, Kensington, London, W8
Client: Iona Brown

Campden Hill, Kensington, London, W8
Client: Sir John and Lady Riddell (Gordon
Richardson's daughter)

80 Cannon Street, London, EC4
Client: Exco International

Canonteign Manor, Ashton, Exeter, Devon
Client: Viscountess Exmouth

14 Carlos Place, Mayfair, London, W1
Client: Mr Hugh Ross

Carton, Maynooth, Co. Kildare, Eire.
Client: Mrs Peter (Miranda) Sellers
Country Life, vol. 80, pp. 488, 514; vol. 147, p. 636;
vol. 153, p. 1539
English Decoration in the 18th Century, pp. 65, 79, 132,
225
Note: a stable block conversion attached to Carton

120 Cheapside, London, EC2
Client: Schroders
Note: offices for Gordon Richardson before he
became Governor of the Bank of England

Chelsea, London, SW3
Client: Signora Pallavicini (a lady from Florence)

Chequers, Princes Risborough, Buckinghamshire
Client: The Chequers Trust
With John Fowler

Chesham House, 30 Chesham Place, Belgravia,
London, SW1
Client: Mrs E. Hopton

Chesham House, 30 Chesham Place, Belgravia,
London, SW1
Client: Sir Neville and Lady Pearson
Note: George Oakes painted a mural in the dining
room.

Chesham Place, Belgravia, London, SW1
Client: Mrs Carney

Chesham Place, Belgravia, London SW1
Client: Mrs Trusted

Chesham Place, Belgravia, London SW1
Client: Mrs Lomnitz

Chesham Street, Belgravia, London, SW1
Client: Mr and Mrs Paul D'Ambrumenil

3 Chester Square, Belgravia, London, SW1
Client: Mr and Mrs Julian Faber (the daughter of
Harold Macmillan)

Chester Square, Belgravia, London, SW1
Client: Mrs Nigel Campbell (Barbara Goalen, the
model)

Chester Square, Belgravia, London, SW1
Client: Lady Cleminson

Chester Square, Belgravia, London, SW1
Client: Mrs Hilary David

Chester Square, Belgravia, London, SW1
Client: Mrs P. Ross

Chester Street, London
Client: Mr and Mrs Christopher Birch

Chevening, Sevenoaks, Kent
Client: Chevening Trust
With John Fowler
Note: just the hall and staircase

Cheyne Walk, Chelsea, London, SW3
Client: Mr John Craven

Cheyne Walk, Chelsea, London, SW3
Client: Lady Kleinwort

Chicago, USA
Client: Mrs Ann Bartram

Chicago, USA
Client: Mrs Sissy Bunn

Chicago, USA
Client: Mr and Mrs Jack Crowe

Chicago, USA
Client: Mr and Mrs Plato Foufas

Chicago, USA
Client: Mr and Mrs Fred Krehbiel

Churchill House, Ireland
Client: Mr Fred Krehbiel

45 Circus Road, St John's Wood, London, NW8
Client: Mr J. B. C. Danny

Clerical Medical General Assurance, Bristol

Cold Blow, Oare, Marlborough, Wiltshire
Client: Mr A. P. Rollo
Country Life, vol. 53, p. 195

Coolmore Stud, Fethard, County Tipperary, Ireland
Client: Mr and Mrs John Magnier

Cornbury Park, Cornbury, Oxfordshire
Client: Lady Rotherwick
In succession to John Fowler

6 Cottesmore Gardens, Kensington, London, W8
Client: Viscountess Ednam (Earl Dudley)

Cottesmore Gardens, Kensington, London, W8
Client: Miranda, Countess of Iveagh

Cowdray Park, Midhurst, West Sussex
Client: Viscountess Cowdray

Cranborne Manor, Cranborne, Dorset
Client: Viscount and Viscountess Cranborne
Note: library only

Cutler's Gardens, Devonshire Square, London, EC2
Client: Lehman Brothers

Dalkeith, Earl and Countess of (London home)

Derbyshire
Client: Mr and Mrs Barr

20 Devonshire Place, London, W1
Client: London Clinic
Note: entrance hall only

Dock House, Woodbridge, Suffolk
Client: Mr John Quilter

Dorneywood, Burnham, Buckinghamshire
Client: H. M. Government
With John Fowler

39 Dovehouse Street, Chelsea, London, SW3
Client: Miss Mary Brassey
Note: companion to Dolly Rothschild

The Dower House, Buntingford, Hertfordshire
Client: Mr and Mrs 'Jack' Profumo

Dummer Down Farm, Dummer, Hampshire
Client: Mrs R. Ferguson (stepmother to the Duchess of York)

Dunecht House, Aberdeenshire, Scotland
Client: Viscount and Viscountess Cowdray

Duntisbourne, Duntisbourne Abbotts, Cirencester, Gloucestershire
Client: Lord and Lady Richardson

The Durdans, Epsom, Surrey
Client: Mrs Bruce McAlpine

Durham Cottage, 4 Christchurch Street, London, SW3
Client: Mr Michael Mosley
Note: house that had once belonged to the Oliviers

Eaton Close, Belgravia, London, SW1
Client: Viscount Bearsted

107 Eaton Place, Belgravia, London, SW1
Client: The Hon. Mrs Reggie Ward

Eaton Place, Belgravia, London, SW1
Client: Lady Miranda Nuttall (former wife of Peter Sellers)

36 Eaton Square, Belgravia, London, SW1
Client: Ruth, Lady Fermoy

72 Eaton Square, Belgravia, London, SW1
Client: Mr and Mrs Douglas Wilson

80 Eaton Square, Belgravia, London, SW1
Client: Sir Leon and Lady Bagrit

100 Eaton Square, Belgravia, London, SW1
Client: Mr N. F. Mavroleon

100 Eaton Square, Belgravia, London, SW1
Client: Mr and Mrs Harry Hyams

Ebury Mews, Belgravia, London, SW1
Client: Mrs W. Stirling

Eccleston Mews, London
Client: Dowager Duchess of Hamilton
Note: the mews was converted in the Gothic style by Philip Jebb.

Edwards Square, Kensington, W8
Client: Mr and Mrs Stephen Joseph

Egerton Crescent, Knightsbridge, London, SW3
Client: Mr and Mrs Bershad

Egerton Crescent, Knightsbridge, London, SW3
Client: Mr and Mrs Merton

Egerton Terrace and Egerton Crescent, Knightsbridge, London, SW3
Client: Mr and Mrs John Goodwin

36 Elder Street, London, E1
Client: Mr Paul D'Ambrumenil
Note: his office at Norman Frizzell Ltd

Elvetham Hall, Hartley Wintney, Basingstoke, Hampshire
Client: Sir Emmanuel and Lady Kaye
Note: a large conference centre

Ennismore Gardens, South Kensington, London, SW7
Client: Mrs Ferragamo

Ennismore Gardens, South Kensington, London, SW7
Client: Lady Marjorie Stirling

Exbury, Hampshire
Client: Mr and Mrs Marcus Agius

Eydon Hall, Eydon, Northamptonshire
Client: Lady Ford

Eyford Manor, Stow-on the-Wold, Gloucestershire
Client: Lady Kleinwort

Ferry House, Old Isleworth, Richmond, Surrey
Client: Lady Caroline Gilmour

The Folly, Gatley Park, Leinthall Earls, Herefordshire
Client: Mrs Peggy Willis
In succession to John Fowler

Freefolk House, Whitchurch, Hampshire
Client: Mr Julian Sheffield

Friar's Well, Roundtown, Aynho, Banbury, Oxfordshire
Client: Lady Ward (formerly Mrs Michael Astor)
In succession to John Fowler

Garden Cottage, Logan Place, South Kensington, London, SW7
Client: Sir Robert Wilson

Garrowby Park, York, North Yorkshire
Client: Earl and Countess of Halifax
Note: library only

Gatley Park, Leinthall Earls, Herefordshire
Client: Mr Thomas and Mrs Henrietta Dunne

Glebe House, Whitsbury, Hampshire
Client: Mr Anthony Hobson (of Sotheby's)

46 Green Street, Mayfair, London, W1
Client: Mrs J. Moffett
Note: George Oakes painted a mural on the staircase.

Grey Abbey House, Newtownards, Co. Down
Client: Mr William Montgomery

Flat 14, 33 Grosvenor Square, Mayfair, London, W1
Client: Sir Martin Lindsay
Note: he married Loelia, Duchess of Westminster.

Grosvenor Square, Mayfair, London, W1
Client: Mr and Mrs Angus Mackinnon

27 Grove End Road, St John's Wood, London, NW8
Client: Mr J. Burns

Hambleden Manor, Hambleden, Buckinghamshire
Client: Maria Carmela, Viscountess of Hambleden
In succession to John Fowler

Hambro Magan Ltd, 32 Queen Anne's Gate, London, SW1
Client: Mr George Magan

Hans Place, Knightsbridge, London, SW1
Client: Mrs Miller-Munday

Hans Place, Knightsbridge, London, SW1
Client: Sir Gerrard and Lady Peat

Hartley Place, Hartley Wintney, Hampshire
Client: Sir Emmanuel and Lady Kaye

Haseley Court, Little Haseley, Oxfordshire
Client: Mrs Desmond Hayward
Note: saloon only

Hatton Grange, Shifnal, Shropshire
Client: Mr R. Kenyon-Stanley
Country Life, vol. 143, pp. 466–70

Hayes Hill, Twyford, Berkshire
Client: Lady Elizabeth Godsall

43 Hays Mews, Mayfair, London, W1
Client: Mrs Dennis; Mrs Heinz
With John Fowler
'My favourite London house', by Loelia, Duchess of
Westminster, *The Sketch*, 9 March 1955, pp. 204–5
Colefax & Fowler, pp. 9, 20, 21

Hennells Jewellers, Bond Street, London, W1

Hilborough Hall, Thetford, Norfolk
Client: Mrs Mills

Hoare's Bank, 37 Fleet Street, London, EC4

Hobe Sound, Florida, USA
Client: Mr and Mrs Whitney Payson
'Hobe Sound Heirloom', *Architectural Digest*, March
1997

Holland Park, London, W11
Client: Viscount and Viscountess Blakenham

Holme Pierrepont Hall, Holme Pierrepont,
Nottinghamshire
Client: Mr Robin Brackenbury

Holybourne House, Chadlington, Oxfordshire
Client: Mr M. Wigley

Home Farm, Upper Basildon, Berkshire
Client: Sir Gerrard and Lady Peat

Horsted Keyne, Sussex
Client: Mr and Mrs Julian Faber

Hunton Down House, Hunton, Sutton Scotney,
Hampshire
Client: Mrs Angus Mackinnon

Hunton Manor, Hunton, Sutton Scotney, Hampshire
Client: Mr and Mrs Angus Mackinnon
With John Fowler
Note: drawing room by Raymond Erith, garden by
Russell Page

Hurlingham Club, Fulham, London, SW6

6 Hyde Park Crescent, London, W2
Client: Mrs Al Sabah

6 Hyde Park Gardens, London, W2
Client: Mr and Mrs Anthony Thesiger

15 Hyde Park Gardens, London, W2
Client: Mary, Duchess of Roxburghe

Jamaica
Client: Mr and Mrs Steve Schwarzman

Jeddah, Saudi Arabia
Client: Sheikh Mahfooz

Keir, Stirling, Scotland
Client: Mrs Susan Stirling
In succession to John Fowler

Kensington Palace, London, W8 (Wren House)
Client: Sir John and Lady Riddell

Kensington Palace, London, W8
Client: Sir Michael and Lady Peat

Kilboy, Tipperary, Ireland
Client: Mr Tony Ryan

Kitzbühel, Austria
Client: Mr and Mrs Dumba

Knowsley, Liverpool
Client: Earl of Derby
With John Fowler
Country Life, vol. 34, p. 54; vol. 81, p. 276

Kuwait
Client: Mr Al Bahai

Kuwait
Client: Mr and Mrs Al Fulaig

Kuwait
Client: Mr and Mrs Al Sagar

Kuwait
Client: Sheikh Badria Al Sabah

Lansdown Road, Kensington, London, SW7
Client: Mr and Mrs Oppenheim

Lansing Bagnall Ltd, Basingstoke, Berkshire (offices)

Lennoxlove, Haddington, Scotland
Client: Earl and Countess of Haddington
In succession to John Fowler

Linden House, West Drive, Wentworth, Surrey
Client: Mrs T. Thornton

Lower Dryton Farm, Blunsdown, Wiltshire
Client: Mrs E. Barker
Note: mother of Fred Barker of Lushill

Lowesby Hall, Leicester
Client: Sir Nicholas Nuttall
Country Life, vol. 18, pp. 342–8; vol. 37, pp. 626–33;
vol. 39, p. 105

Lowndes Close, Belgravia, London, SW1
Client: Mr and Mrs Paraschos

Lullenden Manor, East Grinstead, Sussex
Client: Mrs Floor

Lushill, Hannington, Wiltshire
Client: Mr and Mrs Fred Barker
In succession to John Fowler
Note: Venetia Barker was the sister of Princess
Victoria von Preussen later became Venetia, Lady
Wimborne

Madrid, Spain
Client: Mrs March

Madrid
Client: Mrs Maria Davila

Maine, USA
Client: Mr and Mrs Joseph Ledbetter

Maperton House, Wincanton, Somerset
Client: Princess Victoria von Preussen (sister of Lady
Wimborne and Lady Nuttall)

Maysmead Place, Churchill, North Somerset
Client: Lieutenant Colonel J.K.L. Mardon

Mellerstain, Gordon, Berwickshire, Scotland
Client: Countess Haddington
With John Fowler
Country Life, vol. 38, p. 648; vol. 102, p. 380; vol.
124, pp. 416, 476

Miami, Florida, USA
Client: Mrs Maria Davila

Miami, Florida, USA
Client: Mr and Mrs Umberto da Costa

Moissac, Lot et Gasonne, France
Client: Mr and Mrs Vincent Paravicini

Mount Street, Mayfair, London, W1
Client: Mrs Rhodes

Munstead House, Busbridge, Godalming, Surrey
Client: Lord and Lady Freyburg

Nashville, Tennessee, USA
Client: Mr and Mrs Joseph Ledbetter

Nassau, Bahamas
Client: Mrs Maria Davila

Netherton, Andover, Hampshire
Client: Mr J. Charrington

New York, USA
Client: Mr and Mrs S. Bershad

New York, USA
Client: Mrs Wyser-Pratte

New York, USA
Client: Mrs Vida Belton

New York, USA
Client: Mrs Cox

New York, USA
Client: Mr and Mrs Galin

New York, USA
Client: Mr and Mrs Kahn

New York, USA
Client: Mr and Mrs Whitney Payson

New York, USA
Client: Mr and Mrs Steve Schwarzman
'Export Quality', *House & Garden* (USA), November
1990

New York, USA
Client: Mrs Katz (formerly Mrs Schwarzman)

New York, USA
Client: Mr Staunton

New York, USA
Client: Mr and Mrs Joseph Ledbetter

Norman Fuzzell (offices), Elder Street, London, E1

North Port House, Haddington, Scotland
Client: Dowager Duchess of Hamilton

Notley Abbey, Thame, Oxfordshire
Client: Mr and Mrs John Danny

Oakly Park, Ludlow, Shropshire
Client: Earl and Countess of Plymouth

Pallinsburn, Cornhill-on-Tweed, Northumberland
Client: Mrs C. Mitchell

Palm Beach, Florida, USA
Client: Mr and Mrs Alan Dayton

Palm Beach, Florida, USA
Client: Mr and Mrs Fred Krehbiel

Paris, France
Client: Lady Wimborne

The Pavilion, Hampton Court, Middlesex
Client: Mrs Cecil King (Dame Ruth King)

14 Pelham Crescent, South Kensington, London,
SW7
Client: Lady Gunston
With John Fowler

Pelham Crescent, South Kensington, London, SW7
Client: Mr and Mrs Gelardine

Penny Holme, Fadmore, Yorkshire
Client: Countess of Feversham
With John Fowler
Country Life, vol. 124, p. 774

Lady Richard Percy
Address unknown, Northumberland

Philadelphia, Pennsylvania, USA
Client: Mr and Mrs Christopher Birch

Phillimore Gardens, Kensington, W8
Client: Mr and Mrs Alan Dayton

Phillimore Gardens, Kensington, W8
Client: Mrs Steel

Plumpton Place, Lewis, Sussex
Client: Lady Manton (later Lady Brownlow)
Country Life, vol. 73, pp. 522–8
Note: Lord Manton bought the estate in 1938 for
£9,000; he died in 1968 and in 1969 Lady Manton
married Lord Brownlow; the property was bought in
1972 by Robert (Jimmy) Page of Led Zeppelin.

Pont Street, Belgravia, London, SW1
Client: Sir Gerrard and Lady Peat

Prestons, Ightham, Kent
Client: Sir Gerrard and Lady Peat

Ramsbury Manor, Ramsbury, Wiltshire
Client: Mr and Mrs Harry Hyams

Regent's Park, London, NW1
Client: Mrs Al Ghanim

Regent's Park, London, NW1
Client: Mrs Solemani

Robinson, Geoffrey MP – London

St Anselm's Place, Mayfair, London, W1
Client: Lord and Lady Richardson

St James's Place, London, W1
Client: Sir Emmanuel and Lady Kaye
In succession to John Fowler

15 St James's Square, London, W1 (Lichfield House)
Client: Clerical Medical Insurance

5 St Leonard's Terrace, Chelsea, London, SW3
Client: Mrs E. Dugdale
With John Fowler
Note: one of John Fowler's pre-war clients; house
redecorated exactly as he had originally done it

St Michael's Mount, Penzance, Cornwall
Client: Lady St Levan

Sandbeck Park, Doncaster, South Yorkshire
Client: Earl and Countess of Scarbrough
Country Life, vol. 138, pp. 880–83, 966, 1024–7
Colefax & Fowler, p. 156

Sandwich Bay, Kent
Client: Mr and Mrs Julian Faber

Schroders Bank, London
Client: Gordon Richardson (office)

Scotlands Farm, Cockpile Green, Wargrave,
Berkshire
Client: The Hon. Mrs Michael Payne

Seymour Court, Marlow, Buckinghamshire
Client: Mrs Merton

Sezincote, Moreton-in-Marsh, Gloucestershire
Client: Lady Kleinwort
Dining room only
Colefax & Fowler, p. 89
Country Life, vol. 85, pp. 502, 528; vol. 160, pp.
600–2
English Decoration, pp. 102, 116, 120, 165
Inspiration of the Past, pp. 88, 89, 167 176

Somerton House, Winkfield Row, Berkshire
Client: Lady Bridget Garnett

Somerley House, Ringwood, Hampshire
Client: Lady Normanton
Note: also a dower house for her

70 South Audley Street, Mayfair, London, W1
Client: Mr Charles Sweeney

South Terrace, South Kensington, London, SW7
Client: Mr and Mrs Marcus Agius

Squerryes Court, Westerham, Kent
Client: Mrs Anthea Warde

Stanley House, Newmarket, Surrey
Client: Earl and Countess of Derby

Stenigot House, Market Raisen, Lincolnshire
Client: Mr and Mrs Peter Dennis

Stone Green Hall, Merston, Sussex
Client: Sir Robert Wilson

Stowell Park, Yanworth, Gloucestershire
Client: Lady Rothschild

Strattom House, Strattom, Co. Kildare, Ireland
Client: Mr Kevin McLory

Swan Walk, Chelsea, London, SW3
Client: Mr and Mrs Crispin Odey

Swerford Park, Chipping Norton, Oxfordshire
Client: Mr and Mrs Christopher Harris

Syon House, Middlesex
Client: Duke of Northumberland

Thorp Perrow, Bedale, North Yorkshire
Client: Colonel Sir Leonard Ropner
Country Life, vol. 169, pp. 566–8

Thurloe Square, Kensington, London, SW7
Client: Baroness de Gunsberg

Tidcombe Manor, Tidcombe, Wiltshire
Client: Earl and Countess Jellicoe

Madame Tussauds, Marylebone Road, London,
NW1

Tyninghame, Dunbar, Scotland
Client: Countess of Haddington
With John Fowler
Colefax & Fowler, p. 47
Country Life (garden), vol. 12, p. 208; vol. 158, p. 336;
vol. 181, issue 43, p. 80; (conversion of house) vol.
183, issue 35, p. 80
Inspiration of the Past, pp. 174, 193, illus. XLI, XLII

86 Vincent Square, London, SW1
Client: Lord and Lady Duncan Sandys

Villalba Herres, Tenerife, Spain
Client: Don M. C. Kabana

Waddesdon Manor, Aylesbury, Buckinghamshire
Client: Mrs James 'Dolly' de Rothschild

Walton Place, Belgravia, London, SW1
Client: Sir Gerrard and Lady Peat

Warwick Avenue, Little Venice, London, W9
Client: Lord Rothschild

Warwick Square, Pimlico, London, SW1
Client: Lady Duncan Sandys

Warwick, Square, Pimlico, London, SW1
Client: Mrs Winston Churchill

Waverton House, Waverton, Gloucestershire
Client: Mr and Mrs Hambro
'Architecture: Quinlan Terry', *Architectural Digest*,
June 1986

Weinstock, Simon

West Horsley Place, East Horsley, Surrey
Client: Mary, Duchess of Roxburghe

West Wycombe Park, West Wycombe,
Buckinghamshire
Client: Sir Francis Dashwood

Weybridge, Surrey
Client: Mr and Mrs Peter Janssen

Whitney, Mrs Jock: London flat
Note: in succession to John Fowler

Wilbury Park, Salisbury, Wiltshire
Client: Miranda, Countess of Iveagh

Willis Faber, Tower Hill, London, EC3

6 Wilton Crescent, Belgravia, London, SW1
Client: Mrs Lanahan

Wilton Crescent, Belgravia, London, SW1
Client: Mr and Mrs Fred Krehbiel

Winchester, Hampshire
Client: Mrs Paul

Winkburn Hall, Newark, Nottinghamshire
Client: Mr and Mrs Craven-Smith-Milnes

17 Woronzow Road, St John's Wood, London, NW8
Client: Sir George Solti
Note: just an armchair

MY ASSISTANTS
Birdie Fortescue, The Hon.
Camilla Brown
Caroline Edwards
Celine Franassovici
Colin Orchard
Daphne Wilbraham
Emma Berry
Fenella Smith
Fiona Merritt
Fiona Moglove
Francine Preston
Gillian Lyster
Guy Oliver
Holly Seaward
Jane Eustice
Jane Stourton
Joanna Harper
Lucilla Berliand
Lynette Pearson
Marlene Stoddart
Nikki Atkinson
Nina Campbell
Pierre Serrurier
Piers Northam
Ros Walker
Sally Jeffreys
Samantha Kingcome
Sarah Gillespie
Serena Forbes
Sophie O'Connell
Susie Faulkner
Ursula Culverwell

INDEX
Page numbers in *italic* refer to illustrations.

ACKNOWLEDGMENTS

My deepest thanks must go to Fred Krehbiel, whose encouragement, kindness and generosity has been amazing. My thanks also to David Green, Trudi Ballard and Barrie MacIntyre of Colefax and Fowler for allowing me to have access to the archives and for all their help. And to the team at Pimpernel Press, the publisher and editor Jo Christian, Sue Gladstone the picture editor and Becky Clarke the designer. They have all been very helpful and encouraging to me as a first-time writer.

Most importantly, the book would not have happened without the support and hard work over years of Martin Wood, who somehow transcribed my tapes and writing into a presentable form and did so with great patience, much encouragement and a sense of humour. I owe him an enormous debt of gratitude.

And then I have to say that without the training and inspiration that I gained by working with John Fowler, none of this – neither the book, nor, indeed, the life in decorating – would have come about. He opened the door into a fascinating career. I hope he would have approved.

PICTURE CREDITS

All the illustrations are the author's, with the exception of those listed on this page.
The publishers have made every effort to contact holders of copyright works. Any
copyright holders we have been unable to reach are invited to contact the publishers
so that a full acknowledgment may be given in subsequent editions.

Peter Atkins: 70, 80

Bill Batten © *The World of Interiors*: 207

Donald Church/author: 4

Colefax and Fowler: 1, 2, 6, 8, 14, 24, 30, 31, 38, 42, 44 *below*, 46, 47 *left*, 48, 52, 53 *right*, 55, 59, 60, 65 *above right, below left and right*, 73, 74, 75, 76, 82 *below left and right*, 85 *above right*, 87, 90, 100, 101, 102, 103, 104, 105, 106, 110 *right*, 111 *above left and right and below left*, 112, 113, 114, 115, 120, 121, 122, 123, 124, 130, 158, 168, 169, 170, 171, 176, 178, 182 *right*, 183 *right, top to bottom*, 188, 189, 204

Courtesy of the Library of Congress: 50

© *Country Life*: 61, 81

Andreas von Einsiedel/*House & Garden* © The Condé Nast Publications Ltd: 175

© Mark Fiennes/Bridgeman Images (by kind permission of the Chequers Trust): 72

Getty Images/Hulton Archive/Photoshot: 69 *right*

Lynette Hood: 34

Gavin Kingcome; 190, 192, 193, 196, 197, 198, 199, 200 *below*, 201, 202, 203, 208 *below*

Fred Krehbiel: 132, 133, 134, 135, 136, 137, 138, 139, 140 *below*, 141, 143, 144, 145, 146, 147, 148, 149, 150, 151, 152, 153, 154, 155

Barrie MacIntyre; 200 *above left*, 209

Duncan McNeil/*House & Garden* © The Condé Nast Publications Ltd: 180, 181 *left*

John Mason: 77, 78, 95 *right*, 110 *centre*, 127 *above left and centre right*, 186

Tania Melich Crowe: 110 *left*

Derry Moore: 96

© The National Trust, Waddesden Manor (The Rothschild Collection): 40

George Oakes: 49

Private collections: 33 *above and below right*, 37, 39, 53 *left*, 54 *right*, 56, 57, 82 *above*, 88 *left*, 194, 195, 208 *above left*

Christopher Simon Sykes © *The World of Interiors*: 187

Marianne Topham/author: 7

Mark Uriu: 84, 85 *above left and below*, 127 *below right*

William Waldron: 127 *above right and below left*, 128

Elizabeth Winn/Martin Wood: 43 *above*

www.zuber.fr: 89